Pelican Books
VOLCANOES

D0734928

Peter Francis was born and brought up in Northern
Rhodesia (Zambia), but was educated in England. After
graduating in geology at the Imperial College of Science
in 1966 he took part in an expedition to the Bolivian
Andes. It was this journey that first fired his interest in
volcanoes, but it was not until he had spent three
wind-swept years preparing a Ph.D. thesis on the rocks
of the Outer Hebrides of Scotland that he was able to
devote his attention to volcanoes. While writing his
thesis, he organized a seven-month-long research project
in the Andes, which enabled him to examine volcanoes at
first hand in Chile, Peru, Ecuador, Colombia, Guatemala
and Mexico.

On returning to England, he joined the staff of the
Open University, where he was able to combine his
interests in writing about geology with a continuing
volcanic research programme, which has involved field
work in Italy, the Sudan, Mexico and the Andes. Apart
from volcanoes, his main interests lie in flying and music.

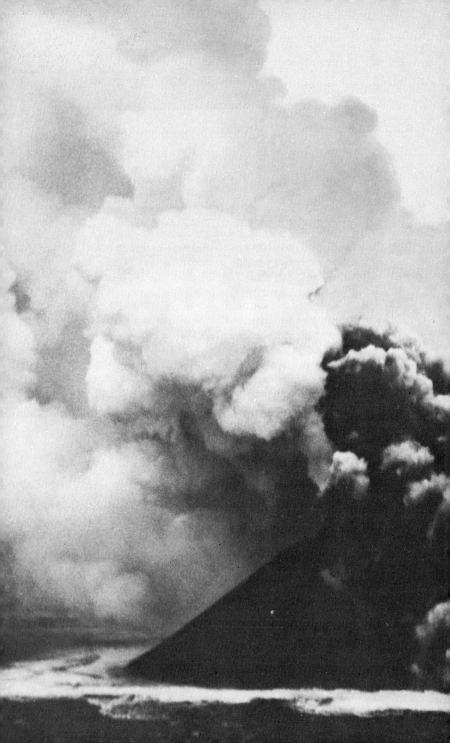

Peter Francis

# *Volcanoes*

 Penguin Books

Penguin Books Ltd,
Harmondsworth, Middlesex, England
Penguin Books,
625 Madison Avenue, New York, New York 10022, U.S.A.
Penguin Books Australia Ltd,
Ringwood, Victoria, Australia
Penguin Books Canada Ltd,
41 Steelcase Road West, Markham, Ontario, Canada
Penguin Books (N.Z.) Ltd,
182–190 Wairau Road, Auckland 10, New Zealand

First published 1976
Copyright © Peter Francis, 1976

Designed by Geoffrey Terrill

Made and printed in Great Britain by
Hazell Watson & Viney Ltd, Aylesbury, Bucks
Set in Monophoto Bembo

For my cat Jeoffrey

# Contents

# List of Plates

# *Preface*

There are many other books on the market called *Volcanoes*, and some of them are much weightier and more respectable tomes than this one, and cover the subject in greater depth. So why write yet another? It is always difficult to determine what are an author's motives in writing a book, but in the present case, three factors were involved. First, the profound developments in the geological and geophysical knowledge of both the Earth and the Moon in the last few years have left most of the earlier books hopelessly out of date, and I felt that there was a need to show how some of these developments have made volcanoes and their relevance to the Earth as a planet a lot easier to understand. Second, and more important, although my many predecessors have shown clearly just how spectacular volcanic eruptions can be, I felt that they often failed to show just how fascinating and important volcanoes can be in other, broader, ways. Third, most of the better earlier books were written mainly for the textbook market. This one has less academic pretensions, though I hope, of course, that 'students' of all kinds will find it interesting. I shall only be disappointed if readers put it down with a yawn, and wish they hadn't bought it.

The book stems from a visit made by a group of Imperial College post-graduates to South and Central America in 1969 and 1970, when I first acquired my interest in volcanoes. I owe a great deal to my companions on that trip, particularly to George Walker, from whom I have learned much. I am also grateful to Richard Thorpe, of the Open University, for making valuable, if sometimes pungent, comments on the manuscript.

P.F.

# *Chapter 1*  Volcanoes in their global setting – Plate Tectonics

If mountains can have personalities, then volcanoes are schizophrenic – they have split personalities. For most of their life, they are dormant, and one tends to think of them as graceful upsweeping cones, delicately capped with snow, dreaming serenely over the cherry-blossom-draped landscapes of calendars and travel posters. Sometimes, perhaps not very often during their lifetimes, volcanoes erupt and present a wholly different character. Convolute eruption clouds tower above them, raining hot ashes on the helpless humans who live on their flanks, and glowing tongues of liquid rock ooze inexorably downwards, engulfing the flimsy structures which stand in their way. Not surprisingly, it is for these displays of nature's most powerful forces at work that volcanoes are chiefly known, and in almost all primitive societies they have been regarded with fear and identified with deities and evil spirits.

Although today volcanoes are no longer regarded with such religious awe, their violent aspects are still widely publicized; deservedly, since volcanic eruptions are amongst the finest of natural spectacles. There are thousands of metres of film of eruptions and hectares of accounts in newspapers and books, almost all of it devoted to the 'human interest' situations that arise whenever natural events interrupt the pattern of human life. Some eruptions have become major historical events, since many of the world's greatest natural disasters have been associated with volcanoes, either directly through the effects of explosions and suffocation by volcanic gases, or indirectly through the much further-reaching effects of tidal waves triggered off by an eruption, such as those resulting from the great eruption of Krakatoa in 1883. This book will of course deal with the familiar aspects of volcanoes and with the different kinds of eruptions that take place, but in addition to this, it will cover some of the quieter, less well-known aspects, and try to explain why volcanoes exist at all, why they occur where they do, and how they fit into the history of the Earth as a whole. To do this will involve discussion of concepts which you may not immediately associate with volcanoes: the fact that Africa and South America were once joined and later drifted apart; that the direction which is customarily thought of as 'north' would, a few million years ago, have appeared to be 'south' on an ordinary magnetic compass; that the very rocks on which we live – no matter where – may have originated through volcanism; that much of the gold and many of the other economic minerals that we use every day are linked with volcanic activity; that most of the world's best coffee and tea come from volcanic areas, and that there may be areas on the Moon and Mars which are analogous to terrestrial continents and oceans. Before embarking on these widely different topics, however, it is essential to consider volcanoes in their global setting.

## The world distribution of volcanoes

Volcanoes are not scattered randomly around the world. If you were asked to name countries in which volcanoes occur, you would probably think of places such as Japan, Iceland, Hawaii, Italy, New Zealand and so on. At first, these areas may seem quite unrelated, but no matter what countries you think of, the volcanoes in them have one rather odd thing in common – they are all very near the sea. This isn't such an irrelevant statement as it may sound – it is a fact that almost *all* the volcanoes in the world are within a couple of hundred kilometres of the sea. There are remarkably few active volcanoes in the *centres* of continents – none at all in South or North America, away from the Andean–Rockies mountain belt, none in central Asia, none in Australia, and only one away from the coast in Antarctica. There are some important exceptions in Africa, and also some recently-dead volcanoes in France and Germany, but these form a rather specialized, distinct group, and we'll see how they fit in later on.

Given, then, that volcanoes have a predilection for the seaside, let's now pin down more precisely where they occur. If one plots the sites of all the recently-active volcanoes in the world on a map, one finds that several distinct, narrow chains exist, some of these running along the edges of continental land masses, some along island arcs and some of them through the sea (Fig. 1). We'll follow two of these chains in a sort of volcanic Cook's tour since they are of fundamental importance to our story, and will crop up repeatedly throughout the rest of the text. Before commencing it should be emphasized that when a geologist talks of a volcano having been *recently* active, he means that it has been active within the last ten thousand years. That may seem anything but recent, but remember that a million years is a relatively insignificant span of time compared with the age of the Earth, at present reckoned at about 4,600 million years. An 'active' volcano is usually regarded as one which has erupted at least once in historic times.

*Continental margin volcanoes*

The first chain starts off right down in the Antarctic, a few hundred kilometres from the South Pole. Here in the lonely isolation of the Antarctic ice cap is Mt Early, the world's southernmost volcano. Further to the north, along the ice-bound coast of Marie Byrd Land are more volcanoes, and a well-defined belt soon becomes established, swinging away into the long, crooked arm of the Graham Land Peninsula, and then eastwards into a scatter of desolate, little-known volcanic islands, the South Sandwich Islands. This line of islands swings round to the north, and finally back to the west through South Georgia, describing a great loop, and then heads off for the extreme south of South America. Here, in the tangle of islands and fjords that is Patagonia, the volcanic chain becomes established on the South American continent with Mt Burney, an obscure, almost unknown volcano which has only once been visited by a geologist, in 1911.

From Mt Burney northwards, volcanoes occur intermittently

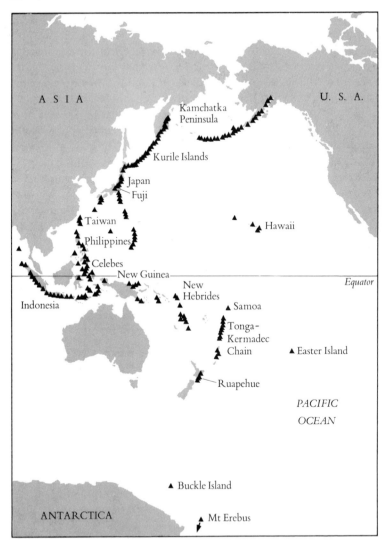

*Fig. 1 (Parts 1 and 2) The distribution of active volcanoes round the Pacific.*

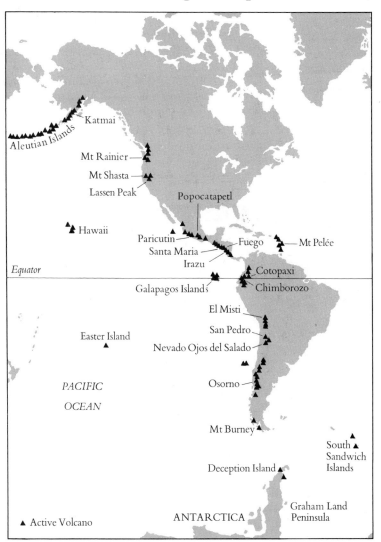

Katmai

Aleutian Islands

Mt Rainier —

Mt Shasta —

Lassen Peak

Popocatapetl

Hawaii

Paricutin —
Santa Maria —
Irazu

Fuego — Mt Pelée

*Equator*

Galapagos Islands

Cotopaxi
Chimborozo

El Misti

San Pedro —

Nevado Ojos del Salado —

Osorno

*PACIFIC*

*OCEAN*

Easter Island

Mt Burney

South
Sandwich
Islands

Deception Island

*ANTARCTICA*

Graham Land
Peninsula

▲ Active Volcano

along almost the entire 7,000-kilometre length of the Andes. In all, there are thousands of extinct or dormant volcanoes, but only forty-five are considered to be 'active'. Right in the northern part of South America, in Colombia, the volcanic chain and the Andean mountain chain get a bit mixed up. The mountains swing away to the east, running into Venezuela, but the volcanic chain after a short gap in the dreary and fever-ridden jungles of the Isthmus of Panama, reappears in full vigour in Costa Rica, and extends throughout the Central American republics of Nicaragua, El Salvador and Guatemala, which are by reputation as unstable and explosive politically as the many volcanoes that they contain.

1. *The 6,000-metres-high San Pedro volcano in the Andes of northern Chile. This doesn't look much like the 'conventional' conical volcanoes, but it is active, and a small plume of steam is visible near the summit.*

The Caribbean islands present a slight complication to this simple picture of a single volcanic chain running up the Americas. They form another chain, looping up from the coast of Venezuela through Jamaica and Cuba, heading towards the Yucatan peninsula of Mexico. The West Indian islands contain less than a dozen active volcanoes, all of them congregated in a small arc at the east of the chain, but one of these, Mt Pelée, was responsible for the most lethal eruption of this century.

Mexico contains many active volcanoes, a quantity of them burdened with tortuous Aztec names such as the well-known Popocatepetl. Moving further north, the United States has rather fewer volcanoes, and although there are some impressive cones such as those of Mt Shasta and Mt Rainier, both over 4,000 metres high, there have been only a few minor eruptions in historic times. Further north still, Canada has no major volcanoes, but there have been some eruptions in prehistoric times.

In the south west of Alaska, the volcanic chain picks up again strongly, and swings out to sea to form the long arcs of the Aleutian and Kurile Islands. These curve back up northwards towards the Kamchatka peninsula of the U.S.S.R., an intensely active volcanic province, and then the chain sweeps down southwards, heading for Japan. From Japan, the chain goes on, through the island of Taiwan (Nationalist China), through the Philippines and into the Celebes. Here there is a kind of volcanic 'T' junction. One branch runs north-westwards up into the Indonesian archipelago, where volcanoes have killed more people than anywhere else on earth, and peters out before reaching the Asian mainland. The other branch runs south-eastwards through New Guinea and the New Hebrides and through a scatter of small Melanesian islands, before making an abrupt dog's leg northwards to the Samoan islands to join the Tonga–Kermadec chain which extends southwards again into New Zealand.

Sadly, there are no volcanoes on the South Island of New Zealand, and the volcanic chain we have been following all round the Pacific seems to fizzle out there. The only volcanoes further south are in Antarctica, over 1,500 kilometres away. These include Buckle Island, just off the Antarctic coast, and Mts Erebus and Terror, only a few kilometres from Scott's original base camp, from which he set out on his last heroic journey. One shouldn't strictly include Erebus and Terror in the same chain as those of New Zealand – the gap is rather large – but they do bring us conveniently back to Antarctica, from where we began our journey of some 40,000 kilometres round the entire Pacific Ocean. The chain of volcanoes which girdles the Pacific is known appropriately enough as the 'Ring of Fire', and although it's a much more complex, disjointed affair than it may seem from this brief summary, it is unquestionably one of the Earth's greatest physical features, and contains a large proportion of all the world's volcanoes. And not one of them is more than 300 kilometres from the sea.

## Mid-ocean volcanoes

Our second tour begins nearly at the opposite pole, with Jan Mayen, a small, ice-gripped island in the Arctic Ocean, roughly half-way between Greenland and Arctic Norway. On this bleak island is a volcano, Beerenberg, which last erupted in 1970. Southwest of Jan Mayen is Iceland, built entirely of volcanic rocks, and famous for both its volcanoes and its geysers. The Icelanders called one of their finest gushers of boiling water and steam *Geysir*, and this name was applied subsequently to all those depressing pieces of gas-fired plumbing which used to be a familiar part of the British bathroom scene.

Iceland has twenty-two volcanoes, but the ones which have been most in the news are located on the Westmann Islands, just off the south coast. A new island, Surtsey, was built up by an eruption which started in 1963 and continued intermittently until 1967. In February 1973 an eruption suddenly burst out on the tiny island of Heimaey, and for a time it seemed as though the town of Heimaey, Iceland's biggest fishing port, would be destroyed. Fortunately, though, the eruption petered out in July 1973 before irrevocable damage had been done.

South of Iceland, the Atlantic Ocean stretches out devoid of even the tiniest of islands for thousands of kilometres. In 1884, sightings of a submarine eruption were reported by the officers of ships, right in the middle of the ocean, half-way between Ireland and Newfoundland. This may have been an eruption similar to that which built Surtsey, but it came to nothing, and no island succeeded in raising its head above water.

Just about level with the Straits of Gibraltar and 1,300 kilo-

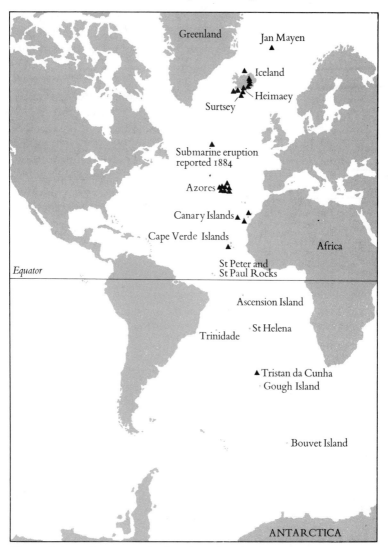

*Fig. 2  Active volcanoes in North and South Atlantic Oceans.*

metres from the Portuguese coast are the Azores, a small group of islands which are entirely built of volcanic rocks, where eruptions took place in 1957 and 1973. South of the Azores, but only about 100 to 150 kilometres from the African coast are the Canary Islands, also volcanic, and also the scene of recent eruptions. South and west of the Canaries, the Atlantic extends emptily for thousands of kilometres, broken only by the Cape Verde Islands (also volcanic) and two tiny specks of land, St Peter and St Paul's Rocks, which are not strictly volcanic, oddly enough, but are composed of material that must have been derived from much deeper levels in the Earth than most volcanic rocks. South of this tiny pair are a few lonely islands separated from one another by hundreds of kilometres of sea – first, Ascension Island, then St Helena, and then over towards the Brazilian coast, Trinidade. Further south still is Tristan da Cunha, notorious for its eruption

2. *The lava flow on the island of Tristan da Cunha which caused the evacuation of all the islanders in 1962. The crater from which the lava emerged is at the bottom, and some of the islanders' boats and fields can be seen at the top left.* (Photo courtesy of I. G. Gass)

in 1962 which precipitated the evacuation of the unfortunate islanders to Britain. Tristan has two near neighbours, both un-inhabited, Nightingale and Inaccessible, and a third a couple of hundred kilometres further south, Gough Island; all of them are the battered remains of extinct volcanoes.

Further south still, the Roaring Forties begin – those empty ex-panses of the 'Southern Ocean' which stretch right around the world at this latitude. The last link in our tenuous volcanic chain lies even further south: south of latitude 50°; Bouvet Island, deso-late, inaccessible and almost entirely icebound. Little is known of eruptions there, but there may have been one in the last decade, since sets of aerial photographs of the island taken many years apart show some slight changes.

## Continental drift and Plate Tectonics

In the days before modern oceanography, the story would stop short at this point, with just a long, tenuous chain of widely-separated volcanic islands running down the middle of the Atlantic with no obvious connection between them. The link, however, was discovered soon after systematic depth soundings were taken, when it was discovered that there was a long submarine mountain range running down the middle of the Atlantic from Arctic to Antarctic. This range, although covered by many hundreds of metres of water for most of its length, breaks surface in a few places to form the chain of apparently unconnected volcanic islands. (But not all; some, like the Canaries, although related to the ridge, lie well to one side of it.) More important, the range almost exactly bisects the Atlantic Ocean from north to south following closely the profile of the African and South American coasts, so it's always called the *Mid-Atlantic Ridge*. Specimens re-covered from the sea floor showed that this ridge consists entirely of volcanic rocks, and similar ridges were soon found to be present beneath many of the oceans. Not all of them are strictly mid-ocean – some of them run right up to the continents – but together they form a world-wide network of mountain belts far higher (above ocean floor level) and more extensive than any on dry land. The Mid-Atlantic Ridge will play an important part in our study of the nature of volcanism, and so will another, the *East Pacific Rise*, which runs up the eastern Pacific, and eventually intersects the North American continent in the vicinity of California.

After Francis Bacon first drew attention to it in 1620, there was endless speculation on the reason for the striking similarity in shape between the coastlines of Africa and South America. Cardboard cut-outs of the two continents were made and fitted together, computer programmes written to devise the most perfect match between the two continents, similarities and the differences in the geology of corresponding areas studied *ad nauseam*, and even details of the animal life in each continent compared, but without reaching any firm conclusions on whether or not the two continents had ever been united. The remarkably faithful matching of the Mid-Atlantic Ridge to the shapes of the continents was a great boost to the theory of *continental drift*, which postulated that Africa and South America had originally formed a supercontinent, which subsequently split up, with the two parts moving away in opposite directions. But even the presence of the ridge proved nothing – it merely made the problem at once more difficult and more fascinating, and debate over the possibility of continental drift raged fiercely, with geologists divided into two opposing camps.

So long as no viable *cause* for continental drift could be demonstrated, however, belief in it remained an act of faith. The elegant solution to the uniquely challenging problem of finding a cause was first suggested in 1929 by Arthur Holmes, one of the greatest of British geologists, but it was not until 1960 that the late Professor Harry Hess of Princeton University in the U.S.A. developed Holmes's idea into a convincing hypothesis. Although he did not know it at the time, Hess's work was to initiate a revolution in geological and geophysical thinking, and ultimately it became the foundation of a major new theory about how continents and oceans are related, and what part volcanoes play in the evolution of the Earth. This new approach to world geology is generally known as the *Plate Tectonic Theory*, or just Plate

Tectonics. Although geology is a fairly elderly discipline, as sciences go, in its 150-year history there have been no sudden 'breakthroughs' of the sort beloved of journalists. It has advanced slowly, by the patient amassing and interpretation of data in many varied fields, ranging from the study of fossils (palaeontology) to the chemical and physical properties of rocks themselves (petrology). Plate Tectonics, however, was truly a great leap forward since it helps to explain the interrelationships of almost all geological phenomena. As such it must rank as one of the most fundamental scientific advances of the century. Apart from its intrinsic interest, Plate Tectonics is also an excellent example of how many major scientific advances are made: the starting point is a bright idea in the mind of some unusually-gifted scientist, an intuitive feeling probably based on thoroughly shaky evidence rather than some great intellectual *tour de force*. The first idea is refined into a hypothesis by collecting more evidence to see if it really works, and ultimately it may be elevated into the rather grand status of a Theory, if successful predictions can be based upon it. Any theory must be useful; it must be able to explain how or why things happen. If in the course of its development observations are made to test the theory, and the theory fails to explain some of them, then it has to be refined to take account of the new observations. Before considering the Plate Tectonic Theory and its evolution, however, a short background description of the overall structure of the Earth is necessary.

Our planet has three main parts: an inner *core* which is believed to consist of a mass of iron and nickel; a *mantle*, composed of dense dark silicate rock, rich in iron and magnesium, known as *peridotite*; and a very thin *crust*. Since we live on the crust, it is important to us in more ways than one, but we are only going to consider it in its relationship to events in the mantle, since these explain how Plate Tectonics works.

The crust can be divided into two types, oceanic and continental. The continental crust, taken as a whole, consists of rocks fairly light both in colour and density which contain a lot of silica, $S_iO_2$. (Silicon and oxygen are by far the most abundant constituents in the Earth's crust.) Broadly speaking, the rocks of the continental

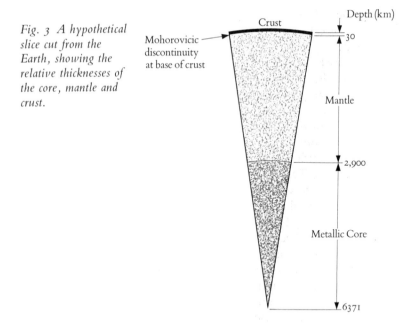

*Fig. 3  A hypothetical slice cut from the Earth, showing the relative thicknesses of the core, mantle and crust.*

crust have the composition of granite, the rather coarse-grained pink- or grey-speckled rock beloved of the more respectable banks and monumental masons. This should not be taken too literally – not *every* rock in the crust is a granite – things like limestones are vastly different in composition – but the average composition of *all* the rocks on the continents is about that of granite and contains over 60 per cent of silica. In most areas the continental crust consists of a thirty-kilometre-thick slab of such rocks, but under high mountain ranges it is fifty or more kilometres thick. Continental crust is also present beneath most of the shallow seas of the world, such as the 200-metre-deep North Sea, which is in geological terms just a temporarily-flooded bit of the European continent.

The oceanic crust, which forms the floor of all the deep oceans of the world, is much thinner, only about eight to ten kilometres thick, but since the oceans cover a much greater proportion of the

Earth's surface than the continents – the proportion is roughly three to one – they are quantitatively just as significant. The rocks of the oceanic crust are different in many respects from the 'average' rocks of the continents: they are black, dense rocks, usually very fine-grained, contain much less silica (less than 50 per cent), and are remarkably uniform, even monotonous in appearance. These are the archetypal volcanic rocks, called *basalts*.

Both the oceanic and the continental crust are separated from the underlying mantle by a sort of boundary, or discontinuity, known after its Yugoslavian discoverer as the Mohorovicic discontinuity, or Moho for short. This discontinuity was recognized by studying the behaviour of shock-waves from earthquakes: above the Moho, shock waves travel relatively slowly; below it, in the denser rocks of the mantle, they travel much faster.

Now what happens in the mantle is extremely important, because it is in the mantle that we have to look for the *mechanism* behind Plate Tectonics. The rocks of the mantle are rather curious in one respect – they appear to have the properties of both liquids and solids. Where geologically instantaneous events such as earthquakes are concerned, they are rigid enough to transmit the shock waves, like any solid. But on a much longer time-scale, involving thousands of years, they behave differently and can 'flow' like a highly-viscous liquid, millions of times more viscous than even the stickiest treacle. In this respect the mantle rocks resemble pitch or brittle toffee, which will shatter at a sudden blow, but will bend easily if flexed slowly and continuously. Pitch, of course, gets progressively softer as it is heated, and similarly, since the rocks of the mantle are also at high temperatures – the temperature in the earth increases downwards at a rate of about 30°C per kilometre – they can also be thought of as being rather 'soft'. Accepting then that the material making up the mantle can behave as a viscous liquid, this raises an interesting possibility. If a body of liquid is at the same temperature throughout, it will remain still, unless someone comes along and stirs it up. But if the lower parts of the liquid are hotter than the upper parts, then it will be anything but still. The hottest parts of a liquid are also the least dense or 'lightest' and so they tend to rise upwards to float above the denser, cooler liquid. As the liquid ascends, though, it cools down and thus gets denser, so that it must sink again. A continuous cycle soon gets established, with hot liquid rising and cold descending – the effect can be seen in any hot liquid that has particles in it, even tea or coffee made with instant milk. The process is known as convection, and it is widely, but not universally, believed to work on a huge scale in the mantle. In a cup of tea, the particles whizz round at a great rate; in the mantle the flow is so slow that it would be barely perceptible over the course of a human lifetime.

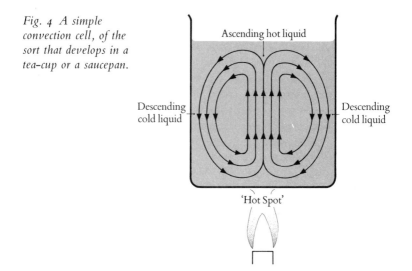

*Fig. 4 A simple convection cell, of the sort that develops in a tea-cup or a saucepan.*

Ascending hot liquid

Descending cold liquid

Descending cold liquid

'Hot Spot'

It was Arthur Holmes who first suggested that mantle convection currents might be responsible for continental movements, but he lacked any direct geophysical data that might have supported his views. An upwelling current of hot liquid, be it tea or mantle, carries a lot of heat with it, and this factor provided one of the starting points for the new Plate Tectonic ideas. It was found that the *heat flow*, or rate at which heat is moving upwards through

the Earth's crust, is several times higher along the Mid-Atlantic
Ridge than on the ocean floor on either side. This is where Hess
started in his attempt to explain the nature of global processes. He
suggested that beneath the volcanic Mid-Atlantic Ridge there was
an upwelling convective current of hot, partly-liquid rock in the
mantle and that as this column approached the surface it would
split, turning away from the ridge in two branches. Both branches
would move steadily outwards to form the oceanic crust, which,
as it got progressively further away from the ridge would rapidly
acquire a thin veneer of deep sea sediments (muds and clays,
mixed up with myriads of tiny shells from planktonic organisms).
Hess mistakenly thought that the oceanic crust consisted of altered
peridotite, the material of the mantle itself. It is now known,
however, that it is made up of basaltic rocks, derived indirectly
from peridotite, and erupted by volcanic action along the ridge
itself, building up the long submarine mountain range and giving
rise to the relatively few volcanoes which poke their heads above
sea level. Hess's outstanding contribution was the suggestion that
new oceanic crust is actually generated at a mid-ocean ridge, and
spreads out laterally away from it.

This suggestion, which was made in 1960, is at the root of all
that follows; we can label it the 'sea-floor spreading' hypothesis.
Right from the beginning, it had some obvious implications. Hess
thought that the spreading rate at the ocean ridge was of the order
of one centimetre per year. If this were true, and if oceanic crust
was being generated at all the oceanic ridges in the world at this
rate throughout geological history, then the entire present oceanic
crust could have been formed in a mere couple of hundred million
years, and therefore, without some other kind of process acting,
there would be a vast quantity of spare oceanic crust lying around.
(Remember that the age of the Earth is 4,600 million years.) It was
obvious that oceanic crust must be continually destroyed somewhere at a rate comparable with that of its creation at the oceanic
ridges in order to maintain a balance. Hess suggested that this took
place along the deep ocean trenches, such as the Chile–Peru
Trench, which runs parallel to the west coast of South America,

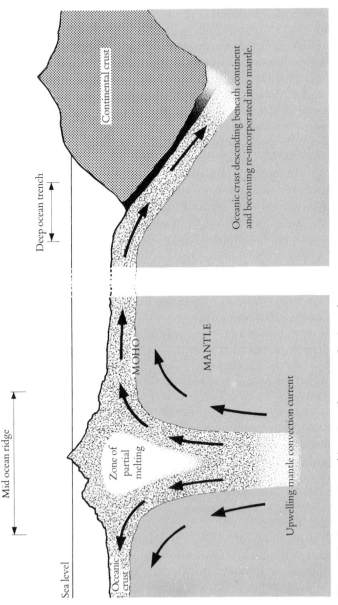

Fig. 5  *Hess's conception of how 'sea-floor spreading' works.*

and that the relatively 'cold' oceanic crust dived down beneath the continents in these zones, descending deep into the mantle to complete the convective cycle. Continental drift could therefore be easily explained by Hess's hypothesis, since the rocks of the mantle under the continents are identical to and continuous with the rocks of the mantle underlying the thin oceanic crust. The continents just drift around passively on the backs of the mantle convection cells, like great rafts, with the 'leading' edges of the rafts being dragged down and thickened where they encounter descending oceanic crust. The thickened edges of these rafts are of course the mountain chains such as the Andes.

A great deal of evidence from many different fields of research was required to turn Hess's 'sea–floor spreading' idea into a theory. Strangely enough, the most critical discovery had already been made, *before* Hess published his idea, but it was left to two other geologists, F. J. Vine and D. H. Matthews, to demonstrate three years later how this pre-existing evidence supported the new hypothesis. The evidence was of the way in which the rocks of the oceanic crust are magnetized; it's not the kind of thing that one comes across every day, so it will take a bit of explaining. Rocks may not seem initially to be particularly magnetic. They aren't on the whole, though some will affect the needle of a compass brought up near to them. All rocks, however, and especially basaltic rocks which contain a lot of iron minerals, are weakly magnetized, and this magnetism can be detected by sensitive instruments. The magnetism is built into the basalt when it is first formed, and it records the nature of the Earth's magnetic field *at the time of formation*. This record is retained permanently, so if a specimen of rock is put into the detecting instrument, and various careful measurements made, it is possible to find out what the Earth's magnetic field was like at the time when the basalt cooled from its original molten state.

We are all used to thinking of the Earth as some kind of large magnet, with two magnetic poles located quite near the geographic North and South Poles, so that the needle of a compass always lines up in the same direction. We are so sure of this that we go out confidently into the hills, or sail away in boats armed only with a magnetic compass, certain that it will always point in the same north–south direction, so we can judge our own direction of travel from it. Over the period of a man's life, small changes *are* in fact detectable – the magnetic poles wander very slowly around the geographic poles, so the direction of 'magnetic' north varies slightly from year to year. To all intents and purposes, though, magnetic north remains north. But if we were gods, and immortal, and could sit ourselves comfortably to watch the years slide by, with a magnetic compass conveniently to hand next to the ambrosia and nectar, we'd see something extraordinarily interesting. After about 100,000 years or so, the needle of the compass would abruptly become unstable and then swing round to face in the *opposite* direction, so that what was once compass north would become compass south, and vice versa. Nothing else would change, though, the north *geographic* pole wouldn't move, and if we were to go outside to check up, the sun would still rise and set in the same place, and the Pole Star would appear at night over the local gas works. All that would have happened is that for some reason the Earth's magnetic field would have reversed itself. If, after a stiff swig of nectar, we were to watch further developments, we'd find that in another 100,000 years or so, or even longer, exactly the same thing would happen again, and the compass would swing back suddenly to its original position. This process would continue indefinitely, with reversals taking place at intervals of as little as 100,000 years or as much as one million years, but with the overall result that the compass spent about as much time pointing in one direction as it did in the other.

No one yet knows quite why these reversals occur, but they were the keystone to Vine and Matthews's modification of Hess's 'sea-floor spreading' concept. Reversals have, so far as is known, been taking place throughout geological time, and the evidence of these reversals is stored up in the magnetic fabrics of the rocks of both the continents and the oceanic crust. A group of geophysicists who were working on the rocks of the floor of the north-east Pacific had discovered, before Hess's suggestion was published, that instead of a random pattern of reversals, such as were common on land, the oceanic crust in the Pacific exhibited a pattern of 'strip reversals'; the rocks in each strip were magnetized in one fixed direction, but the rocks in alternate, parallel strips were magnetized in the reverse direction, like this:

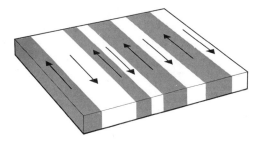

*Fig. 6 A hypothetical slab of oceanic crust, showing alternatively-magnetized strips.*

Hess did not appreciate the significance of these strip reversals, but Vine and Matthews did, and they suggested that while the 'sea-floor spreading' concept was basically right, it could be refined and that instead of the simple kind of gigantic conveyor belt that Hess had conceived, with oceanic crust being generated at the ridges and moving away in opposite directions, the situation was much more like that of a conveyor belt-cum-tape recorder. As the moving convection cell carries basaltic crust away from the ridge, slowly but continuously, the magnetic reversals taking place every few hundred thousand years or so leave their imprints on the newly-formed rocks emerging from the ridge; as every reversal occurs, so it is recorded in the formation of reversely-magnetized strips on each side of the ridge. Once a strip of new ocean floor has been formed, and acquired its magnetic recording, nothing further happens to it, but it continues to move away slowly from the ridge, at a rate of anything up to several centimetres per year.

Three implications followed immediately from Vine and Matthews's brilliantly original modification of sea-floor spreading: first, the 'strips' should always be parallel to the ridge axes; second, they should be symmetical about the ridge, so that the strips on one side are mirror images of those on the other; third, and most important, the rocks furthest away from the ridge should be *older* than those nearest to it. A great deal of effort was put into the collection of new data on the magnetic patterns of the ocean floors in the 1960s and this quickly demonstrated the correctness of the first two points: the strips certainly were parallel to the ridges, and symmetrical about them. One of the classic studies of this time was that of the Reykjanes ridge, part of the Mid-Atlantic Ridge, just south of Iceland. The map shows clearly how the magnetic pattern relates to the ridge:

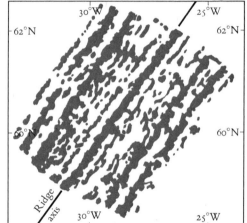

*Fig. 7 Magnetic strip reversals recorded over the Reykjanes ridge. The black areas of oceanic crust are magnetized in the opposite direction to the white areas.*

The strips of course are not complete, exact rectangles; that would be asking too much, but they obviously are strips, and obviously are symmetrical about the ridge axis – each black strip left of the axis can be matched with a similar black strip of equal width on the right of the axis, at the same distance from it.

The third implication, that the rocks furthest from the ridge should be the oldest, was less easy to test. However, in 1969, a large-scale American project, JOIDES (Joint Oceanographic Institutions Deep Earth Sampling) was able to confirm it, in the course of a programme of drilling into the deep ocean floors to sample the rocks and sediments there. Thirty bore-holes were drilled in the Atlantic at various carefully-selected sites, and in each hole the drill first passed through a thin surface layer of sediments into the basaltic rocks of the oceanic crust. The material obtained

*Fig. 8  This JOIDES map shows the ages of specimens collected from different points on the Atlantic Ocean floor; the specimens furthest from the ridge are the oldest, broadly speaking.*

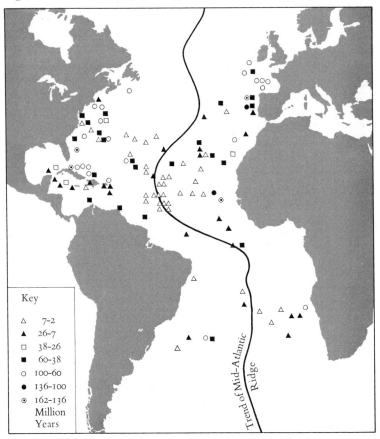

Key

| | |
|---|---|
| △ | 7-2 |
| ▲ | 26-7 |
| □ | 38-26 |
| ■ | 60-38 |
| ○ | 100-60 |
| ● | 136-100 |
| ◉ | 162-136 |
| | Million Years |

Trend of Mid-Atlantic Ridge

from the drill holes could then be dated, both by sophisticated radio-isotope methods, and by the more ordinary, down-to-earth method of examining the kinds of fossil organism present in the sediments. (Different fossils are characteristic of different periods in the Earth's history.) In splendid confirmation of Vine and Matthews's hypothesis, it was found that the age of each sample was proportional to its distance from the mid-ocean ridge. The bore-holes nearest the ridge gave ages below seven million years, while those furthest away gave ages of over 160 million years.

With this discovery the concept of sea-floor spreading was home and dry, and almost universally accepted. Many scientists saw at once its far-reaching implications and a whole spate of major papers were published in 1967 and 1968, which quite suddenly added up together to make a completely new way of looking at the Earth's main working parts: Plate Tectonics. It would probably be unfair to single out a single worker as the 'discoverer' of Plate Tectonics, but the term 'plates' was first used by an American, W. Jason Morgan, who was following up earlier work by J. Tuzo Wilson of Toronto University. Almost at the same time D. P. McKenzie of Cambridge and R. L. Parker of the Scripps Institution in America had come to much the same conclusions as Wilson and together these scientists were responsible for what they called the 'New Global Tectonics'. That term didn't last long, though, and 'Plate Tectonics' really came into being when scientists all over the world, such as Isacks, Oliver, Sykes, Le Pichon and Morgan (to name but a few), began to apply the new way of thinking to specific parts of the globe.

They demonstrated that the crust of the Earth can be divided into six large *plates*, and many smaller ones, and that *all* major crustal processes can be related to the relative movements between these plates. Thus, the oceanic ridges are sites of intense seismic activity: a huge number of earthquakes occur along and beneath them. Many thousands of earthquakes can be recorded along the ridges in any one year and a few of these are quite severe, but since they are generally a long way from anywhere, they don't hit the headlines. For us, though, they are important, because if one plotted a map to show the distribution of *all* earthquake centres in

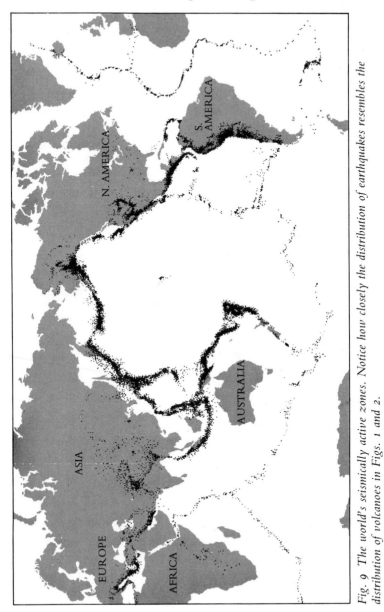

*Fig. 9 The world's seismically active zones. Notice how closely the distribution of earthquakes resembles the distribution of volcanoes in Figs. 1 and 2.*

the world for the last ten years, a large proportion of them would be scattered along the oceanic ridges. And the rest? Most would be congregated around the circum-Pacific 'Ring of Fire'. The earthquakes in these Pacific coastal areas, of course, are notorious, since they occur at sites beneath the continental crust, with all too familiar effects on human life.

These major linear belts of earthquake or seismic activity are used to divide the Earth up into major plates, each plate being bounded by *plate margins*. There are three types of plate margin, two of which we have already come across. The mid-ocean ridges where oceanic crust is being continuously created are known as *constructive plate margins*, while the deep ocean trenches which define the sites where the oceanic crust dives down again into the mantle are known as *destructive plate margins*. There is also a third type, called *conservative* or *passive* plate margins which are margins between plates at which nothing special happens – the two plates merely slide sideways past each other without fuss or bother. It would be quite impossible to discuss all the plates and sub-plates making up the Earth's crust in this book, and it wouldn't be very useful either, since some of them are extremely complex and not at all well understood. But to get over the main ideas, we will consider just two plates, and the margins between them: the East Pacific Plate and the South American–Atlantic Plate. We'll make a hypothetical traverse from Easter Island on the East Pacific Rise (an oceanic ridge, remember) right across South America as far as the Mid-Atlantic Ridge, so we'll be starting at one plate margin, crossing a second and ending up at a third, each of them, of course, marked by a major belt of seismic activity. Notice that there is *no* seismic zone along the east coast of South America, the continental crust merely sits passively on top of the mantle.

The East Pacific (or Nazca) Plate, between the East Pacific Rise and the west coast of South America, consists entirely of oceanic crust, but the other plate consists of *both* continental crust (South America) and oceanic crust (the bit of the South Atlantic Ocean floor between South America and the mid-Atlantic ridge). Easter Island, where the traverse starts, is entirely volcanic but it is really only an insignificant scrap of land in the vast Pacific. Geologically,

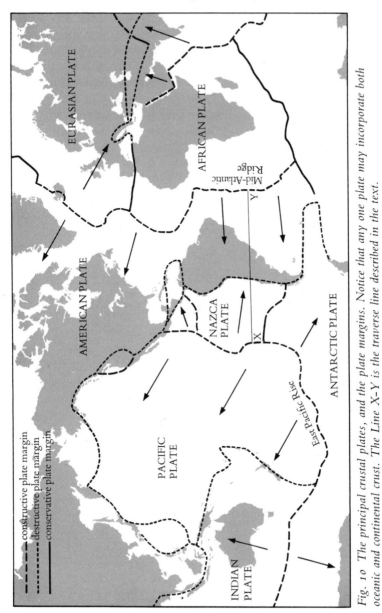

Fig. 10 *The principal crustal plates, and the plate margins. Notice that any one plate may incorporate both oceanic and continental crust. The Line X-Y is the traverse line described in the text.*

the most critical zone is the junction between the two plates, which is defined by two major physical features; the extreme depths of the Chile–Peru Trench, which runs along just off-shore of the continent, and the extreme heights of the Andes mountains, the crest line of which runs parallel to and 350 kilometres east of the Trench. There is a vertical difference of something like fifteen kilometres between the two extremities. Using sensitive earthquake-detecting instruments (seismographs or seismometers), it is possible to pin down quite precisely the sites where the shock waves originate in this region, and it can easily be shown that these sites are confined to a narrow belt which dips steeply down under the continental margin at about 60°, and which hits the surface just where the ocean is deepest, in the Chile–Peru Trench. These steeply-inclined belts or zones of earthquake sites are known

*Fig. 11  The sites at which earthquakes occur at the South American Plate margin. The scatter of dots reveals the well-defined 'Benioff zone', dipping steeply eastwards.*

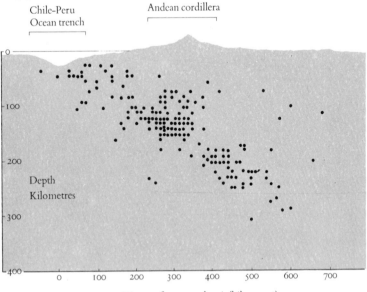

Distance from trench axis (kilometres)

now to exist all round the Pacific; they are called *Benioff zones*, after their discoverer, the seismologist Hugo Benioff. Now sea-floor spreading tells us that the oceanic crust of the Pacific is moving away from the East Pacific Rise *towards* South America. But South America itself is moving *away* from the Mid-Atlantic Ridge, since the Atlantic Ocean is widening steadily as new oceanic crust is generated at the ridge. So what happens when the two plates meet? A sort of steady-state continuous collision – and the site of the collision is marked by a major belt of active volcanism, the Andean part of the 'Ring of Fire'!

More fully, it looks as though what happens is this. The oceanic crust of the East Pacific Plate does collide with the continental mass of South America but instead of piling up in a heap, it ducks down, and dives under the continent; the site of the 'bend' being below the 7,500-metre-deep Chile–Peru Trench, while the zone of actual sliding contact between oceanic and continental crust is defined by the 60° dipping earthquake belt, the Benioff zone.

A colossal amount of energy is involved in the process of the two massive plates sliding over one another and most of the energy is manifested in the form of heat. Any two surfaces rubbing together produce frictional heat, such as a brake shoe pressing against a brake-drum. Along the Benioff zone so much heat is generated that some of the rocks of the oceanic plate and the lower part of the continental plate melt, and the molten material then moves upwards and away. To escape, it has to travel up through quite large thicknesses of continental crust, and a large proportion does not get very far; instead, it comes to rest and solidifies a few kilometres below the surface, forming enormous masses of igneous rock which have been forced or intruded into the crust and are known as *batholiths* (Greek origin, meaning something like deep stones). The rest of the melted material reaches the surface and is erupted as lava and ashes, building up the narrow chain of volcanoes that runs the whole way up the South American continent.

So Plate Tectonics, with its underlying concepts of constructive and destructive plate margins, explains very elegantly why volcanoes exist where they do, in distinct chains. So far, though, volcanoes have been discussed in rather general terms as though

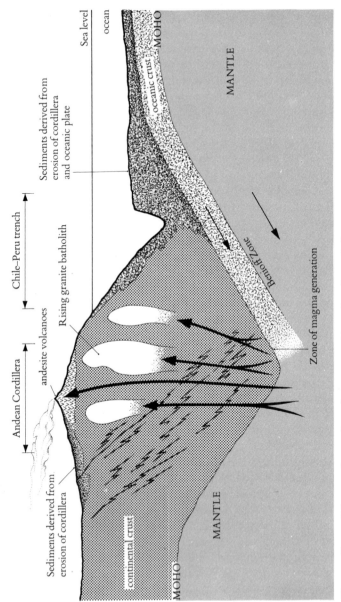

Sea level

ocean

MOHO

oceanic crust

MANTLE

Sediments derived from erosion of cordillera and oceanic plate

Benioff Zone

Chile–Peru trench

Rising granite batholith

Zone of magma generation

andesite volcanoes

Andean Cordillera

Sediments derived from erosion of cordillera

continental crust

MANTLE

MOHO

*Fig. 12 Some of the complex geological processes taking place beneath the Andean cordillera.*

the volcanoes of the constructive plate margins were identical to those of the destructive. This isn't the case at all, and to see why, one need only to look at the composition of the rocks involved.

Hawaii and Iceland are nearly as far apart as it is possible to get on Earth, but both are composed of basalts, and oceanic volcanoes everywhere in the world are composed of almost identical basalts. There are small variations in composition from one island to another, of course, but these are insignificant, and should not obscure the underlying fact that basalt constitutes a fundamental rock type, common to all parts of the Earth. Basalts form the entire oceanic crust of the Earth, and all of this basalt originates in the same way, from the melting of rocks in the upper part of the mantle, underneath the ocean ridges. These source rocks are the peridotites, and since geophysics tells us that the mantle consists of the same kind of material all over the world, it's clear that melting part of the mantle beneath Hawaii should produce the same kind of rocks as those produced by melting part of the mantle beneath Iceland.

The 'continental' volcanoes are a different kettle of fish. The lavas of which they are built appear to come from three separate source areas. Some comes directly from the upper mantle *above* the descending oceanic plate, some from partial melting of the oceanic plate itself, and some from the lower part of the continental crust. Some of the sea-floor sediments, muds, and oozes sitting on top of the oceanic plate also get melted.

The upshot of this is that, while melting of the rocks of the oceanic plate by itself might produce rocks similar to those of the oceanic volcanoes, when it gets melted at the Benioff zone, a great deal of other material is added, from the mantle (peridotitic) and from the continental crust (granitic). Thus the volcanic rocks formed are drastically different from their oceanic counterparts. They are the *andesites*, named after the Andes where they make up almost all of the major volcanoes. Andesites come half-way between basalts and granites in almost every property: silica content, density, colour and so on, so they are known as *intermediate* rocks. A typical andesite is light grey in colour, contains about 60 per cent of silica ($S_iO_2$) and has a conspicuous number of small white crystals, a few millimetres across, scattered throughout a fine-grained homogeneous matrix. These small crystals are known as *phenocrysts* and are one of the most characteristic features of andesites.

To sum up, remember that basalts are produced at constructive plate margins (oceanic ridges) and andesites at destructive margins (the 'Ring of Fire' type). The two rocks are different in chemical composition, and this difference manifests itself in a number of intriguing ways; ways which a fair part of this book will be devoted to exploring.

## Rift valleys, continental collisions and submarine fractures

Before leaving it, a few words on how Plate Tectonics explains three other features of the Earth's global framework: first, the volcanoes which *don't* occur in either of the two major kinds of zone that have deen discussed so far; second, what happens where two continental plates come together, as opposed to a continental or oceanic plate margin; and thirdly, the major faults and fractures which disrupt the neat linear trends of the ocean ridges and what these imply.

Much the most important area where volcanoes are *not* related to either constructive or destructive plate margins is Africa. Some of the African volcanoes are quite well-known – Kilimanjaro and Mount Kenya are probably most famous, while the Ngorongoro crater is probably better-known as a wildlife sanctuary than as an extinct volcano. These three, and a whole host of less well-known volcanoes are not just randomly distributed round Africa; they are intimately related to the East African *rift system*, which can be traced for thousands of kilometres up Africa, into Ethiopia, and even into the Red Sea. A rift is a long, narrow valley, with straight sides formed by geological faults, the bottom of the valley having been dropped down along these faults, relative to the country on either side.

It's the presence of these bounding faults which gives the rifts

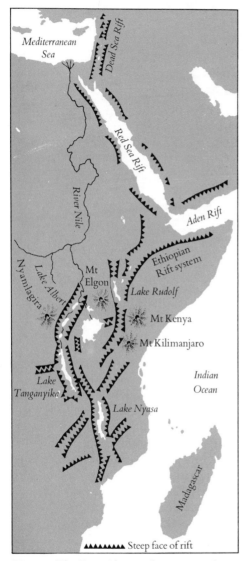

Fig. 13 *The East African rift system, and some of the important volcanoes.*

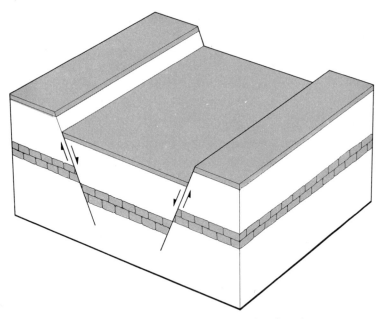

*Fig. 14  A simple rift valley. Most are more complex than this.*

their very distinctive linear character and it explains why the coasts of the Red Sea are so conspicuously straight and parallel – it too is part of a rift system. Volcanoes are dotted at intervals along the East African rift system, usually in areas where the surface of the surrounding countryside is elevated into a kind of dome, with the centre of the rift valley often in the highest part of the dome. The rift valleys are very important structures, and although the valleys themselves are not particularly deep – only a thousand metres at most – it is generally considered that they reflect deeper level structures which probably extend down as far as the mantle. The volcanic rocks erupted by the rift valley volcanoes are also distinctive. Most of them are basaltic, but many contain much more sodium and potassium than the 'ordinary' basalts of the oceanic volcanoes, so they are known as *alkali basalts*. (Similar alkali basalts do in fact occur on oceanic volcanoes, but only in small amounts.) One of the volcanoes on the Tanzanian part of the rift system, Oldonyo Lengai, is thoroughly odd in that it is so alkaline that it erupts lavas which are more like washing soda (sodium carbonate) than respectable rocks. So characteristic are alkaline volcanic rocks of the rift valleys that for a long time they were summed up as a whole with a convenient label such as 'rift valley alkaline volcanics', and our understanding of them did not advance much further, until the ideas of Plate Tectonics and sea-floor spreading began to seep through, to throw light on what this distinctive group of volcanic rocks was doing in the middle of Africa.

One of the most interesting discoveries to emerge after the introduction of these concepts was that the Red Sea was in fact not a sea at all, but an ocean! More seriously, since the Red Sea is so narrow, one might be justified in thinking that it represents a strip of continent that has been simply dropped down below sea level, and that the sea has flowed in to fill the trough produced. Oceanographic work, however, showed that there was much more to it than this – the Red Sea is *not* floored throughout by continental material, but in part by basaltic rocks identical with those of the 'ordinary' ocean floors. It immediately became clear that the Red Sea is a kind of 'proto-ocean' – although no mid-ocean ridge has yet developed, oceanic crust *is* being generated somewhere beneath the Red Sea, and, by implication, the Red Sea is widening, with Africa and Arabia moving steadily further apart. This is just the kind of situation which may have prevailed about 200 million years ago when Africa and South America were beginning to split up, and the Atlantic Ocean was only a long, sinuous, ribbon-like sea separating the two.

If this *is* the case, and there is still plenty of argument about it, then Mts Kenya, Kilimanjaro and all the rest immediately fall into place. Before the Red Sea became an ocean, it probably started off as a rift valley, along which a lot of volcanic activity took place for tens of millions of years, before splitting apart some twenty million years ago. Thus the present East African rift system, along which volcanism has also been going on for tens of millions of years, may mark the site of a great new split across

Africa, which would produce two new continents, separated by a new ocean. One of these new continents would be very large, consisting of most of west and north Africa; the other would be relatively small, consisting only of eastern and south-eastern Africa. The latest thinking, however, is that this may not happen. The Atlantic appears to be widening so rapidly that, instead of rifting taking place to form a new ocean, Africa is being pushed up so hard against Arabia that the Red Sea may get closed up once more!

Europe has its own rift system, and its own volcanoes, though these are not nearly so impressive as the great African structures. The valley of the river Rhine is in part a rift valley, and there are some small volcanoes associated with it, particularly in the Eiffel area of Germany. In the centre of France there is another small cluster of volcanoes in the Auvergne area, which may occupy a site where rifting made a half-hearted attempt to get started, but failed dismally. Both the French and German volcanic provinces have been active relatively recently, although there have been no eruptions in historic times.

The massive programme of oil exploration drilling in the North Sea has revealed a much bigger, though very much older, rift valley system, with at least one major volcanic centre, located off the coast of Scotland. This discovery proved to be something of an embarrassment to the oil companies, since volcanic rocks are about the least promising rocks in which to find oil. From a geologist's point of view, though, the volcanic rocks are fascinating since they show that, when the Atlantic Ocean was beginning to widen in Jurassic times, about 170 million years ago, Europe was rifted in the same way that Africa is at the present day, with a complex, branching rift valley running for hundreds of kilometres beneath the present North Sea, extending as far as Norway, while the volcanic rocks off Scotland must once have looked very much like the great East African volcanoes such as Mt Kenya.

Apart from volcanoes formed along rift valleys, there are also a few which occur right in the middle of plates, far away from any plate margin. Strangely, these 'mid-plate' volcanoes can occur either in continental *or* oceanic plates. In Africa the isolated mountain ranges in the central Sahara, such as the Tibesti, Hoggar and Jebel Marra, are all major mid-plate volcanic complexes, with some of the volcanoes reaching over 3,000 metres in height. Without doubt the most famous examples of mid-plate volcanoes are those of the Hawaiian Islands, in the middle of the Pacific Ocean.

It is not easy to understand why these volcanoes exist; they don't fit in with the Plate Tectonic theory. One of the most popular ideas to account for them maintains that these isolated volcanoes are sitting above 'hot spots' in the mantle, sites where a rising plume of hot material is moving upwards through the mantle, perhaps originating deep down near the core. The plume effectively burns a hole through the overlying crustal plate (oceanic or continental) and a volcano results. This idea has been strongly criticized, but it does find some support from the intriguing fact that some mid-plate volcanoes, particularly those of Hawaii, are arranged in chains, with the youngest at one end and the oldest at the other. This, the 'hot spot' supporters argue, is where the oceanic plate drifted over a stationary mantle hot spot, so that, instead of a hole, a sort of long thin slot was burned through the oceanic plate!

Let us consider now what happens when continental plates collide. It has been shown that Plate Tectonics provides an acceptable explanation for the process of continental drift, but so far little mention has been made of the arrangement of the continents before drifting occurred. The general consensus is that before the major episode of drifting took place the continents were joined up in a great mass clustered around the South Pole, and, more important for our present purpose, the Indian sub-continent was not attached to the main mass of Asia – it's generally thought that it was tucked in neatly between Africa and Antarctica while Asia was somewhere vaguely off to the north.

When continental drift was initiated, about 200 million years ago, and the huge ancestral continent split up, India began to move rapidly northwards and ultimately piled up into the Asian mass,

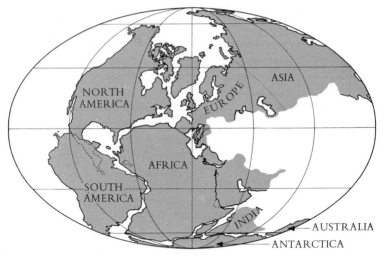

*Fig. 15  One possible arrangement of the continents as they may have been 200 million years ago, before they started sliding around.*

about sixty million years ago. At about the same time Africa closed up on Europe, narrowing the gap of sea between the two to the width of the present Mediterranean. The result of this mammoth collision between continents was the Alpine–Himalayan mountain belt. This runs from the Pyrenees, through the Alps proper, through the Middle East into the Himalayas, and eventually into the sea in the Far East. In its many thousands of kilometres the range contains a great wealth of different kinds of rocks and geological structures, but it is more interesting for what it does *not* contain: in all its immense length there is not a single volcano actually *within* the mountain range. In the Mediterranean, there are some famous volcanoes, such as Vesuvius, Stromboli and Etna which lie well to the *south* of the Alpine mountain chain. Although the detailed geology of the Mediterranean is very complex, these volcanoes can be fitted into a Plate Tectonic setting, since when the African continent began closing up on Europe, the oceanic crust which had floored the original, much wider

Mediterranean was forced down beneath the continental crust of Europe, and thus a destructive plate margin was formed. This plate margin is more complex than the Andean one, where the volcanoes are located along the highest parts of the mountain range, but it can be traced in a series of arcs through the Italian and Greek islands into Asia Minor.

The situation in the Himalayas is rather more involved. There must once have been oceanic crust between India and Asia, but only recently has evidence been found that a simple destructive plate margin once existed parallel to the line of the present mountain chain along which the oceanic crust was consumed. It seems that there was once a chain of active volcanoes there, but that these became extinct millions of years ago, and have since been eroded away, so that little trace remains. But whatever happened in the past, the processes operating at the present day at the continental plate boundary between India and Asia are quite different from the processes operating where oceanic and continental plates come together. The most important difference in fact is that beneath the Himalayas there is not a great slab of oceanic material diving down into the mantle, and no simple Benioff zone, as there is beneath the Andes. It is something of a problem to determine exactly what *is* going on beneath the Himalayas, but we will leave that problem severely alone, because what we are going to look at next raises some even more difficult ones!

So far, oceanic ridges have been discussed quite glibly, as if they

*Fig. 16  Transform faults along the Mid-Atlantic Ridge.*

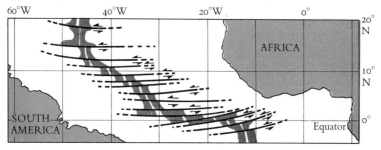

were simple continuous linear features. In fact they're not, they are broken up into dozens of smaller segments by major fractures which run almost at right angles across them.

These fractures clearly off-set the axes of the ridges, and they are known as *transform faults*. Now an ordinary geological fault would do just the same thing if it cut across a marker band of some kind. If movement on the fault were to continue, so that the two sides were moving past one another, then clearly the off-set of the marker band would steadily increase with time. This is where transform faults are different; although 'the two sides are constantly moving past one another, the two halves of the ridge axis on either side of the fault maintain the same off-set. This strange situation arises because in a transform fault such as the one in the diagram, oceanic crust on both sides is moving in the same direction (to the left) and at the same rate, at point A; in *opposite* directions between A and B; and in the *same* direction (to the right) and at the same rate again at B. So though there is continuous movement on the fault between A and B, the relative positions of the two ridge axes remain unaffected.

*Fig. 17　A comparison between an 'ordinary' fault and a transform fault.*

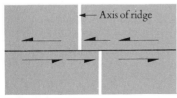

Ordinary fault initially

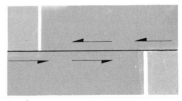

At a later stage

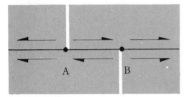

Transform fault

Transform faults may seem a bit obscure, but they are important. Remember that Hess's original suggestion was that upwelling convection cells in the mantle reached the surface at the mid-ocean ridge. But since pieces of oceanic crust are sliding past one another in opposite directions along transform faults this implies that the same must be happening in the convection cells underneath. This in turn would mean that the convection cells would have to be extraordinarily narrow compared to their length, and throws some doubt on the validity of convection cells as the driving mechanism for Plate Tectonics. This is a bit unfortunate since it undermines some of our thinking about how Plate Tectonics works. There's more to come, though. Imagine (to provide a fixed reference point) that Africa was firmly locked in its present position, unable to go drifting around the globe. Now Africa is surrounded on both sides by mid-ocean ridges, one in the Atlantic and one in the Indian Ocean, and as we have seen, South America is moving away from Africa and the Atlantic is widening. But since we've fixed Africa in place, this means that the Mid-Atlantic Ridge must also be migrating *away* from Africa. Of course, if we 'fixed' the Mid-Atlantic Ridge instead of Africa, and used that as our reference point then nothing would seem amiss. But don't forget that Africa then would be moving away from the Mid-Atlantic Ridge, and *towards* the Indian Ocean ridge – which would have to migrate away from Africa even faster to keep its distance. The point about all this is that to postulate the migration of ridges is also to postulate the migration of the convection cells beneath them, and there is no obvious reason why convection cells deep in the mantle should move about in any regular fashion.

Worse still, recent geophysical work has shown that only one layer in the mantle is likely to be fluid enough to contain moving convection cells. This layer, known as the Low Velocity Zone or L.V.Z. (because the velocity of seismic waves in it is lower than in any other part of the mantle) means that the diagram of the Earth's structure that we started off with is a little over-simplified. A better version would be:

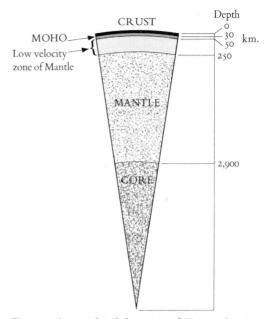

*Fig. 18  A more detailed version of Fig. 3, showing the Low Velocity Zone in the mantle.*

Now although the L.V.Z. is about 150 kilometres thick, that's still not very much compared with the total thickness of the mantle, nearly 3,000 kilometres. So if convection cells are confined to this one layer, they must be rather improbably thin compared with the size of the plates which they are thought to transport.

It's clear, then, that there are some substantial objections to the relatively straightforward concept first put forward by Hess, that mantle convection cells provide the driving mechanism for sea-floor spreading. In fact, as far as we know at the moment, there can be no *simple* relationship between the movements of the crustal plates and convection cells in the mantle, but so far no one has come up with any better ideas, so we will have to leave this problem rather in the air, and go on to look at volcanoes themselves, since these are a good deal easier to get at than mantle convection cells. But don't forget in reading the following chapters that while we still have a great deal to learn about *how* Plate Tectonics works, it certainly *does*.

## *Chapter 2* Three classic eruptions

In the few thousand years that civilized man has lived on Earth, there has been an extremely large number of volcanic eruptions. Of this number the great majority went unrecorded, probably even unobserved, but a very few made such an impact on human affairs that they have become significant historical events, and have been described and discussed in the minutest detail. The eruption which probably had the most far reaching effect on civilization was that of Santorin (Thera) in the Aegean, in about 1470 B.C. This abruptly extinguished the highly-developed Minoan culture centred on Crete, and, because the eruption caused the submergence beneath the sea of a large part of the island of Santorin, it may have given rise to the age-old legends of Atlantis, the 'lost' or 'drowned' continent. Most of the evidence for these legends is drawn from some rather vague references by the Greek historian Plato, in particular a passage in his *Timaeus*: 'But at a later time there occurred portentous earthquakes and floods, and one grievous day and night befell them when the whole body . . . of warriors was swallowed up by the earth, and the island of Atlantis in like manner was swallowed up by the sea and vanished.'

Although this written account is extremely tenuous, patient archaeological excavations that have been going on for many years on Santorin are beginning to reveal a story to rival that of Pompeii. The eruption of the volcano buried a town, Akrotiri, which is thought to have had a population originally of about 30,000. The eruption itself was preceded by at least two major earthquakes, which seem to have scared off the inhabitants, since they stripped the town of all movable objects and fled – no bodies have been found in the ruins. When it came, the eruption was of massive proportions and deposited a great thickness of ash which completely buried the town, and it set off great tidal waves which may have been responsible for the termination of the Minoan civilization by ravaging the coastal towns all around Crete. The excavations on Santorin are far from complete, but already some of the wall paintings that have been recovered from the ruins and preserved in the museum at Athens have been ranked as amongst the most important artistic discoveries of the century.

Since there still remains so much more archaeological work to do on Santorin, three more completely documented eruptions will be described in this chapter. These can be regarded as classics of their kind, and are important not only because of their intrinsic interest as dramatic events in history, but also because they illustrate some of the facets of volcanic eruptions which will be discussed in later chapters. The three volcanoes concerned are about as widely scattered around the world as possible – Vesuvius in the Mediterranean, Krakatoa in Indonesia, and Mt Pelée in the Caribbean. The latter two are simple destructive plate margin volcanoes, but the Plate Tectonic setting of Vesuvius is a bit complex.

## Vesuvius, A.D. 79

On 5 February A.D. 62 a severe earthquake shook the area round what is now Naples, on the west coast of Italy. In Roman times, of course, Naples and its sprawling suburbs did not exist, but clustered around the shores of the bay of Naples there were many small, thriving towns and ports.

Two of them, Pompeii and Herculaneum, which were located on the lower flanks of Vesuvius, were particularly badly shaken by the shocks, and some damage was done, but the townspeople were not especially alarmed. They simply rebuilt the fallen walls, and carried on with their normal efficient and highly-organized lives; they did not associate the earthquake with Vesuvius, and there was no particular reason why they should. Although they

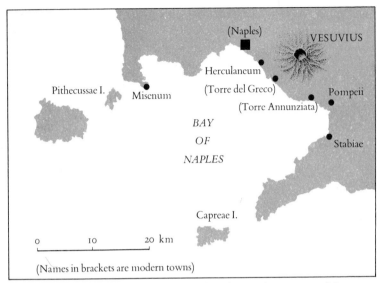

*Fig. 19  The principal towns mentioned by Pliny in his account of the A.D. 79 eruption. The names of modern towns are shown in brackets.*

knew that it *was* a volcano, it had been dormant for centuries, and they had no records whatever of any eruptions. So peaceful had the volcano been, in fact, that its fertile soils were extensively cultivated, vineyards flourished on favoured sunny slopes, and the people living on and around the volcano were enjoying the prosperity and security of the Roman empire at its height. The earthquake, of course, was an expensive nuisance, but earthquakes had never been particularly rare events in Italy, so little significance was attached to it. During the next sixteen years minor earthquakes continued to shake the area spasmodically. We now know that major eruptions are commonly preceded by seismic activity, and these shocks would have provided ample warning of the forthcoming eruption, had anyone been aware of their significance. No one was, however, and life went on normally until the very last moment. On 24 August A.D. 79, with all its preliminary stirrings ignored, Vesuvius burst into life, and one of the most momentous eruptions in history commenced. It lasted two days. At the end of it, both Pompeii and Herculaneum had been obliterated, and thousands of people killed.

One of those to die was a naturalist and an Admiral in the Roman Navy, Caius Plinius or Pliny the Elder, who was a much-respected man and widely-known in his own time. By one of the ironies of history, it was the death of this great man that led to our having an extraordinarily vivid, accurate eye-witness account of the events of 1,900 years ago. Because Pliny the Elder had been so widely-esteemed, the historian Tacitus was anxious to find out more about the circumstances of his death, and about the eruption in general, so he asked Pliny's nephew, who was seventeen at the time and survived the eruption, to provide him with details of what had happened. Pliny the Younger's account took the form of two letters to Tacitus, in which he described the fate that befell his uncle, and how he and his mother had fared. These letters are particularly valuable to us because Pliny was clearly aware of the need to describe objectively what he had experienced, and to resist the temptation to exaggerate. As he wrote himself, *'Nec defuerunt qui fictis mentionisque terroribus vera pericula augerunt.'*★ Well, of course, there always are! The following account is closely based on Pliny's letters.

On the morning of 24 August (the ninth day before the kalends of September) when the various Plinys were all in Misenum, a small town across the bay of Naples from Vesuvius, a curious large cloud was seen in the sky over the volcano. At first it looked harmless enough, and did not even seem to be coming from the mountain. It grew rapidly, however, soon dispelling all doubts. Rising initially in a vertical plume for many thousands of metres, and then spreading out laterally in the upper atmosphere, it took on a shape rather like that of a pine tree, with a trunk and branches. The elder Pliny was full of curiosity at first, and planned to sail across in his galley for a closer look, but his nephew was not so keen on the idea, and turned down his uncle's invitation to go

★ 'There were people, too, who added to the real perils by inventing fictitious dangers.'

along as well, pleading pressure of work. Before he had even set off, however, Pliny the Elder received urgent requests for help from people living nearer the volcano, so his trip which had been intended as something of a scientific investigation rapidly became a rescue mission. Pliny intended to try and evacuate people living on the coast immediately beneath the volcano, in the area which is now Torre del Greco, but as his galley approached the coast it was showered with hot ashes and sizeable lumps of pumice from the volcano. The shore was already becoming inaccessible as piles of ash accumulated, so he was forced to abandon his attempt, and turned to the south, running before the wind to escape from the increasingly heavy rain of ashes. He landed eventually at Stabiae (near the present Castellammare), where things were still fairly tolerable, and there he encountered a friend of his, one Pomponianus, who was making frantic preparations to escape, loading his possessions on to ships and fretting for a favourable wind so that he could put to sea. Full of confidence, Pliny tried to calm down the overwrought Pomponianus, and to demonstrate his own unconcern, went off to freshen up in the local baths, and subsequently sat down to eat a hearty meal.

3. *The present Vesuvius, from Castellammare (Stabiae). The profile of the volcano has changed greatly since A.D. 79; the low peak on the right is part of the crater wall produced by that eruption. The prominent central cone has grown subsequently.*

As night fell on Stabiae, Vesuvius presented an awesome sight, with the oppressively heavy ash cloud above it lit up in a baleful red glare from the many fires that had been started by the rain of hot ash. Remarkably, Pliny slept calmly during the early part of the night, although ashes had begun to pile up outside the house, but he eventually awoke as the situation deteriorated. Pomponianus and his companions were badly worried both by the ash-fall, and by the frequent tremors which were now shaking the house. After a discussion, they decided that their best hope for safety would lie in leaving the house, making for the shore and trying to get away in a ship. Tying pillows to their heads with towels to protect themselves from the larger falling lumps, they set off. It was totally dark, blacker and denser than the darkest night – even after dawn should have come – as the thick cloud of ash hung over them, cutting off the light from the sun. Carrying torches to light their way, they all reached the shore safely, but to their dismay found the wind still unfavourable, and the sea too rough to allow them to get away. At this point apparently, Pliny became unwell; he lay down on a cloth spread out for him and twice asked for water to drink. Later on, when wafts of sulphurous fumes from the volcano were making things even more unpleasant, most of the party that were with him fled. He rose, tried to follow them, but immediately fell dead. His contemporaries thought that he had been poisoned by the volcanic gases, since when his body was found three days later it was completely undamaged, looking more like that of a sleeping man than a dead one. It's now thought unlikely that volcanic gases were responsible since Stabiae was so far from the volcano, and all of his companions survived. It's more likely that Pliny, who was a corpulent man, died from a heart attack brought on by the nervous strain of the eruption.

On the morning when Pliny the Elder died in Stabiae, things were becoming pretty bad for Pliny the Younger and his mother at Misenum, on the other side of the Bay of Naples. Frequent tremors were shaking the house that they were in, and there too a dense pall of dust and ash from the volcano hung over them blocking out the sun, so that the light was faint and uncertain.

They decided for safety's sake to leave the town and set off in chariots, with a large crowd of panic-stricken fellow-refugees jostling and harassing them. They stopped in open country just outside the town, clear of danger from the collapsing buildings, but found that tremors were still so frequent that their chariots were constantly on the move, despite having their wheels chocked with stones. Overhead, lightning flickered frequently as the static electricity accumulating in the ash cloud discharged. At one point, they saw the sea receding from the near-by beaches; sucked away and apparently forced back by the earthquakes, so that quantities of sea creatures were left stranded. Ash began to sift down round them, lightly at first, adding to the horror of the situation. Conditions were not so bad, however, that Pliny and his mother could not have got well away from the town into a safer region, but they were reluctant to leave because they were worried and uncertain about the fate of the elder Pliny. They remained, therefore, on the outskirts of the town, until, terrified of being crushed by the mob, they decided to seek refuge in the open fields, but they had hardly agreed on this when fresh ash clouds, denser than ever, overwhelmed them and brought total darkness. The darkness was so complete that Pliny compared it with a sealed room in which the lamp had been put out. It was infinitely more unnerving than that though, for they were not in a sealed room but out in the open, with the air rent with cries from the crowd: screams of naked terror and prayers for deliverance. The ash fall became heavier, piling up around them, so that they had periodically to shake themselves clear of it, to prevent themselves being buried.

This living nightmare lasted for many hours until a sickly daylight showed again and the sun could be seen once more through the haze of dust. Peace returned, and the dazed survivors were able to collect themselves, find their friends, and look about. Great changes had been wrought by the eruption. Where once the smooth cone of Vesuvius had risen, only a shattered stump now remained; where once there had been fields and vineyards and all the normal clutter of the countryside there now stretched a silent grey carpet of ash, mantling everything like a thick, dirty snow-fall. Amidst it all, not a bird or insect stirred.

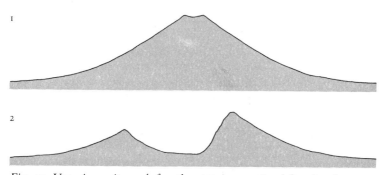

*Fig. 20  Vesuvius as it was before the* A.D. 79 *eruption (above) and afterwards (below).*

Pliny's account naturally didn't go into the details of the mechanics of the eruption, but his account is so illuminating that it is quite clear what happened, and similar eruptions, blasting large volumes of pumiceous ash into the air are still called *Plinian* eruptions. It was the heavy fall of ash from the eruption which brought an abrupt end to the town of Pompeii. It almost disappeared under a carpet of pumice over three metres deep, so that only the upper parts of some tall buildings emerged above it. With most of its inhabitants either dead or financially ruined by the eruption, there was no hope at all of salvaging the buried town, and it was abandoned. So completely was it abandoned that with the passage of time, and the weathering away of what little remained of it, its location was forgotten, although the facts of its existence and its fate were widely known. Centuries passed. The Roman empire declined and fell, the Dark Ages came and went, new peoples settled round Vesuvius, and ultimately new towns began to spring up. In 1595, some remains of the city came to light during excavation work for a new aqueduct – a few coins, and some fragments of marble tablets containing inscriptions referring to Pompeii. In the seventeenth and eighteenth centuries, when noble families all over Europe were becoming increasingly art-conscious in the wake of the Renaissance and anxious to fill their mansions and palaces with pieces of classical statuary and other antiquities, the remains of Pompeii were ravaged haphazardly, with innumerable random pits being dug in the hope of turning up items of value, particularly small carved figures, vases and pieces of jewellery. There was no pretence of archaeological intentions – the subject hadn't evolved by then – Pompeii simply acted as a large open pit mine for works of art. (Sir William Hamilton, Britain's envoy to Naples, was once deeply involved in this pillaging, giving most of his acquisitions to his wife, Emma, better-known as Nelson's mistress.) Herculaneum suffered equally badly, except that there underground shafts and tunnels had to be driven to get at the antiquities.

Things began to improve in the nineteenth century, however, when more coordinated methods were employed, and for the first time, digging began to be directed at finding out about Pompeii, rather than making a profit. It has been said, in fact, that systematic archaeology was born in the ruins of Pompeii. Although the excavations are not yet wholly complete, many hectares of the town have now been revealed to the light of day, and it is now possible to stroll along the abandoned streets once more with the remains of shops, houses and villas on either side. The general impression is rather eerie, but it is more reminiscent of a Second World War bombed city than of one abandoned nearly 2,000 years ago. Judging by the size of the town, it probably had a population of about 20,000 in A.D. 79. Many of these people were able to escape before the town was overwhelmed, but about 2,000 died; some because they elected to remain in what they thought was the safety of their houses, some because they left their escape until it was too late, some because they were too burdened down with prized possessions to move quickly enough, and some because they were just plain unlucky.

It's quite clear that the eruption was totally unexpected. The normal business life of the town continued right up to the last moment and in some houses food was laid out for meals that were never eaten. Many corpses, or rather fossils of corpses, were found by the excavators in the ash. After death the bodies of the victims of the eruption were rapidly buried by the accumulating ash, and rain falling on this ash soon after the eruption cemented it into a fairly hard mass before the flesh of the corpses had decayed. The ash swelled slightly as a result of the wetting and set hard round the corpses, making perfect natural moulds of them, and in some cases preserving even the imprint of clothing and the details of facial expressions. These moulds were found as holes in the ash by the nineteenth-century excavators, and they discovered that by pouring in a setting compound such as plaster of Paris they could obtain a complete three-dimensional cast of the original corpse. Many hundreds of casts of these human fossils have since been made, and from them we can learn a good deal about the last appalling hours in the life of Pompeii.

A few of the victims who sought refuge in their houses were killed when the weight of accumulating ash caused the roofs to collapse, but most were suffocated by the choking sulphurous

4. *One of the streets of Pompeii. The large blocks acted as stepping stones, so that the citizens could cross the road without treading in the ordure left by the many mules and horses pulling carts through the streets.*

5. *The forum of Pompeii. The profile of Vesuvius is dimly visible in the background industrial haze.*

fumes of the ash cloud. The plaster casts demonstrate this with unpleasant clarity; in many of them the hands are still pressed to the mouth, preserving the last hopeless efforts to breathe. Those who died in the streets attempting to get away suffered the same agonizing fate and were stifled by the fumes. The many casts all tell the same sad story. One of the most pathetic is that of a pet

6. *One of the human victims of the eruption.*

dog, which died still chained to a post. It survived for quite a long time, until the accumulating ash had built up to such a thickness that its chain would no longer allow it to keep above the ash, and it died, its dreadful last moments clearly visible in its taut body, arched back and straining neck.

7. *The dog.*

Many of the human victims clearly left their homes feeling full of optimism, carrying bags of gold, pieces of jewellery and other valued objects, which they refused to abandon even at the point of death. They died still clutching them. At least one citizen died through coming *back* into the town after a great thickness of ash had accumulated, and presumably during a lull in the eruption,

either to loot or to rescue his own little hoard of gold. So great is
the lure of material possessions!

Pompeii was not the only town to suffer from the rain of
pumice and ash; the fall-out in fact covered an area of hundreds of
square kilometres and several other Roman settlements, but
Pompeii was particularly badly hit because it was so close to the
volcano and was down-wind of it, so that the ash-laden eruption
cloud was carried towards the town by the prevailing wind.
Neighbouring Herculaneum suffered quite differently. It was upwind of the volcano, so it escaped the worst of the thick ash-fall
that Pompeii experienced, and almost all the population seem to
have escaped unharmed – not more than thirty skeletons have
been found. The main difference, though, was that while Pompeii
was obliterated by the steady accumulation of ashes over a long
period, perhaps as much as two days, Herculaneum was overwhelmed in a matter of minutes, possibly well after the eruption
proper had ceased.

Great thicknesses of pumice and ash had piled up on the slopes
of Vesuvius above Herculaneum, and this loose material very
rapidly became saturated by torrential rainstorms which may have
been triggered by the eruption cloud itself: the dust particles
acting as nuclei on which water vapour could condense to form
droplets. The waterlogged heaps of wet muck soon became unstable and eventually began to slide downwards, quite suddenly
becoming semi-liquid slurries or mudflows, which swept down
the sides of the volcano, gathering speed and more and more
material the whole time. Some of these mudflows rushed through
Herculaneum and engulfed it completely; crushing some buildings and smothering the rest twenty metres deep in a slowly con-
solidating welter of mud, pumice, boulders and debris. So
thoroughly buried was Herculaneum that a new town, Resina,
has been built right on top of the old. The compacted mudflow
presents a much more serious problem to archaeologists than the
relatively soft pumice of Pompeii, and this coupled with the awk-
ward presence of the new town on top of it makes it unlikely that
it will ever be completely excavated. In some respects, however,
Herculaneum is even better-preserved than Pompeii, although it

did not escape the attentions of the treasure seekers of the seventeenth and eighteenth centuries, and it has furnished an even greater wealth of detail than Pompeii on the day-to-day life of a flourishing Roman town.

The social and historical value of both Herculaneum and Pompeii are well known and need not detain us here. The ash-fall which buried Pompeii and the mudflow which covered Herculaneum, however, are first-class examples of two major kinds of volcanic phenomena, which have been repeated scores of times on different volcanoes in different parts of the world and we will be following them up more closely when we come to a detailed consideration of the mechanisms of eruptions.

## Krakatoa, 1883

The Sunda Straits, between the Indonesian islands of Java and Sumatra, are one of the great sea lanes of the world. Even in the nineteenth century, many hundreds of vessels passed through the Straits each year, most of·them small coasting ships but also a good many larger vessels trading between Europe and the East Indies (Java and Sumatra were at that time prosperous Dutch colonies). The Straits, which are only twenty-four kilometres across at their narrowest point, are not particularly deep, averaging about 200 metres, and there are a number of islands dotted about them. Approximately thirty-two kilometres west of the narrowest point of the Straits there lay a small group of rather oddly-named islands: Krakatoa, Verlaten Island, Lang Island and – oddest of all – Polish Hat. Most of the coastal details of these islands were fairly well known to the hydrographers of both the British and Dutch navies, but little was known about their inland geography. The largest of them, Krakatoa, was known to be about nine kilometres across from north to south and the British Admiralty charts showed it to consist of several volcanic cones arranged roughly in a line. At the southern end of the line was a particularly prominent, fresh-looking cone, 798 metres high, known by its Javanese name of Rakata. (Somehow, by the

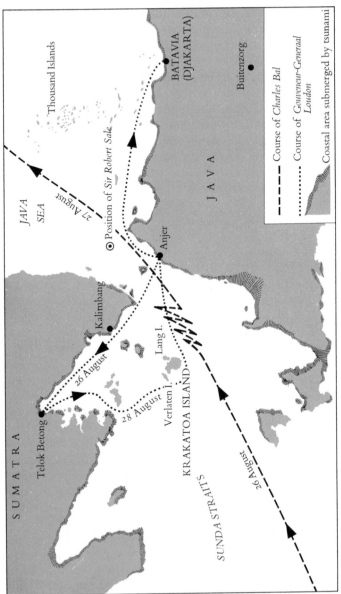

Fig. 21 *The Sunda Straits in 1883, with the courses of two of the ships that were deeply involved in the eruption. The shaded areas were swamped by waves triggered off by the eruption.*

mangling that place-names go through, the name *Krakatoa* was corrupted from *Rakata*.) At the northern end was a much lower, broader cone, Perboewetan, whose crater wall had been breached at some time in the past by a large lava flow.

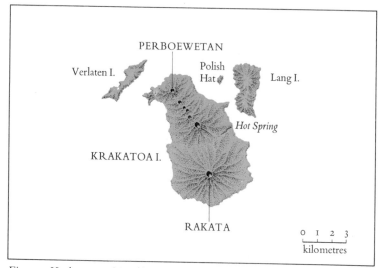

PERBOEWETAN

Verlaten I.

Polish Hat

Lang I.

Hot Spring

KRAKATOA I.

RAKATA

0  1  2  3
kilometres

*Fig. 22 Krakatoa and its adjacent islands before the eruption.*

None of the islands was inhabited, nor were they often visited, except by woodcutters from both shores of the Straits who landed periodically to fell timber in the luxuriant tropical forests that clothed the islands. From time to time, too, native fishermen would anchor in their sheltered bays to take on water or ride out storms. Some of the Naval survey parties may also have landed briefly on Krakatoa, because a hot spring is marked on some maps, but apart from this we know remarkably little about the islands or their volcanic history. There are some reports of a major eruption which took place between May 1680 and November 1681, and this eruption is said to have stripped bare the rich vegetation and ejected vast quantities of pumice that covered all the surrounding seas, but this is all that is known. It isn't even known where on Krakatoa the eruption was centred, but the chances are that it was Perboewetan, since the lava flows in the crater looked extremely fresh when they were examined in the nineteenth century. It's possible that some other minor eruptions occurred between 1681 and 1883, but if they did, there is no record of them, and all of the reports and descriptions made by ships passing Krakatoa suggest that it was quite dormant. The islands were well-known for their beauty to the passengers of the steamships passing up and down the Straits, but few of those who leant on their ship's rail on sultry moonlit evenings, gazing out at the serene islands could ever have conceived that they were to be the site of some of the most catastrophic events that the world has ever seen.

The first intimations that the forces which had lain dormant for two centuries would soon be unleashed came in the late 1870s, when frequent minor earthquakes began to shake the areas round the Sunda Straits. A particularly big tremor on 1 September 1880 damaged an important lighthouse on the Java coast, and was perceptible as far away as northern Australia. But Indonesia, in common with Vesuvius and almost all volcanic areas in the world, is located in the middle of an intensely active seismic zone, so earthquakes in the area were far from uncommon, and the local people did not attach much special significance to this latest bout of tremors. The seismic activity gradually increased in intensity until on Sunday, 20 May 1883, Krakatoa abruptly came to life, announcing its re-awakening with a series of explosions audible in towns over 150 kilometres away. These went on for several hours, rattling doors and windows almost continuously. On the following day, a sprinkling of ash fell over a wide area, and a great column of steam was seen rising above Krakatoa, leaving no doubt that a major eruption was under way. This vigorous phase continued for a few days, with the column of steam and ash climbing eleven kilometres high above the volcano and showering ash over points up to 480 kilometres distant.

By 27 May, though, things had quietened down sufficiently for a daring (or foolhardy) party to charter a steamboat from Batavia (now Djakarta) and sail out to the islands to see what was going on. The noise at one point as the party approached the island was quite deafening. In the words of one of them, the background noise was so loud that a rifle shot sounded comparable to 'the popping of a champagne cork amid the hubbub of a banquet'. (Sophisticated crowd, these Dutch colonials.) From their boat, they saw that everything on the island was entirely covered with fine white dust, like snow, and that the trees on the northern part of Krakatoa and Verlaten Island had been stripped of their leaves and branches by the rain of falling pumice, while those growing on Lang Island and Polish Hat seemed to have got away without much damage. Scrambling ashore, and scuffing their way inland through ankle-deep ash, the party were able to see that the centre of all the excitement was the small cone of Perboewetan, at the northern end of Krakatoa. This was in a state of semi-continuous eruption, with minor explosions taking place every five or ten minutes, showering fragments of pumice 200 metres into the air, and occasionally revealing the cherry-red glow of liquid lava in the crater, while all the while a great banner of steam rose 3,000 metres into the air. The visiting party, who were the first and last ever to get a good look at the crater of Perboewetan, found it to be about 1,000 metres in diameter and about fifty metres deep, with a small pit, also about fifty metres deep in the centre of the crater floor; it was from this pit that the steam cloud was escaping with a great roar.

After this remarkable visit, the volcano continued to be active for a week or two, but the explosive activity died down somewhat, and it began to look as though the eruption was going to be just a nine-days'-wonder, and would soon fade away and be forgotten. On 19 June, however, things began to warm up again, and the plume of steam and ash, which had been showing signs of flagging, rose higher and higher as more and more powerful explosions shook the air. By the end of June, observers on the mainland of Sumatra reported that all the higher parts of Perboewetan had been blown away, and that a *second* eruption column was now rising from the centre of the island. During the month of July, many areas in Java and Sumatra were rocked both by explosive blasts of exceptional violence, and by many minor earthquakes. Even this severe shaking, however, failed to cause alarm amongst the local people; they had by that time been living with the eruption for many weeks, and it is remarkable just to what extent familiarity of even something as exceptional as a volcanic eruption can breed contempt.

On 11 August a Dutch government surveyor, Captain Ferzenaar, made another examination of the island at close quarters, but he prudently stayed on his boat. He reported that all of the formerly rampant vegetation on Krakatoa had now been destroyed, with only a few of the thicker tree-trunks still rising above the thick mantle of ash, and that there were now *three* major eruption columns carrying clouds of dust and pumice high into the air, escaping from three separate vents. One of these was the original pit at the centre of the Perboewetan crater; the other two seemed to be more in the centre of the island. From the northeast side of the island Captain Ferzenaar also reported that he could see no less than eleven other minor centres of activity, which were either emitting small columns of steam, or occasionally ejecting dust in small explosive bursts. There may well have been others on other parts of the island, but unfortunately the heavy curtain of dust and fumes being carried by the wind prevented him getting right round. Captain Ferzenaar's observations on the state of Krakatoa in early August, even though made only from a boat keeping to the upwind side, are particularly useful because they provide the last reliable account of the situation before the culminating events which ensued fifteen days later.

Volcanic eruptions are sometimes compared with the drama, colour and spectacle of Wagner's operas – the 'Ride of the Valkyries' had been used very effectively as the background music to a film of some particularly lurid eruptions. Wagner's operas are remarkable for their length, their tedium, and the magnificence of their occasional climaxes. The eruption of Krakatoa has some parallels in these respects, for after an impressive opening, the eruption dragged on for a full three months before reaching its climax on 26 and 27 August. So extensive was the havoc wrought in those two days that it was only many months afterwards that a complete picture began to emerge of what had happened. The Dutch government appointed a fact-finding Scientific Commission in October 1883, and they published a preliminary report some six months later. The Royal Society in Britain also set up a committee to investigate the scientific aspects of the eruption and published a weighty tome containing the committee's findings in 1888. These two reports remain the source of almost all the information about the eruption; the Royal Society in particular went to great lengths to amass every possible scrap of information and even inserted a notice in *The Times* requesting anyone who had seen or heard anything to come forward.

Part of the difficulty in compiling these accounts was that there were so few survivors from the coastal towns in the Sunda Straits which were most directly affected, and those who had survived were often too distraught and confused to give an accurate description of what they had experienced. The best eyewitness reports came from European officials living in the two important towns of Batavia and Buitenzorg, where there were even some useful scientific recording instruments – one of them at the Batavia town gasworks – and from the officers on board the various vessels that were on passage through the Straits at the time of the eruption. There were a great number of these at different points along the Straits, but there were three that found themselves right in the thick of things. First, there was the British ship *Charles Bal*, under Captain Watson, on voyage to Hong Kong, which was sailing eastwards through the Straits on 26 August, keeping to the south of Krakatoa, and passing about sixteen kilometres distant. Second, there was a local Indonesian vessel, the *Gouveneur-Generaal Loudon*, which was plying back and forth across the Straits between Anjer in Java and Telok Betong in Sumatra. She passed about forty-eight kilometres north of Krakatoa on the evening of the twenty-sixth, spent the night of the twenty-sixth to seventh anchored in Telok Betong, tried to sail again for Anjer in the morning, but was prevented from doing so by the violence of the eruption. Third, there was another British vessel, the *Sir Robert Sale*, which was at the eastern, narrower end of the Straits, sixty-four kilometres from Krakatoa on the twenty-sixth, and attempted to sail westwards (towards Krakatoa) on the twenty-seventh, but was quite unable to do so. Apart from these three, reports came in to the Royal Society from more than fifty other vessels, whose log-books provided a valuable source of information, particularly since officers-of-the-watch habitually keep a note of the time at which observations are made.

After months of sifting through scores of reports from observers at sea and on dry land, the geologist in charge of the Dutch investigation, R. D. Verbeek, was able to piece together a comprehensive account of the events of the two fateful days, Sunday 26 and Monday 27 August. All the reports agreed that there had been a gradual but marked increase in the intensity of activity on Krakatoa during the three days preceding the twenty-sixth. At 1 p.m. on the twenty-sixth explosions loud enough to be heard well over 150 kilometres away were taking place at intervals of about ten minutes, and at about 2 p.m. an English ship, 120 kilometres from the scene, sighted a black cloud, rising to an altitude estimated to be about twenty-five kilometres above the volcano. By 3 p.m., the explosions were so loud that they were audible 240 kilometres away; by 5 p.m. they were so stupendous that the sound was carrying all over Java. In towns such as Batavia, 160 kilometres from Krakatoa, the din was terrific, the noise being compared with 'the discharge of artillery close at hand . . . causing rattling of windows and shaking of pictures, chandeliers and other hanging objects'. The same pattern of events continued throughout Sunday evening and most of the night. The *Charles Bal*, which was at its closest to the volcano at this time, reported:

. . . sounds like discharges of artillery at intervals of a second of time, and a crackling noise, probably due to the impact of fragments in the atmosphere . . . the whole commotion increasing towards 5 p.m. when it became so intense that the captain feared to continue his voyage, and began to shorten sail. From 5 to 6 p.m. a rain of pumice in large pieces, quite warm, fell upon the ship.

Captain Woolridge on the *Sir Robert Sale*, rather further away, reported seeing the eruption column rising above the volcano: '. . . a most terrible appearance, the dense mass of clouds being covered with a murky tinge, with fierce flashes of lightning'. A little later, at 7 p.m., the whole scene was lit up from time to time by electrical discharges, and at one time the cloud above the mountain presented 'the appearance of an immense pine tree, with the stem and branches formed with volcanic lightning'. (There's an interesting analogy here with Pliny's description of the great cloud at the A.D. 79 eruption of Vesuvius.)

Things became so bad for the *Charles Bal* later on in the evening that she had to spend the entire night tacking back and forth south east of Krakatoa, probably remaining within twenty kilometres of it – the ash-fall from the eruption was so thick that Captain Watson could not see well enough to steer away to safety, but ironically, the glare from the volcano provided a weird and somewhat improbable lighthouse. A less pleasant night can scarcely be imagined, with a steady rain of hot ashes falling on the ship, and the air laden with hot, choking fumes of sulphurous gases. To make matters worse, peculiar pinky glows of static electricity lit up the mastheads and rigging of the ship with an unearthly light. On the *Gouveneur-Generaal Loudon*, this phenomenon (known to mariners as St Elmo's Fire) was even more extensive, and the native crew 'engaged themselves busily in putting out this phosphorescent light with their hands . . . and pleaded that if this light . . . made its way below, a hole would burst in the ship; not that they feared the ship taking fire, but they thought the light was the work of evil spirits . . .' The peculiar phosphorescent glow was the result of the atmosphere around the ship being highly-charged with static electricity, generated by the rush of the steam through the volcanic vent, and the friction between the myriads of fragmentary particles that were blasted up with it.

After 4 a.m. on the morning of the twenty-seventh the eruption appeared to die down a little, but the grandest moments were yet to come. They came in the form of series of explosions on a far greater scale even than any of the preceding ones, and greater than anything that man has experienced before or since. According to the painstaking analysis of the records by Verbeek, the largest of these took place at 05.30, 06.44, 10.02 and 10.52 Krakatoa time, on the morning of 27 August; of these the third was much the most violent. The sound of these great explosions was audible over a large part of the Earth's surface: at Elsey Creek in South Australia, 3,224 kilometres from Krakatoa, the noise was loud enough to wake sleeping people, who described it as being similar to the sound of rock being blasted. At Diego Garcia Island, 3,647 kilometres away (in the Indian Ocean), the sounds of the explosions were at first thought to be coming from a ship in distress, firing its guns to attract attention, so the people ran out to vantage points on the coast of the island to try to see it. The furthest point to which the sound carried was Rodriguez Island, 4,811 kilometres distant, near Mauritius in the Indian Ocean, where the sounds were also taken for gunfire at first. Nearer Krakatoa, the effects were much more serious. At Batavia and Buitenzorg, the blast blew in dozens of windows, and even cracked walls. A barograph used to record the pressure of gas in the gasholder in Batavia enabled the times of arrival of the pressure waves from the explosions to be recorded accurately, but the blast produced by the greatest of the explosions was such that the gasholder leapt out of its well, causing the gas to escape. Much the most destructive effects of the explosions, however, were a series of *tsunamis* (often wrongly called tidal waves) which swept up and down the shores of the Sunda Straits. It was these, not so much the explosions *per se* that made the Krakatoa eruption the most lethal on record. Very few people are known to have been killed directly by the explosions, great though they were, but no less than 36,000 died when the *tsunamis* ripped over low-lying areas all along the coasts, overwhelming towns and villages. The port of Anjer quite simply ceased to exist as the succession of great waves washed over it, carrying away all the flimsy wooden buildings that made up the town.

The climactic series of explosions of 27 August added volumes of fresh material to the already huge eruption column above the volcano, and some estimates suggest that it rose as much as eighty kilometres into the air. The ash raining down from it added to the misery of the people in the area – the *Sir Robert Sale* reported lumps the size of pumpkins falling on her decks, and she was at least forty kilometres distant. At Batavia, the pall of ash took a fair while to arrive; in the early morning of the twenty-seventh, the sky was clear, but by 10.15 it had become lurid and yellowish as the ash spread across the sky; by 10.30 the first fine ash was actually sifting softly down on to the streets. At 11 a.m. a heavy rain of ash was falling, and by 11.20 the air was so thick with ash and pumice dust that the sun was blotted out, and total darkness fell on the city, remaining until 1 p.m. The ash-fall itself ceased two hours later. Since Batavia was over 160 kilometres from Krakatoa, it escaped fairly lightly; in some places, nearer the volcano, total unrelieved darkness lasted nearly two days. These awful conditions naturally made it quite impossible to tell what was happening actually on Krakatoa, but it is thought that some milder explosive activity continued. The *Charles Bal* and *Sir Robert Sale* were beating about in the darkness for the whole of the twenty-seventh, and ash rained down on them so steadily that the crews had to spend hours shovelling it off the decks and shaking it clear of sails and rigging. On the *Gouveneur-Generaal Loudon*, it was reported that at one time dust and water were falling together, as mud, and a thickness of fifteen centimetres accumulated in only ten minutes. Fortunately, this soon declined to a more tolerable rate.

At 7 p.m. on the twenty-seventh, another outbreak of fairly violent explosive activity occurred, and got progressively more and more vigorous until 11 p.m. when it started to decline. These outbursts marked the end of the entire eruption, for at 2.30 p.m. on the twenty-eighth, after being active for a hundred days, the last, mild explosion echoed out over Krakatoa, and silence returned.

Slowly, life returned to something like normal in the Straits, and the bewildered survivors were able to bury their dead, and salvage what they could of homes in towns and villages that had been swept by *tsunamis* and showered with ash. Initially, the great masses of floating pumice which had piled up on the sea made it difficult for ships to force their way through the water – rafts three metres thick were reported in places – but eventually parties were able to reach the islands and determine what changes had taken place. The Royal Dutch Navy made a detailed survey of the whole group of islands immediately after the eruption, and the maps they produced revealed the full extent of the effects of the explosions which had reverberated round so much of the world. The whole of the northern part of the island of Krakatoa had disappeared, with the exception of a bank of pumice and a small isolated rock, about ten metres square, which was left standing above the ocean with deep water on either side. Not a vestige remained of the cone Perboewetan, and the whole of the northern part of the cone Rakata had been blown away, leaving a semi-vertical cliff. A great crater had been formed, most of it below sea level, and soundings showed that where land had once stood 300 metres above sea level, the water was now 300 metres deep. In all, about two thirds of the island of Krakatoa had disappeared and Verbeek estimated that about fifteen cubic kilometres of matter had been ejected by the eruption. This fell as pumice and fine ash over an area of nearly four million square kilometres, but most of it, of course, fell in the immediate vicinity of Krakatoa. So while the island of Krakatoa ended up considerably smaller, Verlaten

*Fig. 23 After the eruption. The outlines of the islands as they were originally are shown dotted.* (From the Royal Society report of the eruption)

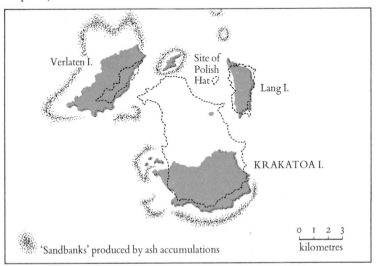

Verlaten I.

Site of
Polish
Hat

Lang I.

KRAKATOA I.

0  1  2  3
kilometres

'Sandbanks' produced by ash accumulations

Island and Lang Island ended up much bigger, due to the accumulation on them of enormous volumes of ash, which also piled up in the sea to form 'sand' banks. And Polish Hat? Not a trace remained.

## Mt Pelée, 1902

The mighty Krakatoa eruption was compared in some ways with a Wagnerian opera. In the case of the 1902 eruption of Mt Pelée there is no need to resort to such artificial comparisons, because the eruption does in fact form the basis of an opera, known as *The Violins of St Jacques*, which has been performed in London within the last few years. The opera, by Malcolm Williamson, was itself based on a novel of the same name by Patrick Leigh Fermor, who wove a complicated plot of romance and intrigue against the colourful background of a sultry Caribbean town in the midst of a hectic carnival, while above the town a volcano rumbled threateningly. The volcano ended up by destroying the entire island. In the book Mt Pelée is thinly disguised as the volcano Salpêtrière, while St Pierre, the town which was actually involved in the eruption, appears as St Jacques, but the actual events of Thursday 8 May 1902 were so dramatic in themselves, and the tragedy so complete, that it seems a little unnecessary to dress up the facts in a romanticized account. But this is probably better than some of the attempts that have been made deliberately to exploit the natural human interest in such a tragic event with supposedly factual accounts of the eruption, in which accurate reportage takes second place to lurid, entirely hypothetical detail. A recent offender makes its intentions of arousing morbid curiosity perfectly clear on its front cover, proclaiming '30,000 people burned, boiled and suffocated to death', 'A whole thriving city levelled to the ground in seconds', and 'The world best-selling account of one day when the earth exploded'.

At the time of the eruption, St Pierre was the principal town on Martinique, a small island in the Caribbean, and a prosperous French colony. Six kilometres north of the town rose the gentle slopes of Mt Pelée, not a particularly impressive volcano, only 2,250 metres high. The island and the volcano were renowned for their beauty. To quote a contemporary description, which reads rather like a modern travel brochure:

It has the softest of summer zephyrs blowing across its fields and hill-sides; swift and tumbling waters break through forest and plain; and mountain heights rise to where they can gather the island's mists to their crowns. There are pretty thatched cottages, nestling in the shade of coco-nut, mango and breadfruit, and decked out with bright hibiscus and bougainvillaea.

The town of St Pierre itself was no less appealing, stretching for some three kilometres along the shores of the Caribbean. It boasted a number of imposing public buildings, including a town hall, cathedral, military hospital and a theatre, and even had electric lighting, unusual in those days. Most of the town, how-ever, consisted of a picturesque maze of narrow, rambling streets, lined with old-fashioned houses with steeply-pitching red-tiled roofs. The population of this delightful little town was estimated in the official census of 1894 to be 19,722, most of them Martini-quians – a hybrid mixture of creole, mulatto, negro and coolie – with a few French government officials and civil servants.

Like Krakatoa, Mt Pelée had been active for quite a time before disaster struck. Whereas, however, the Krakatoa eruption was the first for two centuries, Mt Pelée had previously erupted within the living memory of some of the older residents of St Pierre; a mild affair in 1851 which did little apart from sprinkling a bit of ash about. The first signs of the new eruption were seen on 23 March 1902 when a rambling party were making an ascent of the volcano. Looking down below them from the top, they saw that a small crater with the remains of a dried-up lake in it was emit-ting sulphurous vapours from several points. This crater was known as the Étang Sec, or dry tarn, a name worth remembering because it was later to become the focus of the eruption proper. On 25 April things began to liven up, and minor explosive activity in the Étang Sec hurled ashes and bits of rock into the air, and the eruption gradually increased in vigour. On 27 April, an

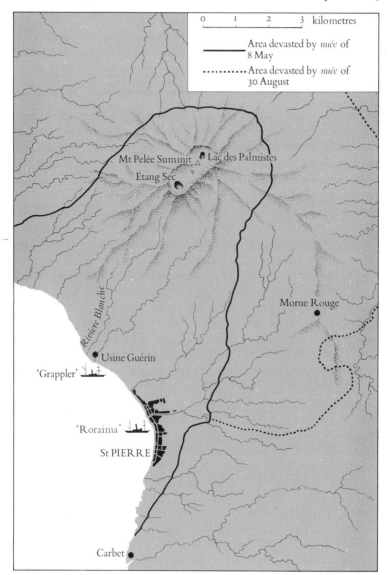

*Fig. 24 Mt Pelée and the area devastated by the* nuée ardente *of 8 May 1902*. (After La Croix)

investigating party climbed up from St Pierre to find out what was happening, and found that the Étang Sec now contained a small lake, in the middle of which a small volcanic cone had begun to grow. The days that followed this discovery saw a steady increase in activity, with the town of St Pierre now being showered with light falls of ash and subjected to unpleasant wafts of sulphurous fumes. Mrs Prentiss, the wife of the American consul in St Pierre wrote a letter home: 'The smell of sulphur is so strong that horses in the street stop and snort, and some of them drop in their harness and die of suffocation. Many of the people are obliged to wear wet handkerchiefs to protect themselves from the strong fumes of sulphur.' By 3 and 4 May the situation was really bad, with frequent loud explosions, and substantial amounts of ash accumulating in the streets. The St Pierre local newspaper, *Les Colonies*, carried an article saying: 'The rain of ashes never ceases . . . the passing of carriages is no longer heard in the streets. The wheels are muffled . . . puffs of wind sweep the ashes from roofs and awnings, and blow them into rooms, the windows of which have imprudently been left open.'

The first major blow in the events of 1902 struck on 5 May, when the crater lake in the Étang Sec burst through the crater walls, and rushed down the valley of the Rivière Blanche. The mass of new, hot rock forcing its way up through the crater floor had both helped to displace the water from the crater, and heated it up to nearly boiling point, so it was a scalding torrent that flashed down the valley, travelling at a speed of something like ninety kilometres an hour. As it flowed, it incorporated into itself masses of loose debris, mud, rubble and boulders, some of them reported to weigh fifty tons. This peculiarly unpleasant mixture combined to become a mudflow, which over-ran everything in its path; in particular a large sugar processing plant, the Usine Guérin, which stood on a tongue of flat land in the valley of the Rivière Blanche, surrounded by sugar-cane plantations. Thirty workmen died in the factory, of which nothing remained but a tall chimney stack, sticking up like a post above a desert of black boiling and seething mud. As if this were not bad enough, the great mudflow rolled on into the sea at the mouth of the Rivière

Blanche, setting up a series of waves as it did so, one of which was powerful enough to capsize the yacht *Prêcheur* moored off the river mouth. All on board died. Some accounts also suggest that these waves swept over the low-lying parts of St Pierre, near the waterfront, causing some damage and casualties.

As the situation went from bad to worse, the people living near the volcano became increasingly distressed, and many tried to leave St Pierre, heading for Fort-de-France, Martinique's second town. The local authorities, however, did not welcome the prospect of a large-scale evacuation. Apart from the problem of dealing with large numbers of frightened refugees, there was also an election coming up on 10 May, and the political factions in the town were anxious that nothing should interfere with it, so there was a concerted effort to play down the possible risk. A 'scientific commission' comprising some of the most learned people on the island was set up, and they produced a report designed to set fears at rest. One of the members of this commission and principal of the Lycée, Monsieur Landes, was rather worried by events, but when interviewed by the local newspaper, made a cautious, non-committal statement, and warned that some of the areas nearest the volcano should be evacuated. The nub of Monsieur Landes's thinking was that Mt Pelée presented no more danger to St Pierre than Vesuvius did to Naples, a distinctly ambiguous conclusion! The editor of *Les Colonies*, however, seized on this statement, and in an editorial in the very last issue his paper was ever to publish, tried to use it to encourage people to stay in St Pierre. 'Where,' he asked, 'could one be better than at St Pierre? Do those who invade Fort-de-France believe that they will be better off there than here, should the earth begin to quake? This is a foolish error against which the populace should be warned.' His appeal must have met with some response because although some hundreds of people did leave for Fort-de-France, many hundreds *more* sought refuge in St Pierre itself, flocking in from the surrounding countryside, so that on the morning of 8 May, as many as 30,000 people were probably crowding the town. Mrs Prentiss, the American consul's wife, in her last letter to America, said that she had the opportunity of leaving St Pierre with her husband on an

American schooner, but decided that the situation did not warrant it. She died with her husband on the next day, only a few hours after writing her letter.

At 07.52 (St Pierre time) on 8 May, the telegraph operator in St Pierre tapped out the single word 'Allez' to his opposite number in Fort-de-France, meaning that he was ready to receive a message. It was the last word to come out of St Pierre. We shall never know exactly the sequence of events in St Pierre on that morning, but we can build up a fairly accurate picture from the physical evidence of the ruins, and the reports of eye-witnesses. We can at least be sure of the time when the town died, because apart from the abrupt halt in telegraph traffic, the big clock on the Military Hospital was found intact in the smouldering ruins, with its hands stopped at 07.52.

8 May was Ascension Day and many faithful Catholics had assembled in the Cathedral, to celebrate the day, and to pray for deliverance from the volcano. At about 07.50, a series of deafening detonations was heard, and a great black cloud was seen to issue out from near the top of Mt Pelée. The cloud rolled effortlessly and relentlessly down the slopes of the volcano, spreading out into a broad fan which rapidly engulfed St Pierre, and in the next two or three minutes killed all but two of the population, and set the town ablaze from end to end. The eye-witness accounts of what happened in those few minutes naturally vary in many details, but one of the most reliable descriptions of the actual eruption of the cloud was that of Monsieur Roger Arnoux, a member of the Astronomical Society of France, who was observing from a vantage point well above and away from the town. He was awakened by a minor earth tremor during the night of the seventh to the eighth, but went back to sleep again and experienced nothing else untoward during the night. The following morning, however, at about 8 o'clock:

. . . while still watching the crater, I noticed a small cloud pass out, followed two seconds later by a considerable cloud. This latter cloud rolled swiftly down towards St Pierre, hugging the ground, but extending upwards at the same time, so that it was almost as high as it was long. The vapours . . . were of a violet grey colour, and seemingly very dense, for although endowed with an almost inconceivably powerful ascensive force, they retained to the zenith their rounded summits. Innumerable electrical scintillations played through the chaos of vapours, and at the same time that the ears were deafened by a frightful fracas.

The phenomenon that M. Arnoux had observed and described so graphically was new to science, and subsequently when other examples were observed on Mt Pelée, they became known as *nuées ardentes*, or glowing clouds. These turbulent masses of super-heated gases and incandescent solid particles present some fascinating problems to vulcanologists, which will be discussed in a later chapter.

8. *A classic photograph taken by A. Lacroix on 16 December 1902, showing a well-developed* nuée ardente *descending the valley of the Rivière Blanche. Mt Pelée itself is hidden by the clouds of dust and ash. It was a closely-similar* nuée *that overwhelmed St Pierre, but that one may have been even bigger, and spread further laterally.*

The sailing ship *Roraima* arrived at St Pierre early in the morning of Thursday, 8 May, and anchored a little way off shore. She could not have come at a worse time; a few hours after she arrived, she was a helpless burning hulk, with most of her passengers and crew dead. A few survived, though, and were able to describe their experiences. They had seen that the volcano was in eruption even before dropping anchor; many of them had come up on deck to see the spectacle. At about 7.45 (ship time), they heard a major explosion and a few minutes later a searing hot blast of gas roared over St Pierre and the ships lying off shore, capsizing the steam ship *Grappler*, and rolling the *Roraima* so severely that she lost all her masts and smokestacks. The fiery blast killed everyone on deck instantly, with the single exception of the captain, who lived on for a short time before becoming unconscious and falling overboard. The force of the blast was such that skylights were blown in, and boiling hot mud and ashes rained down on those below decks, killing many and scalding others. The 'fiery blast', or *nuée ardente*, did not itself last long, but it set St Pierre ablaze. Some of the damage was done by the thousands of casks of rum which were stored in the town, and which exploded in the heat and caught fire immediately. The *Roraima* survivors described burning rum running down the streets and even into the sea, spreading out as far as the ship and causing small fires on her. The conflagration raged for many hours throughout the town, spreading rapidly through buildings already torn open by the blast, and with not a single person left alive to check it. It is possible that a 'fire storm' condition developed in the town, similar to that which occurred in several German cities during the last war, when saturation bombing raids started so many fires that the city became effectively one big fire, sucking into itself hurricane force winds to bring fresh oxygen to the heart of the inferno. One consequence of the blaze in St Pierre was that it is difficult now to diagnose how much of the damage was a *direct* result of the *nuée ardente*, and how much a result of the fires it started. This is a matter of considerable importance, since it is clearly desirable to know as much as possible about the conditions within the *nuée ardente*.

One of the first to go ashore at St Pierre after the disaster was the Vicar-General of Martinique, Monsieur Parel, who was at Fort-de-France on the morning of the eighth, having left St Pierre only the afternoon before. He was able to join a rescue party which set off by boat from Fort-de-France, and he returned to St Pierre a scant twenty-four hours after he had left. Let him describe the scene that met his eyes in his own words:

Thursday 8 May. Ascension Day. This date should be written in blood . . . When, at about 3 o'clock in the afternoon we rounded the last promontory which separated us from what was once the magnificent panorama of St Pierre, we suddenly perceived at the opposite extremity of the roadstead the Rivière Blanche with its crest of vapour, rushing madly into the sea. Then a little further out blazes a great American packet [the *Roraima*], which arrived on the scene just in time to be overwhelmed by the catastrophe. Nearer the shore, two other ships are in flames. The coast is strewn with wreckage, with the keels of the overturned boats, all that remains of the twenty to thirty ships which lay at anchor here the day before. All along the quays, for a distance of 200 metres, piles of lumber are burning. Here and there around the city . . . fires can be seen through the smoke. But St Pierre, in the morning throbbing with life, thronged with people, is no more. Its ruins stretch before us, wrapped in their shroud of smoke and ashes, gloomy and silent, a city of the dead. Our eyes seek out the inhabitants fleeing distracted, or returning to look for the dead. Nothing to be seen. No living soul appears in this desert of desolation, encompassed by appalling silence.

The blast that struck St Pierre was remarkable not only for its searing heat but also for its sheer force – masonry walls one metre thick were blown down, heavy cannon torn from their mounts, and a three-ton statue carried sixteen metres. Angelo Heilprin, an American geologist who visited the scene a few weeks later and wrote a book about the tragedy, described 'twisted bars of iron, great masses of roof sheeting wrapped like cloth about posts upon which they had been flung, and iron girders looped and festooned as if they had been made of rope'. Amidst all this evidence of the effects of unlimited destructive powers unleashed, there were small pockets in which some remarkable things survived – delicate china cups, corked bottles of water, still drinkable, little packets of starch in which the granules were untouched; even a street fountain still splashed cold drinking water in one of the ruined streets.

Because the actual physical damage was so variable in its extent, it was immediately obvious to the early investigators that the almost total mortality was not solely the result of the *force* of the blast, since there would have been at least a few survivors in areas where the blast was less severe. Evidence that the heat of the blast was the cause of death was abundant – there were many poignant scenes of entire families dead in rooms where glass bottles, jugs, bowls and cutlery stood perfectly undamaged on tables where they had been set out. The many thousands of bodies in the ruins all told much the same story, of practically instantaneous death when the searing hurricane from Mt Pelée reached them. There had been no time to attempt to flee, or even to struggle; hundreds simply died in their tracks. The hot gas did its work swiftly, extinguishing thousands of lives in the space of two or three minutes. Many of the victims, of course, were badly burned *after* death by the fires that swept the town, but even those that died in the open showed severe burns on their bodies, even though in many cases their clothes were not even singed. This suggests that

9. *The ruins of St Pierre, still smouldering one week after the eruption. A few centimetres of ash can be seen on the pavement in the foreground.*

although the blast that killed them was intensely hot, it lasted only a few moments, not long enough to ignite fabrics.

The story that the survivors from the town itself told (the number varies in different accounts, between two and four) confirms this interpretation. The most famous tale of all is that of the 'prisoner of St Pierre', a murderer who was incarcerated in the town jail at the time of the disaster. Fortunately for him, his cell was extremely secure, partly below ground level, without even a window – the only aperture into it was a tiny grating above the door. The prisoner, a negro stevedore called Augustus Ciparis, remained locked up in his cell for four days after St Pierre had been laid waste, without food, half-dead from burns and shock, until his cries for help were heard by two negroes picking through the ruins of the town. When he had recovered from his ordeal, Ciparis was able to tell of what had happened – and he went on telling the story for the rest of his life, for he was given a free pardon, joined a travelling circus, and became something of a celebrity.

On the morning of 8 May, Ciparis had been waiting as usual for his breakfast to be brought to him, when it suddenly grew dark, and immediately afterwards, hot air laden with ashes began to come through the grating over the door. It was not a strong gust, but it was fiercely hot, and he was severely burned all over his back and legs. He was wearing a shirt and trousers at the time; these were unmarked. The heat did not last for more than a few seconds, and when it had passed, Ciparis was left in an awful solitude, his cries for help going unanswered as the city burned above him. Had he not had a bowl of water in his cell, he too, would have succumbed before his rescuers found him.

A second survivor, a negro shoemaker called Leon Leandre, had an equally lucky escape, but in circumstances more difficult to understand, since he was not below ground like Ciparis, and several companions around him were all killed outright:

On 8 May, about 8 o'clock in the morning, I was seated on the doorstep of my house . . . all of a sudden I felt a terrible wind blowing, the earth began to tremble, and the sky suddenly became dark. I turned to go into the house, made with great difficulty the three or four steps that separated me from my room, and felt my arms and legs burning, also my body. I dropped upon a table. At this moment four others sought refuge in my room, crying and writhing in pain, although their garments showed no signs of having been touched by flame. At the end of ten minutes, one of these, the young Delavaud girl, aged about ten years, fell dead; the others left. I then got up and went into another room, where I found the father Delavaud, still clothed, and lying on the bed, dead. He was purple and inflated, but the clothing was intact. I went out and found in the court two corpses interlocked; they were the bodies of the two young men who had before been with me in the room . . . Crazed and almost overcome, I threw myself upon a bed, inert and awaiting death. My senses returned to me in perhaps an hour, when I beheld the roof burning. With sufficient strength left, my legs bleeding and covered with burns, I ran to Fonds-Saint-Denis, six kilometres from St Pierre.

There are certain inconsistencies in Leandre's story, but he was obviously describing what he had experienced as well as he could remember it. It seems likely that he owed his remarkable escape to the fact that his house lay right on the fringe of the *nuée ardente*, in the extreme south-east of the town, so that he escaped its worst effects. He was also a strong, well-built man, so his good physique may have helped him.

So much for the death of St Pierre. The eruption did not stop after the destruction of the city, though, and the *nuée* that was responsible for the tragedy was in volcanic terms a relatively minor affair and it was by no means the last from Mt Pelée. On 20 May, a second powerful *nuée* swept through St Pierre, flattening many of the ruins left by its predecessor, but taking no lives – there were none left to take. Several other *nuées* swept harmlessly down the valley of the Rivière Blanche during the next couple of months, but on 30 August death came again to Martinique, where a powerful *nuée* blasted out from Mt Pelée and rolled down in a new direction, engulfing the small village of Morne Rouge. Two thousand people died, in circumstances almost identical to those of St Pierre. After this final fatal episode the eruption dragged on for many months, lasting well into 1903. The ash which had been falling on St Pierre since the beginning of May

1902 continued to accumulate, sifting down softly to cover the ruins of St Pierre in a grey pall and burying many of the bodies that still lay in the debris. One should not attribute human qualities to natural phenomena, but in a strange way the gentleness with which Mt Pelée buried its victims seemed like a sort of atonement for their deaths. A stranger gesture was to follow. In November 1902, a great spine or pillar of solidified lava began to rise above the crater of the Étang Sec, forced upwards by the pressure of the magma below. Growing at a rate of about ten metres a day, by May 1903 the spine was no less than 310 metres high, rearing up above St Pierre like a memorial obelisk, a tribute to the thousands that had died below.

# *Chapter 3* Types of volcanic eruption

Volcanic eruptions are difficult things to classify. Most of the difficulty stems from the fact that an eruption is an extremely complex phenomenon. A single eruption may not only last for months, but it may also consist of a series of separate, different phases, and in many cases different things may be going on on different parts of the same volcano at the same time. However, so long as one is aware of their limitations, classifications are useful, since they provide a series of labels to attach to different eruptions, aiding recognition and simplifying the job of describing them.

There are two principal ways in which eruptions can be grouped. The first, purely spatial method groups eruptions according to the shape of the volcanic vent and where this is situated relative to the volcanic edifice as a whole, while the second depends on the character of the eruption itself, and the nature of the deposits it produces. Both of these methods will be discussed briefly, but it's important to remember that any particular grouping should only be applied to individual recognizable phases of an eruption, and that it doesn't necessarily apply to the whole thing.

## Spatial groupings

By far the most important division here is between *central* and *fissure* eruptions. If one had to define a volcano, the definition would have to be something like 'a site where molten rocks (magma) have been erupted at the surface of the Earth'. Central vent and fissure eruptions represent the two basic ways in which magma can reach the surface. Central vent eruptions are the best-known kind. Basically what happens is that lava and other material is ejected from a hole in the ground, or crater, which is fed by a single pipe-like supply channel extending deep down below ground. As the eruption continues the ejected material piles up round the vent, building up that heap of material that is called a volcano. The standard Fuji-like conical volcanoes are constructed in this way, but a host of other forms can also develop in different circumstances. Central vent eruptions occur all over the world, on the mid-ocean ridge volcanoes, at destructive plate margins, and along the African rift valleys; there is no particular environment which is specially favourable to them.

Fissure eruptions are different in this respect. They occur in areas where the Earth's crust is subjected to tensional forces, trying to pull it apart. Where this happens, the crust may actually break, gaping open in long, narrow, slot-like vertical cracks. At the surface these cracks may remain open and empty, forming deep clefts, but deeper down, magma forces its way up into the crack,

*Fig. 25  A fissure eruption. Magma forcing its way upwards in a dyke reaches the surface, and a line of small cones builds up over the vents, from which large volumes of lava are erupted.*

widening it considerably by hydraulically wedging the walls apart. These magma-filled cracks are known as *dykes*. If the magma pressure is great enough, it will force its way right up the dyke to the surface, spilling out to form lava flows. This will happen more or less simultaneously at several points along the length of the dyke, hence the name *fissure* eruptions.

If you reflect for a moment on which areas are likely to have rocks under tension, and where cracking and dyke intrusion are likely, you will realize that the mid-ocean ridges are hot favourites

*Fig. 26 Hypothetical section across a constructive plate margin, where lateral spreading is taking place as more and more dykes are intruded in the active zone.*

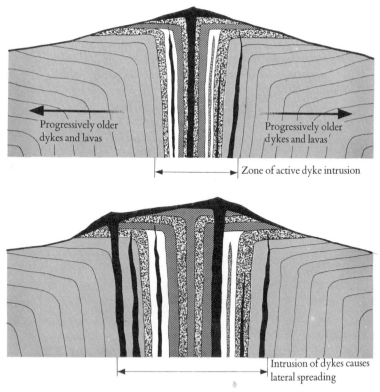

Progressively older dykes and lavas

Progressively older dykes and lavas

Zone of active dyke intrusion

Intrusion of dykes causes lateral spreading

for this kind of activity. Iceland, astride the Mid-Atlantic Ridge, provides an excellent example. With the Atlantic Ocean floor spreading away in opposite directions from the ridge, Iceland is getting wider at a rate of about half a centimetre per year, so a lot of new material has to be added continuously in the zone of tension in the middle, or else the two halves would soon be completely separated. Most of the material is injected in the form of dykes which don't reach the surface, and it's been estimated that the total thickness of dykes intruded in the last ninety million years is over 400 kilometres! Since each dyke is quite narrow, averaging only ten metres wide, that's an awful lot of dykes, and a cross-section through Iceland would reveal hundreds and hundreds, sometimes so closely spaced together that there would be scarcely any non-dyke material present and many dykes would be intruded up the middle of earlier ones. A few of these dykes reach the surface; when they do so, a fissure eruption takes place, and basalt lavas pour out over the surface.

When particularly large volumes of basalt are involved, such eruptions are commonly known as *basaltic flood eruptions*. The most recent example of this kind took place in 1783, when lava was erupted from the twenty-five-kilometre length of the Laki fissure in southern Iceland. The eruption lasted between June and November of that year, and in those six months about eleven cubic kilometres of lava flowed out from the fissure, covering an area of nearly 600 square kilometres. Most of the lava followed the courses of river valleys, principally the Skaftar and the Hverfisfljot, and formed glowing rivers of rock over fifty-six kilometres long. So much lava flowed into the Skaftar valley that it was completely filled and lava began to spill out over the surrounding countryside. The long-term results of this eruption were profound: it proved to be Iceland's worst ever disaster. We'll see why later.

Apart from oceanic areas such as Iceland, fissure or basaltic flood eruptions have also occurred in several important continental areas: the western United States, India, South Africa and South America. Most of these are rather old, and don't relate to the present Plate Tectonic picture, but rather to the situation ten or twenty million years ago. It's thought, in fact, that they represent

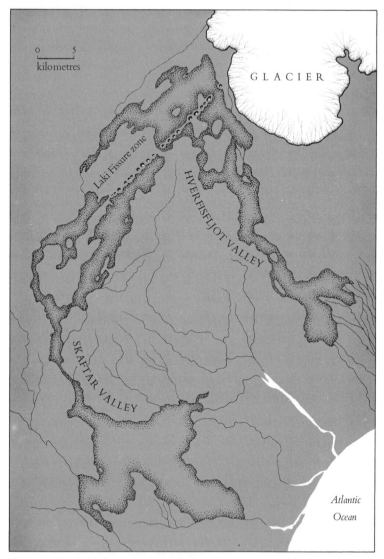

*Fig. 27  The Laki fissure in Iceland, and the areas covered by basaltic lavas erupted from it.* (After S. Thorarinsson)

areas where 'mid-ocean' ridges once formed below the continents, in the late stages of continental rifting, but before an ocean proper had opened (cf. chapter one), so in a sense the kind of volcanic activity that is typical of oceanic areas in fact took place on dry land. Although they are now inactive, these old regions of continental flood basalts are impressive because of the sheer quantity of lavas involved.

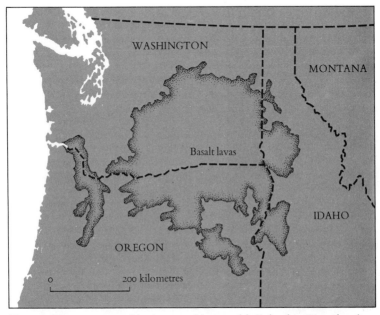

*Fig. 28  The area covered by lavas making up the Columbia River basalt plateau.*

In the Columbia River area of the western U.S.A. where most of the lavas were erupted about twenty million years ago, such vast amounts of basalt were poured out on to the surface that hills 1,500 metres high were drowned in lava! This didn't happen during a single eruption, of course; the individual flows average only ten metres thick, so many hundreds of individual flows are piled up one on top of the other, covering an area of about 130,000 square kilometres. It's not now possible to identify the fissures from which each of these thousands of lava flows were erupted, but it is likely that each was produced by an eruption broadly similar to that of the Laki fissure.

It may seem initially that differentiation between a central and a fissure eruption is the simplest thing in the world but, unfortunately, it's not. A lot depends on the scale that is considered. For example, the Laki eruption taken as a whole constitutes a splendid example of a fissure eruption, but along its twenty-five kilometre length dozens of small volcanic cones were built up, none of them

10. *In a basalt plateau, many hundreds of individual lava flows are piled up on top of one another. There are just three such flows in this photo, none of them more than a few metres thick.*

very big, although each one, if considered separately, could be called a central vent volcano. More important, the big volcanoes which make up the Hawaiian Islands all seem at first sight to have central vents – they are mountains thousands of metres high, with craters right at the top. But the summit craters are situated on a

*Fig. 29 A sketch map of the island of Hawaii showing in black the lavas which have been erupted in the last two centuries. Almost all have come from the prominent north-east south-west fissure or rift zone, giving the whole Mauna Loa volcano an elongate shape. (After G. A. MacDonald)*

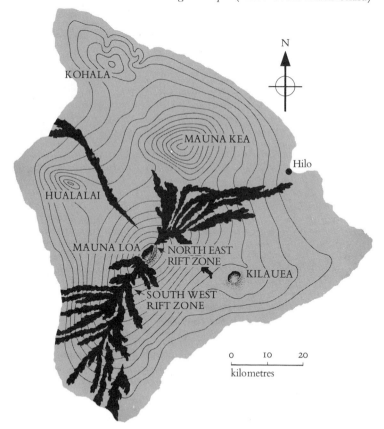

fissure zone, and most of the lavas that are erupted actually emerge from fissures. This means that as the volcano grows, it becomes elongated in the direction of the fissure zone.

11. *An aerial view of a line of cones built up along a fissure in Hawaii. The cones almost certainly overlie a dyke at depth, but this fissure did not produce anything like the volume of lava of the Laki fissure eruption of 1783.* (Photo courtesy of I. G. Gass)

So it's impossible to make a hard and fast distinction between fissure and central eruptions. That isn't particularly important in itself, but it does illustrate some of the difficulties involved in dealing with volcanoes. Let's leave that problem, though, and look at a few of the more important kinds of places in which eruptions occur, relative to a pre-existing volcano.

First, all the activity may be confined to the summit crater at the top of the volcano, just where one might expect it to be.

Second, it's possible for some explosive activity to take place in the summit crater, but for most of the lava to be erupted quietly from a vent or fissure on the flanks of the volcano. Third, there may be very little activity at the summit crater, but the feeder pipe (usually a dyke) may branch off and most of the eruption may take place on the flanks of the volcano, with a small cone being built up, and lavas emerging from it. This is called a *lateral*

*Fig. 30 Some of the more important possible sites of activity on a simple volcano.*

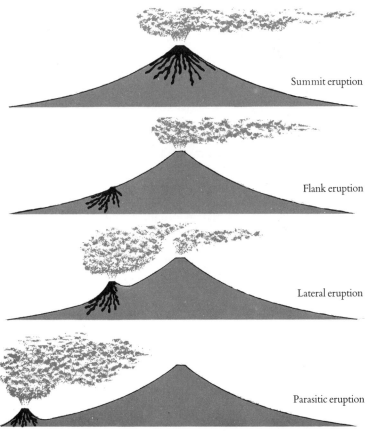

Summit eruption

Flank eruption

Lateral eruption

Parasitic eruption

eruption. Finally, by a natural progression, there may be no activity at all in the summit crater, instead the new eruption may take place completely independently of the main volcano, and a new mini-volcano or *parasitic cone* may be built up. In some cases, such parasitic cones can outgrow their parents, but at that point the term becomes irrelevant.

## Groupings based on the characters of eruptions

In the past, vulcanologists have traditionally grouped eruptions into a sequence of progressively more violently explosive types. This is rather a subjective approach, and has sometimes led to the situation where the same eruption has been given a different label by different observers. It is still useful, though, and is described in this chapter. In the last few years a more objective method, based on the properties of the material erupted has been devised. This method is particularly valuable, since it can be applied to deposits produced by prehistoric eruptions, for which of course there are no observer's records. This method will be discussed in chapter five.

*Hawaiian eruptions* are the mildest of all, and are characteristic of the Hawaiian island volcanoes, which all have soft, peaceful-sounding names such as Halemaumau, Kilauea and Mauna Loa. The important thing about these volcanoes is that since they are right in the middle of the Pacific, they are basaltic, and their basalts are hot and very fluid. When any supply of magma is present below a volcano, it usually contains a great deal of gas, and this gas is often at high pressure. When the magma gets near the surface the gas expands and tries to escape. If it can escape freely, then the eruption will not be violently explosive, since all explosions are the result of the more or less instantaneous expansion of large volumes of gas. Now, since the Hawaiian basalts are so fluid, any high-pressure volcanic gases present can blow off steadily, without much fuss or bother, and the rising magma can reach the surface (to become lava), and flow away quietly from the vent. The Hawaiian lavas are so fluid, in fact, that as they stream away downhill they are often very graphically described as 'rivers of fire'.

Sometimes, when an eruption takes place within a large crater, the lava can't flow away, and gets ponded up in the crater. This has frequently happened on the Halemaumau volcano, which has a deep, circular, pit-like crater about one and a half kilometres across at its summit. This crater often gets filled with lakes of lava which remain molten for amazingly long periods. For a hundred years prior to 1924 the lake was present continually, and has appeared and disappeared again several times since. By night the lava lake presents an unearthly sight, with great slabs of dark, solidified crust shifting about slowly on the surface, allowing the bright lava underneath to gleam through along the cracks between slabs. Sometimes, small lava fountains play in the centre, and these reveal just how completely liquid lava can be, as it splashes and sloshes round the base of the fountain; at other times, small jets of gas blow up through the lava in fiery gouts, churning up the lake into glowing whorls and currents of molten rock. For long periods, this somewhat improbable lake is so safe and tranquil that visitors can come right to the edge of the crater, without the least hazard. Not surprisingly, this lava lake is one of the most photographed features in Hawaii, and the crater has been labelled in suitable post-card terminology 'The House of Everlasting Fire'. This, by the way, is something of a misnomer, since although adjectives like 'fiery' are often applied to volcanic phenomena (count the number of times in this book!) it's not strictly correct, since there is rarely any actual fire, in the sense of combustible material burning to produce flames and smoke. Almost all the red and yellow colours come from the glow of the hot lava, and the 'smoke' consists of steam, dust clouds and fumes of sulphur dioxide and other pungent-smelling gases. Very occasionally true flames are seen, usually small and faint, and these are believed to be produced by the burning of hydrogen gas escaping from the magma.

The ease with which the dissolved high-pressure gases can escape from Hawaiian magmas leads to some very spectacular eruptions. The pressure of the escaping gas sprays liquid lava high into the air, just as a soda siphon squirts water, to form *fire fountains*. These fountains must surely be amongst the most remarkable of all natural phenomena; the plumes of incandescent liquid rock commonly reach many tens of metres in height, and one in 1959 reached not less than 400 metres. They are not just short squirts, either. Some fire fountains play for hours on end. Not unvaryingly, though, like the miserable affairs in Trafalgar Square, but swelling, dying away and surging up irregularly. At the top of the fountain, the spray breaks up into individual droplets which get carried by the wind and fall a long way from the vent, so that downwind of the fountain there is a shifting curtain of glowing droplets showering down.

12. *A lava fountain nearly a hundred metres high which developed during the 1955 eruption of Kilauea volcano, Hawaii. Comparatively-large lumps of material are being ejected in this case.* (U.S. Geological Survey photo courtesy of G. A. Macdonald)

Hawaiian-type eruptions are not confined to Hawaii, although in few other areas are fire fountains quite so beautifully developed. Similar lava lakes to that of Halemaumau have been reported from many strange places: two of the most active volcanoes in Africa, Nyamlagira and Nyiragongo, have both had persistent lava lakes at different times in their history. Generalizing rather, it is probably true to say that Hawaiian-type eruptions are more common on the oceanic island volcanoes than elsewhere (though the examples of Nyiragongo and Nyamlagira emphasize that it *is* only a generalization), since it is in these environments that the fluid basalt lavas are most likely to be found.

*Fig. 31  The four main active Italian volcanoes.*

Slightly more explosive are *Strombolian* eruptions, named after the tiny volcanic island of Stromboli, between Sicily and Italy. Stromboli has been showing the same kind of activity more or less continuously for centuries, and is often called the 'lighthouse of the Mediterranean'. In a typical Strombolian eruption, basaltic lava is again involved, but it is not quite as fluid as in the Hawaiian eruptions and gas escape takes place spasmodically in minor explosions every few minutes or so, sometimes rhythmically and predictably, sometimes irregularly. The explosions usually sound more like thumps and whooshes than proper bangs, and there are sometimes sustained blasts like the din made by a powerful jet engine at close quarters. Each explosion shoots out glowing fragments of semi-solid lava high into the air. These, although they must be travelling very fast initially, seem to move quite slowly, twisting and turning lazily in the air and tracing out elegant parabolic paths as they fall back to earth round the vent. When they hit the ground, they may stop abruptly, embedding themselves still glowing, fuming and sizzling slightly in the loose ash; or they may bounce off, to leap down the steep sides of the cone in a series of great bounds, developing a rapid spin as they do so, and whirring downhill like cannonballs, ending up in a rattling shower of small stones at the bottom. Sometimes, when activity is particularly intense, the wall of the crater is breached and a small lava flow emerges and flows away downhill, and if this happens, the activity tends to quieten down for a while. Large-volume lava flows, though, are not an essential part of a Strombolian eruption; the term is usually used to describe the activity within the crater.

Strombolian activity, then, is a bit noisier than Hawaiian, but it's still not particularly dangerous – there are two villages on Stromboli only a couple of kilometres from the ever-active vent, and the inhabitants rarely have cause to worry about whether they will live to see the sun rise on another day, or on another boatload of visitors coming across to look at the volcano.

This kind of semi-continuous mild activity is quite common on volcanoes all over the world. Etna, on the island of Sicily, has been whooshing and thumping away in one or other of its twin summit craters intermittently for hundreds of years – Milton refers to it as

'Thundering Aetna' in *Paradise Lost* – and the lurid spectacle of gouts of lava being ejected from the crater every few minutes makes an odd contrast with the winter sports going on on the smooth, snowy slopes beneath the summit. In a quite different part of the world, the volcano Pacaya, only thirty-two kilometres from Guatemala City, in Central America, is just as active, if not more so, and the red glare from the volcano can easily be seen from the city on a clear night. This is a relatively small volcano, and so easily accessible that it has even been suggested that a hotel should be built beneath it, to make an especially attractive night spot for jaded Guatemalans, but so far no one has risked the capital.

Mt Erebus, the 4,045-metres-high volcano near McMurdo Sound in the Antarctic also has bouts of mild Strombolian activity. It was in this state when a team consisting of six men from Scott's base camp made an ascent of the volcano in December 1912, with a geologist, Raymond Priestley, in the lead. The party reached the lip of the main summit crater safely, only to find that it was quite docile, and that there was little to see within the crater apart from dense, swirling clouds of pungent sulphurous steam. They took some photographs, left a record of their ascent in a sealed tin in a cairn, and set off back down again. About twenty metres down from the top, Priestley realized that the tin they had left in the cairn in fact contained their exposed photographic plates, and that what they were carrying down with them was the tin containing the record of their ascent. He sent back one of the party to retrieve the proper tin, but no sooner had this poor unfortunate reached the crater rim than the volcano blew up in his face. Fortunately, he survived unscathed, apart from being showered with dust and ash, and inhaling a few lungfuls too many of sulphur dioxide fumes.

Some way to the west of Stromboli, and just to the north of Sicily, are the Lipari Islands. One of these islands contains a small and rather drab, unimpressive-looking conical heap of rubble, with a deep crater at its centre. This is Vulcano, the ancestor of all volcanoes. It has been intermittently active throughout history and may have been even more active in Greek and Roman times than it is now. To the Greeks, Vulcano was known as Hiera, the chimney of the forge of Hephaestus, God of Fire, but it was the Roman God of Fire, Vulcan, blacksmith to the Gods, whose name stuck. Vulcan, by the way, is supposed to have forged the breastplate of Hercules and the shield of Achilles as well as the arrows of Apollo and Diana. And just to cap all this mythological irrelevance, the island of Vulcano is now linked by a small spit of land to another small volcano, Vulcanello, which used to be a separate island, and it has been suggested that this pair comprised the 'Scylla and Charybdis', beloved of Homer and modern politicians, but then so have several other island pairs in the Mediterranean.

Apart from this dubious distinction, Vulcano has also given its name to a type of eruption, the *Vulcanian*, very different from the Strombolian. Several features identify these eruptions. First, they don't occur often during the life of the volcano, but when they do, they may continue intermittently for several months. Second, the magmas involved are much more viscous than those in Strombolian eruptions so that the explosive activity tends to be violent, often demolishing parts of the volcanic structure. In Strombolian eruptions, the red-hot fragments of lava that are hurled out of the vent are usually fairly plastic, smallish, and don't travel far. In a Vulcanian eruption, the ejected material comes in the form of solid blocks and highly-fragmented ash, and the explosions are often powerful enough to heave blocks weighing many tons clear of the crater, while smaller ones may be thrown for a kilometre or more. Third, and perhaps most conspicuous, a great plume of gas and ash rises above the crater, rolling upwards in tight turbulent convolutions often to a height of several kilometres.

A word here in passing about what actually goes to make up a typical volcanic eruption cloud. Three quite separate elements may be involved, all or any of which may be present at any one time. First, there may be a more or less continuous emission of steam and other vapours, not carrying much solid material, which forms a white column rather like the plume above a power-station cooling tower. Next, intermittent or semi-continuous explosions may hurl solid material up in a dense dark mass, with the leading fragments soaring straight up into the air, trailing smaller fragments behind them, and looking from a distance like rockets. These don't usually rise more than a couple of hundred metres before falling back along parabolic paths. The profile of this short-lived low-level blast cloud is supposed to look something like that of a clump of fir trees, so it's sometimes described as 'cypressoid'. Such clouds are usually best developed in eruptions of marine volcanoes.

13. *The cypressoid or 'cock's tail' effect produced by explosions taking place in the partly-submerged crater of the volcano Surtsey, off Iceland. The cock's tails are heavily laden with ash, and therefore dark, but the steam cloud (behind and to the left) is pure white.* (Photo courtesy of S. Thorarinsson)

14. *The magnificent eruption column which formed above Vesuvius on 26 April 1872. The voluted 'cauliflower' texture is well-displayed in the upper parts of the column.* (Photo by G. Sommer)

Last, and most important, is the cloud of fine ash which rises. If there are distinct separate explosions taking place during the eruption, then a fresh ash cloud will develop after each explosion, just like the ones produced by the explosion of a bomb, or after blasting in a quarry. If the explosive activity is more or less continuous, then clearly ash will rise continuously. These debris-laden clouds usually have a dark, solid appearance, often compared with the globular voluted surface of a cauliflower, and rather like the black, towering cumulus clouds that threaten thunderstorms. Often, the three elements are intermingled, so that the result is a mixture of white streaked with the grey or black ashy material. Beneath and down-wind of the ash cloud there is a steady rain of fine ash particles, sometimes falling so thickly that a dark curtain appears to be hanging beneath the cloud, while in and around it electrical storms rage, with lightning flickering frequently, so that the whole effect is much more dramatic than even the most ominous of thunder-clouds.

Vulcanian eruptions sometimes form the first phases of a longer eruption, when the volcano is 'clearing its throat' for the real business, and as such, there may be no *new* magmatic material involved, and all the material that is showered up as ash to form the 'cauliflower cloud' may be merely old, cold, solid lava which was previously blocking up the throat; if this is the case, the eruptions are sometimes called *ultra-vulcanian*. On the other hand, though, it's quite possible for Vulcanian eruptions to continue for long periods, with fresh viscous magma constantly being supplied. Between 1963 and 1965 the volcano Irazu in Costa Rica was more or less continuously active, with frequent explosions raining ash over a wide area and ruining the all-important coffee crop, but throughout this time no lavas were erupted and there was no significant change in the pattern of the eruption.

*Vesuvian* (or sub-Plinian) eruptions are one step further on from Vulcanian, their principal distinguishing feature being that rather than intermittent explosions there is a fairly sustained blast of escaping gas from the throat of the volcano, which carries the cauliflower cloud of ash much higher into the air. These continuous blasts may last for several hours, and in that time they eject large volumes of ash, which is always new magmatic material, rather than shattered bits and pieces of old rock. Vesuvius, which is only about ten kilometres from the centre of Naples and in one of the most densely-populated areas of Italy, has an irregular cycle of eruptions with twenty-five to thirty years of quiet being followed by a major outburst, when a great plume of dust and ash from the volcano rises over the city, reaching many kilometres into the air. The ash-fall from a typical Vesuvian eruption rarely causes casualties, but it did cause problems during the most recent eruption in 1944, when Allied airfields in the

Naples area were carpeted with ash, making the runways temporarily unusable, and gritty particles found their way into the air intakes of aircraft flying in the area.

Pliny the Younger's account of the death of his uncle during the A.D. 79 eruption of Vesuvius has been commemorated in the term *Plinian* eruption, the most violent of all in the sequence we have been considering. Although their effects are more extensive, Plinian eruptions are not basically very different qualitatively from the Vesuvian type. (By the way, don't forget that it is only *types* of eruption, that are being discussed, and that any individual volcano may erupt in any of these ways – or in none.) The one thing above all others which characterizes a Plinian eruption is the sheer volume of the fragmentary material ejected by the gas blast. Pompeii, approximately eight kilometres from Vesuvius, was buried over three metres deep in pumice in A.D. 79, and the total volume ejected in the forty-eight hours or so of that eruption was probably about three cubic kilometres. Frequently, too, there are major structural changes to the volcano, with a large part of it being blown away or collapsing to form a gaping crater, up to several kilometres across. The 1883 eruption of Krakatoa was of this kind, although the four explosions that took place at its climax were so stupendous that a separate type of eruption, the *Krakatoan*, is sometimes referred to.

Probably the best modern example of a Plinian eruption was that of the Bezymianny volcano in Kamchatka, part of the Russian segment of the 'Ring of Fire'. Bezymianny was a rather obscure volcano (the name itself means 'no name') before the eruption and was generally thought to be extinct. The volcano was 3,102 metres high, and had a conical profile. In September 1955 seismic activity began to make itself felt in the surrounding area, gradually increasing in severity until 22 October, when the eruption commenced. For several months intermittent Vulcanian activity continued, hurling ash between four and eight kilometres in the air, but died down somewhat in early 1956. On 30 March, however, an exceptionally violent explosion occurred, blowing off the top 200 metres of the volcano, and propagating a dense eruption cloud which expanded upwards at a speed estimated to be something like 500 metres per second, finally reaching a height of thirty-eight kilometres. About four cubic kilometres of ash were ejected, falling out over an area of 57,000 square kilometres. After the eruption, it was found that almost the whole of one side of the cone had disappeared, and it looked as if a giant bite had been taken out of it. In the bite-shaped hollow, a small mound of viscous lava was growing and continued to do so for a long time afterwards. The significance of this little mound will soon become apparent.

The 1902 eruption of Mt Pelée was the first recognized example of a *Peléean* eruption, a very different kind of phenomenon from the 'ordinary' Vesuvian or Plinian types, although Peléean eruptions often occur as short-lived side-shows to the latter. Only one feature characterizes a Peléean eruption; a *nuée ardente*, or glowing cloud, of the sort that had such lethal effects on St Pierre. (Remember that Mt Pelée unleashed several *nuées* during the eruption of 1902–3, but only two caused casualties.) All of these *nuées* were linked with the growth of a large pile or *dome* of viscous lava on the site of the Étang Sec, where the eruption first started. For the most part, the growth of this dome was accompanied by intermittent Vulcanian activity, responsible for the loud explosions heard in St Pierre and for the ash that was showered down on the town before and after the fateful 8 May. On that date, a part of the side of the dome was blown out, and a large cloud was blasted out sideways, rather than straight up as in a normal Vulcanian eruption. This was a *nuée*. A *nuée* consists of an incandescent mass of solid fragments, buoyed up by the rush of expanding, heated gases. The escaping gases rise upwards, forming a turbulent, dynamic wall, while the denser part, containing most of the solid material, hugs the ground and rolls rapidly over it, travelling at great speed, since each particle of the solid material is in a more or less floating condition, cushioned by escaping gas like a hovercraft.

A *nuée* is at once immensely hot and immensely powerful – the St Pierre *nuée* has often been called a 'tornadic' blast – and its destructive capabilities are all too clear. It's a little surprising, then, that similar phenomena had not been recognized prior to

1902, since they must have occurred on numerous occasions in the past. Since St Pierre, though, *nuées* have been observed in a number of different eruptions, and in a great many of them they are linked with the construction of a lava dome. So often, in fact, that the presence of such a dome is sometimes considered to be a characteristic feature of Peléean eruptions. This is where that small mound of lava on Bezymianny comes in. This eruption could as well be termed Peléean as Plinian, for part of the force of the great eruption of 1956 was expended in powerful *nuées* which swept down the flanks of the volcano with terrific force. Trees twenty-four kilometres from the volcano were felled by the blast, and sandy ash carried by the *nuées* formed deposits over thirty centimetres thick even nine kilometres away.

Not all *nuées* are associated with lava domes, though. Ironically enough, only the day before the St Pierre tragedy, a series of

*Fig. 32 The base surge which develops round the stalk of a typical nuclear 'mushroom' cloud.*

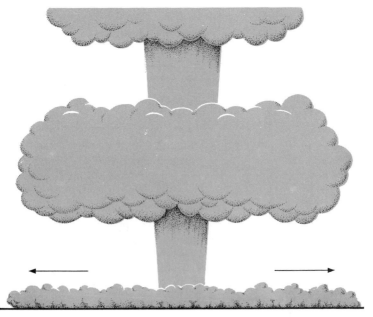

*nuées* were erupted from the volcano Soufrière on St Vincent, 144 kilometres south of Martinique. About one third of the island was devastated but fortunately it was thinly populated, and casualties were relatively few: only 1,350 people were killed. The interesting thing about the St Vincent *nuées* is that they were a side-effect of a conventional Vulcanian-type explosion column. As this rose vertically into the air, the *nuées* rolled away sideways from its base, and down the flanks of the volcano.

These radially-directed *nuées* are an example of a phenomenon known as the *base surge* or ground surge, first recognized in studies of test explosions of nuclear weapons. Next time you see that familiar mushroom cloud rearing up (hopefully on your T.V. screen, not across the road), look at the base or stalk of the mushroom, and you'll almost certainly see a ring of cloud rolling away horizontally from it. That's the base surge. Remember the term, because it will turn up again in a rather odd context.

In 1951 a well-documented eruption of this kind took place on Mt Lamington in Papua, another of those volcanoes which was thought to be extinct until something nasty happened. After a few days of premonitory seismic activity, the eruption started on 15 January and for a few days well-developed Vulcanian activity continued, with frequent explosions and a great eruption cloud reaching up to 10,000 metres. At 10.40 on 20 January a climactic explosion occurred, with a huge ash-laden cloud climbing upwards to a height of 13,000 metres in two minutes. Base surges spread out radially in all directions from the base of the rising ash column, rolling down the volcano at speeds of nearly a hundred kilometres per hour and covering an area of more than 230 square kilometres. Within the affected area the destruction was almost complete and there were no survivors. The force of the blast was impressive. The thick forests growing on the flanks of the volcano were completely levelled, in some cases so completely that it was hard to tell that there once had been trees growing there. To quote the Australian vulcanologist G. A. Taylor, who reached the scene two days later, 'in many places the only evidence of the forest cover was charred roots carved off level with . . . soil surface'. Elsewhere fully grown trees were uprooted, and were found laid out in the direction of the blast. Near the village of Higaturu, the mangled remains of a vehicle were found hanging upside down in a tree. Most of the houses in the village itself were totally destroyed, and 3,000 people were killed.

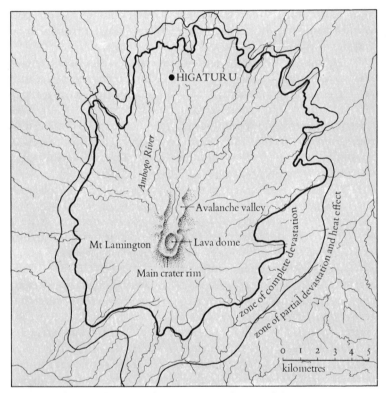

*Fig. 33 The area devastated by the* nuées ardentes *of the 1951 eruption of Mt Lamington in Papua. The* nuées *spread out radially all round the volcano.* (After G. A. Taylor)

Many other examples of Peléean eruptions are now known, especially among the volcanoes in the Philippine Islands, and they have been closely studied, since there is considerable interest in how these eruptions occur and in particular how the material in a *nuée* is actually transported. This is important because it is directly relevant to understanding the mechanism of a type of eruption not yet observed at first hand by any human being, but one that would make the Mt Pelée eruption pale into insignificance if an example were to occur today. These eruptions give rise to rocks known as *ignimbrites*, and they are so powerful that tens of cubic kilometres of ignimbrite can be erupted in *nuée ardente*-like incandescent clouds in the space of a few hours or days. Less than one million years ago an eruption of this sort took place near Naples; the ignimbrites erupted spread out over 5,000 square kilometres, and performed the almost incredible feat of rushing up and over mountain passes 600 metres high. Such eruptions are clearly something rather special, and will be discussed in more detail later.

## Eruptions in general

In discussing the various types of eruption that are generally recognized, it was emphasized that labels such as 'Strombolian' or 'Plinian' should only be applied to recognizable *phases* of an eruption; they may not necessarily apply to the whole thing. To see just how important this is we'll follow the course of one eruption from start to finish. The example we'll consider is that of Mt Etna in 1971. This wasn't an especially spectacular event, although it was the biggest eruption on Etna for some years, and there were no casualties, but none the less it was very instructive.

Etna is a big volcano, much the highest in Europe, and it has a record of activity going well back into history. It's just over 3,300 metres high, so that the top part is snow-covered for much of the year, and the fortunate Sicilians can ride up in a cable car from the warmth of the lower slopes to ski there. Etna has two summit craters, the Main Crater and the North-East Crater (both lying along the line of a fissure), and the North-East Crater had been showing mild Strombolian activity for many years prior to the 1971 eruption. The first evidence that this was on its way was noticed towards the end of March, when a patch of snow just

*Fig. 34 Locality map for the 1971 eruption of Etna, showing the sites of the three main phases of the eruption. None of the villages was seriously damaged by the lavas, although all the best ski slopes (above the Rifugio Piccolo) were permanently ruined.*

below and to the south of the Main Crater began to melt, and simultaneously, activity in the North-East Crater began to die down. On 5 April, a set of fissures opened in the same place, and showers of incandescent fragments of lava were ejected. These rapidly accumulated round the fissure, building up into a conical heap, and then, as more and more new material emerged from the fissures, lava flows were erupted and began to stream down the ski-slopes. This was the first phase of the eruption; it lasted about two weeks. Strombolian activity continued for most of this time in the little cone built up over the fissure, until it was a respectable thirty metres or so in height, while the lavas snaked down-slope in several glowing tongues, permanently ruining many of the best skiing slopes, engulfing one by one the pylons that carried the cable-way, and demolishing the upper cable-station. These flows were relatively small and they didn't get down to the lower, inhabited parts of the mountain. Ironically, though, they demolished an imposing vulcanological observatory built by Mussolini in the 1930s.

The second phase was completely different. A long linear fissure opened abruptly on 13 May, well down on the eastern slopes of the volcano, and at a height of only 1,800 metres. There was no explosive activity, no eruption column, just a crack in the ground opening up, and a few pungent blue sulphurous fumes. Soon, though, lava began to flow freely from the fissure, quite quietly and in much greater volumes than in the first phase. This un-

15. *The ski slopes of Etna after the 1971 eruption. The derelict pylon in the foreground used to be part of a cableway which carried skiers almost to the foot of the summit cone. Aa lavas, visible behind the pylon, now cover the old pistes.*

dramatic release of large volumes of lava, would, if one had to give it a name, probably best be described as a Hawaiian-type eruption. Since they were erupted so low down, it was not long before the rivers of lava were flowing through inhabited areas. They did a great deal of damage to vineyards, roads, bridges and houses and threatened the villages of St Alfio, Fornazzo and Macchia. The people of St Alfio talked the local priest into exorcizing the lava with the help of sacred relics, and, with or without divine intervention, the villages escaped serious damage. The third and final phase was different again. On 18 May a deep pit-like hole opened high up on the volcano, east of the Main Crater, at a height of 2,980 metres. No lava at all was erupted, but great dark cauliflower explosion-clouds rolled out of it, laying a thin carpet of ash downwind of the vent. This was classic Vulcanian activity.

So, not counting the initial Strombolian activity in the North-East Crater, there were three separate sites of activity during the course of the eruption, and each showed different behaviour: Strombolian, Hawaiian and Vulcanian. In part, the difference in behaviour at the three sites reflects the relationship between a lava and its gas content, a topic which will be discussed further in the next section. In the first phase, the gas pressure on the magma was released by the mildly-explosive Strombolian activity. This meant that the magma that fed the fissures of the second phase was almost completely de-gassed, hence its quiet emission. The third, Vulcanian phase, also probably reflects this de-gassing process, with gas escaping from the magma below accumulating in the higher parts of the volcano, and then blasting its way to the surface. This sort of pattern, high-level de-gassing followed by low-level emission of gas-free lavas, is typical of Etna, and many other volcanoes.

## Controlling factors in eruptions

The rather crude criterion that we have used to distinguish between types of eruption, the degree of violence of explosiveness, reflects two more fundamental variables, the viscosity of the lava and the gas content. Let's have a closer look at these two – viscosity first.

In common with all other liquids, from petrol to treacle, molten rocks have a viscosity, and also in common with other liquids, the viscosity decreases with increasing temperature. A 'hot' lava, freshly-erupted, is a great deal less viscous than a 'cold' one, and it can therefore flow faster. The temperature of a lava flow is naturally lower at its far end than at its source, and this means that there are obvious differences in the speed at which the lava moves. At source, a basalt lava may be moving at twenty or more kilometres an hour; at the far end it may be oozing forward like treacle at only a few metres per hour; so the temperature of a magma will obviously affect the style of an eruption considerably. There's a complication, though. Not all magmas have the same composition, and magmas with different compositions melt at different temperatures. Basaltic rocks melt at about 1,100°C, while granitic rocks melt at only about 650–700°C, so magmas of granitic composition are many times more viscous than basaltic ones.

In a Hawaiian eruption, the magmas are basaltic, hot, and of low viscosity, so they can be extruded from a vent as lavas with little effort. Basaltic magmas are usually involved in most Strombolian eruptions, too, but these are slightly more viscous, so there are rather more bangs and thumps, but the material that is ejected is still fairly fluid. As one goes up the scale, though, one finds that magmas of more granitic composition are involved and they and the lavas they produce are more viscous. The more viscous the lava, the more difficult it is to force it through a vent, and the vent may well become blocked with a slow-moving or stationary plug of lava. If this happens, and gas pressure builds up beneath the plug, a potentially highly-explosive situation develops. In Vulcanian eruptions, such a plug may be blown away by repeated explosions, after which lavas may flow away quietly, or if the magma is very viscous, and keeps on coming, explosions will continue. Highly-viscous lavas are always concerned in Peléean eruptions; as we saw earlier, a dome or plug of lava often builds up within the crater concerned, blocking the throat of the volcano, so that the pressures building up beneath can only be relieved by vigorous explosions, which may be directed either upwards or sideways, blasting out as *nuées ardentes*. Evidence of just how viscous the lavas are, and how great the forces involved are, was provided by the great spine which was pushed up out of the vent of Mt Pelée, reaching over 300 metres in height.

A viscous magma, however, is not by itself explosive; it is the gas content which is decisive, and which puts the bang into an eruption. If two magmas have identical viscosities, it's the one with the highest gas content that's erupted most violently. In the case of the 1971 Etna eruption, the magma involved was the same basaltic one throughout, yet its behaviour was quite different in its de-gassed condition in the second phase from its original state in the first, when the eruption was mildly explosive. The contrast between gas-rich and gas-poor magmas is much more pronounced at the viscous granitic end of the scale. If such a granitic magma had a low gas content, it would be erupted at the surface as a viscous lava flow, which would ooze sluggishly out of the vent, travel only a short distance and pile up into massive heaps. If, on the other hand, the same granitic magma had a high gas content, the result would be spectacularly different. As the magma approached the surface, the pressure on it would decrease, and the gas in it would expand; as the gas expanded it would take up more room, and this in turn would force the whole mass to rise faster and higher up the vent. So a violent kind of self-accelerating process would take place, with the magma rapidly blowing itself up into a froth of gas and liquid rock and blasting itself clear out of the vent. It is the myriad solidified fragments of this rock froth which form the large volumes of ash mantling the countryside round the volcano which is definitive of a Plinian eruption. The light-weight rock froth itself is quite familiar, and turns up in British bathrooms; it is, of course, pumice.

## Submarine eruptions

Quite a large proportion of the world's volcanoes are located on the oceanic crust, most of them forming parts of the mid-ocean ridge systems. Inevitably, therefore, there must be a good many eruptions taking place below sea level, so we will conclude this chapter by looking briefly at the sort of activity that results. Two things stem directly from the location of a submarine eruption. First, since the volcano is built on oceanic crust, the magmas involved will be basaltic, so that the sort of eruption that we can expect will be a modification of an ordinary Hawaiian or Strombolian eruption. Second, when red-hot magma comes into contact with a large volume of sea water, the water is converted instantly into steam, and an explosion results. So we can expect our submarine eruption to be much more explosive than its terrestrial counterpart. The power of such underwater explosive activity was demonstrated forcibly in 1952, when a Japanese research vessel, the *No. 5 Kaiyo-Maru*, 211 tons, was sent to investigate reports of a submarine eruption about 420 kilometres south of Tokyo. She never returned from that mission; it is believed that an explosion took place while she was directly over the site of the volcano. There were no survivors from the crew of thirty-one, but some floating debris was found later, with fragments of rock particles from the eruption deeply embedded within it. The ship had clearly been blown apart.

The effect of sea water on a basaltic magma is sometimes clearly displayed in places like Hawaii if there is a long active fissure, extending from inland towards the coast. Along the inland part of the fissure ordinary Hawaiian-type eruptions will take place, with lava being emitted quietly, and perhaps a bit of fire-fountaining. Near the sea, though, where water is able to penetrate inland and downwards through joints and cracks, the activity is much more vigorous, and in many respects resembles Vulcanian activity. A tall, turbulent white steam column rolls upwards above the vent, often becoming grey or black as ash is blasted upwards. Frequent powerful explosions throw showers of fragments into the air, forming the 'cypressoid' eruption cloud mentioned earlier. It has recently been suggested that a good name for eruptions of this type would be 'Surtseyan', after the eruption off Iceland in 1963.

When a volcano erupts actually beneath the sea, a series of stages in the activity can usually be identified. At first, there will be little to see other than an area of dirty, discoloured water, possibly hot or 'boiling', and probably with a good many dead fish floating around in it. Next, explosive activity will start, blasting ashy material in jets a couple of hundred metres above sea level. A more or less permanent steam column will soon establish itself, and a Surtseyan eruption ensues, with ejected material accumulating on the sea floor until there is such a pile that the top of it shows itself above sea level, and an island is born. The style of eruption doesn't change much, though, until the island has grown substantially, and a recognizable cone and crater have developed. By that time, the feeder pipe of magma will have become fairly well insulated from the sea, so for the first time the cherry red glow of liquid lava will be seen, and small lava flows will emerge, cementing the island together. Mild explosive activity usually takes place in the crater, throwing up showers of red-hot lava, and in this condition the style is no longer Surtseyan but Strombolian, and of course the eruption has ceased to be a strictly submarine one. The kinds of deposits that are produced by the submarine and surface phases of the *same* eruption are also quite different, as we shall see.

# *Chapter 4* Volcanic rocks – lavas

In the last chapter, the different types of volcanic eruption were described; in this chapter and the two following some of the different types of rocks that result will be considered. It is important to emphasize how varied volcanoes can be in this respect. Some volcanoes produce only one kind of rock during their entire lives, but others show an impressive diversity. It is hard to imagine a greater contrast between two rock types than that between obsidian, a natural volcanic glass which will shatter at a blow into razor-sharp splinters, and pumice, a rock so light and frothy that it will float on water. Both, however, may be produced by a volcano during the course of a single eruption, and they may be chemically identical. The pronounced *physical* differences between them result only from the contrasted ways in which they are erupted. Obsidian is erupted quietly as lava, forming thick, sluggish flows, while pumice is blasted out rapidly and blown up into a consistency something like expanded polystyrene, with a delicate cellular structure that results from the expansion of large volumes of gas within the magma.

Rocks like pumice, which are ejected as broken, solid fragments rather than in liquid form, are known as *pyroclastic* rocks (pyro – fire, clastic – broken = broken by fire). All volcanic rocks, whatever their composition, may turn up either as lavas or pyroclastics, but rocks of some compositions are more often found as lavas, while others are more common as pyroclastics. This is an important point, and one that will be followed more closely. First, though, a word about the stuff that rocks and minerals are made of.

## The chemistry of rocks

When moving around the surface of the Earth, one cannot fail to be impressed by the diversity of all that one sees, and it is easy to imagine that there is an infinite complexity of different 'things' not apparently related to one another. In chemical terms, though, the situation is much simpler, since all matter is composed of only a hundred or so elements. So the apparently boundless diversity of plant life disappears when one recalls that *all* plants are composed of carbon, hydrogen, oxygen, nitrogen and a few less important elements, and that chemically there is little difference between a daisy and an oak tree. The same is true of rocks. Thousands of different kinds of rocks have been described and separately named, but when one gets down to their chemistry, one finds that they all have a great deal in common. Ninety-two elements exist in nature and another dozen or so have been made by nuclear physicists. Of these ninety-two, only twelve occur in proportions greater than 0·1 per cent in the Earth's crust. Here they are in order of abundance:

|            | *Percentage* |
|------------|------------|
| Oxygen     | 46·6       |
| Silicon    | 27·7       |
| Aluminium  | 8·1        |
| Iron       | 5·0        |
| Calcium    | 3·6        |
| Sodium     | 2·8        |
| Potassium  | 2·6        |
| Magnesium  | 2·1        |
| Titanium   | 0·4        |
| Phosphorus | 0·2        |
| Manganese  | 0·1        |
| Hydrogen   | 0·1        |

Of these twelve, the first eight are much the most abundant, with silicon and oxygen head and shoulders above the rest. Silicon and oxygen, in fact, are the fundamental constituents of almost all the rocks in the Earth's crust.

The two can occur just by themselves, in a compound represented chemically as $Si O_2$; this is silica, and in the form of *quartz* it is one of the commonest rock-forming minerals in the world. Apart from quartz, silicon and oxygen combine together to form an atomic building-block known as the *silicon tetrahedron*, with a single atom of silica surrounded by four atoms of oxygen, like this:

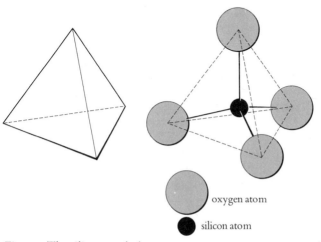

oxygen atom

silicon atom

*Fig. 35 The silicon tetrahedron.*

(To get an idea of what a tetrahedron looks like in three dimensions, look at one of those awkwardly-shaped cardboard milk cartons. They are made up of four triangular sides, and are splendid tetrahedra.) This $Si O_4$ building-block can combine with almost all of the other twelve elements in the list to form *silicate* minerals, and these, with quartz, make up more than 99 per cent of all volcanic rocks. To be academic for a moment, minerals can be defined as 'naturally formed, inorganic substances which possess a definite chemical composition and a definite atomic structure'. Many thousands of separate natural minerals which fit this definition have been described, and, especially in the nineteenth century, scientists spent decades of their lives in searching out new ones. Fortunately, though, all but a few volcanic rocks are built up by various combinations of only seven different minerals, or rather mineral families. Here they are:

$$\left.\begin{array}{l}\text{Olivines}\\\text{Pyroxenes}\\\text{Amphiboles}\\\text{Micas}\\\text{Feldspars}\\\text{Quartz}\\\text{Oxides}\end{array}\right\} \text{Silicates}$$

The first six are all silicate minerals; the last are also-rans, making up the 1 per cent non-silicate content of volcanic rocks, and are almost always oxides of iron and titanium. The olivines, pyroxenes, amphiboles, micas and feldspars are true families, not individual minerals; each family has the same atomic structure, but the chemical composition of minerals in each family can vary widely, within certain limits. The atomic structures which characterize each family are built up in different ways with the basic $S_iO_4$ building-block.

So volcanic rocks are composed of only a few mineral groups, each group having its own characteristic atomic structure. Most volcanic rocks are composed of only four or so of these groups, and there is a steady change in the proportions of different groups present as one goes from one end of the rock spectrum to another. Rocks are classified chemically according to how much silica $(S_iO_2)$ they contain; rocks with a lot of silica are known as *acid*. They consist mostly of quartz and feldspars, with a little mica or amphibole. *Basic* rocks form the other end of the spectrum, they contain much less $S_iO_2$, there is no free quartz (all the silica is present as silicates), but there is a lot of feldspar, and a great deal of pyroxene, olivine and oxide minerals. Apart from quartz and the feldspars, most minerals are dark in colour, so basic rocks with no quartz tend to be dark-coloured, while acid rocks are much lighter and usually have only isolated specks of dark minerals.

As far as actual examples of volcanic rocks are concerned, it was mentioned that the most abundant are basalts, which form at mid-ocean ridges, and andesites, which are formed at destructive plate margins. Basalts are examples of basic volcanic rocks, while andesites are intermediate between basic and acid. To these should be added a third group, which are not so abundant in terms of volume, but which are equally important. These are the *rhyolites*, which are right at the other end of the spectrum from basalts; that is to say they are acid, contain a lot of silica and have the same composition as granite. They are lighter in colour and lower in density than basalts or andesites, and contain fewer dark minerals. Obsidian is a special kind of rhyolite; it is a natural glass, whereas ordinary rhyolites are not. The important properties of these three principal volcanic rock groups can be summarized in a simple table:

| Property | Basalt | Andesite | Rhyolite |
|---|---|---|---|
| Silica content | Least – about 50% (therefore basic) | Intermediate (about 60%) | Most (more than 65%) (therefore acid) |
| Content of dark minerals | Highest | Intermediate | Least |
| Typical minerals | Feldspar Pyroxene Olivine Oxides | Feldspar Amphibole Pyroxene Mica | Feldspar Quartz Mica Amphibole |
| Density | Highest | Intermediate | Lowest |
| Melting point | Highest | Intermediate | Lowest |
| Viscosity as molten rock at surface | Least | Intermediate | Highest |
| Tendency to form lavas | Highest | Intermediate | Least |
| Tendency to form pyroclastics | Least | Intermediate | Highest |

This table illustrates the all-important variations in properties between the two extremes: basalt and rhyolite. Fundamentally, it is the differences in composition that are responsible for all the variations between the extremes, and this produces an interesting chain of cause and effect which can be summed up like this:

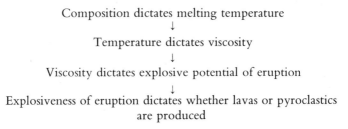

Composition dictates melting temperature
↓
Temperature dictates viscosity
↓
Viscosity dictates explosive potential of eruption
↓
Explosiveness of eruption dictates whether lavas or pyroclastics are produced

So while it may not seem obvious that two magmas, differing only by 5 or 10 per cent in silica content, should behave quite differently on eruption, this chain of cause and effect operates to produce very substantial differences indeed.

## Physical properties of lava flows

Lavas are amongst the most harmless weapons in a volcano's formidable armoury – one can always see them coming, and almost always get out of their way quickly enough. For all their harmlessness, though, they are still absorbingly interesting natural spectacles. A specimen of basalt taken from a cold lava flow, however, is not a particularly inspiring object at all – in most cases, it probably looks like a dirty black lump of clinker. It is usually difficult to see the individual minerals making up a basalt, since they are far too small, so one has to use a microscope. First, though, one has to obtain a very thin section of the rock, thin enough to be translucent. Cutting these sections is a skilled job, requiring the services of a technician in a specially-equipped workshop, so there can be no question of using even the most portable of microscopes to study rocks in the field. When a thin section of a basalt is examined under a microscope, it can be seen to be made up of a closely-felted mass of interlocking needle-like crystals of feldspar, a millimetre or so long, with a scattering of more colourful tiny crystals of olivine and pyroxene and some black opaque specks of iron oxides. It is the word *crystal* that is important. A crystalline substance is an ordered substance: all the atoms in it are arranged in a regular geometrical pattern; so when the lava cooled from its original molten condition, the initial homogeneous liquid melt crystallized out to form well-ordered, identifiable minerals. This may seem quite straightforward, but it is important, because in some cases this orderly process of crystallization does not take place, and the result is a homogeneous lump of rock.

Different minerals crystallize at different temperatures, so that when a basalt magma cools, a sequence of minerals appears. The first mineral to crystallize is usually olivine, which carries on crystallizing as the magma cools until a temperature is reached at which a second mineral, pyroxene, begins to appear, and then, as the temperature drops still further, these two continue to crystallize together. Finally, a temperature is reached when a third mineral, feldspar, joins in. Crystallization then continues until the rock is completely solid. Quite often, olivine and pyroxene begin to crystallize out early on, so they may be present in the final rock as quite large crystals, up to a centimetre across, many times larger than the crystals surrounding them, and easily visible with the naked eye. So there is an important contrast here between the groundmass of tiny, felted crystals and the much bigger, separate *phenocryst* minerals.

Most volcanic rocks contain some phenocrysts – they are a bit like the pips in raspberry jam. The groundmass crystals form when the lava cools on reaching the surface, so the individual crystals are tiny, simply because they don't have the time to grow any larger in the relatively short period that the flow takes to cool. The phenocryst minerals, the pips in the jam, however, crystallize out much earlier, while the magma is still underground. So they have plenty of time to grow to a respectable size and are merely carried passively up to the surface with the rest of the magma when it is erupted, and are distributed uniformly throughout it.

16. *Photograph of a thin section of a typical basalt lava, illustrating the difference in size between the groundmass minerals, and the phenocrysts, which are the large black and white bodies. Here, the phenocrysts are mostly of feldspar, which has a distinctive 'candy-striped' appearance in polarized light. They are about five millimetres across.*

But what about those lavas that solidify into one homogeneous lump, without crystallizing? These are quite common, but instead of being featureless, uninteresting 'lumps', they are highly distinctive natural glasses. When a melt of any kind is cooled rapidly, it does not have time to sort its atoms out into the ordered atomic structures of mineral crystals. The atoms are all 'frozen' into the random positions they occupied in the liquid, producing a material which is neither crystal nor liquid: not crystal because it doesn't have an ordered structure, not liquid because it doesn't flow. It is, in fact, a *supercooled* liquid, and if heated, it would soften slowly over a broad temperature range, rather than melting abruptly. Ordinary window glass is an example of matter in this state; it is made by melting up silicate materials such as quartz sand and allowing the melt to cool under controlled conditions so that crystallization does not occur. Glass, however, may crystallize out or *devitrify* in the solid state if it's left long enough, with myriads of tiny crystals forming and making it opaque. Brittle toffee is another example of a glass; it consists mainly of non-crystalline sugar, while some kinds of fudge are devitrified toffee. When lava flows are erupted at the surface, they are necessarily rapidly chilled, and volcanic glasses are common. The surface layers of basalt flows are commonly glassy; but deeper within, the amount of glass gets less, and more crystals appear, until the whole mass is composed of crystals. The transition from glass to crystals in a basalt may cover a few centimetres, but in andesites and rhyolites it is much broader, and large thicknesses of glass may be present.

## Basalt lava flows

One of the most characteristic features of basalt lavas is that they are often riddled with holes. Large quantities of gas may be involved in the eruption of basaltic lavas; when the lava is below ground, the gas is kept in solution in the molten rock, when the pressure on the lava is reduced the gases come out of solution and bubbles form, just as they do when a bottle of champagne is opened. If the bubbling gas can escape freely, the lava will become de-gassed, or 'flat', and the rock that results will be free of bubbles. If, on the other hand, gases continue to escape while the lava is being erupted, bubbles will go on growing in the lava, and these will be preserved in the rock when it cools. Normally, these bubbles (or *vesicles*) are only a few millimetres across and quite thinly scattered, but sometimes, if the lava has been particularly gas rich, the rock is so honeycombed with large bubbles that it looks like some kinds of Swiss cheese; more holes than solid. Gas bubbles in any liquid tend to rise to the surface, so in any basalt lava flow, it is only the top part which is likely to have a honeycomb texture. In the lower parts of the flow, vesicles are much smaller and scarcer, and are often absent altogether.

There are a great many other possible variables within a single basalt flow, apart from the vesicle distribution. To get an idea of some of the many different features that can be produced, consider what happens to a single, large flow as it is traced from its source to its tip. When it emerges from below ground, a basalt lava is usually at a temperature of about 1,100°C, and it glows fiercely yellow-white, the colour of molten steel poured from a furnace. At this temperature the molten rock is at its least viscous and it flows downhill as a fiery river, splashing and bounding over minor irregularities like a mountain stream, and cascading over larger obstacles in glowing fire-falls. As it flows, the lava cools, and its initial fierce glow subsides to a less intense yellow, and more important, the viscosity increases so that the lava becomes more like treacle. As the viscosity increases, the lava flows more slowly and smoothly, not as boisterously as it did at first. In practical terms, this means that when a yellow–hot lava is first emitted, it can flow at a rate of many kilometres an hour, but lower down on the flanks of the volcano, when it is cooler, it slows to the speed of a run, and then of a fast walk. (The actual rate of flow at any point will, of course, depend on the slope of the ground.) Further away from the source still, the lava flows even slower, and the yellow glow gives way to a bright cherry red, and black streaks and blobs of chilled solid lava appear on the surface. Initially these are no more than tiny wisps streaked out on the surface of the lava, like flecks of foam on a river, which are soon engulfed once more in the main mass. As the lava cools down further, to a dull red, more and more chilled fragments remain on the surface, and these small particles soon agglomerate together, forming progressively larger plates or rafts which cover the surface of the flow, the hot lava itself only glowing through in the cracks between rafts. When the lava has reached this cherry-red temperature, it's extremely viscous, like sticky treacle, and if one can get near enough to the flow to push a pole into it, quite a lot of material can be collected, and this can be carried away while still very hot and soft. In many volcanic areas the locals make a practice of collecting small samples of lava in this way, and then mould it while still hot into ashtrays, medallions and so on, to sell as souvenirs of the eruption.

When a basalt flow has cooled sufficiently for some sort of crust to form, one of two possible things can happen. It can either form a thin, skin-like layer of solid lava over the liquid, rather like the skin that develops on custard or boiled milk, or else it develops a rather thick, rubbly surface layer consisting of loose blocks of solidified lava. This blocky layer is carried along on top of the moving flow, looking for all the world like rocks on a conveyor belt in a quarry.

17. Aa *surface on a lava flow erupted on Mt Etna in 1971. The fumes which partially obscure the surface are rising from part of the flow which was still moving, carrying the rubbly material conveyor-belt fashion. The building is the vulcanological observatory on Etna; a short time after this picture was taken it was destroyed by the lavas.*

18. *This Etna lava flow, erupted during the nineteenth century, is now being quarried. It illustrates clearly how the massive hard rock of the lower part of the flow is overlaid by loose, rubbly material.*

The custard-skin type of surface is not as common as the rubbly type, but it is often particularly well-developed on oceanic volcanoes, and especially on the Hawaiian islands. When lava like this comes to rest or slows down, the 'skin' piles up against itself, buckling up into a closely-spaced series of pleats. These pleats give the lava a ropy appearance, and the flows are called by a name given to them by the Polynesian islanders – *pahoehoe* flows.

The other kind of flow, with the rubbly 'conveyor-belt' surface is also known by a Polynesian name; it is called an *aa* flow. Areas of many square kilometres can be covered by *aa* lavas, and they present severe obstacles to anyone trying to cross them. Every cindery boulder making up the jumbled chaotic surface is loose, irregularly angular in shape, and covered in razor-sharp protrusions. Every step is a balancing act; every slip of the foot means a series of razor-like slashes·on one's boots; to fall means badly

19. Pahoehoe *surface on a basalt lava erupted from Kilauea volcano, Hawaii in 1920. The ropy appearance is quite unmistakable.* (Hawaii Institute of Geophysics photo courtesy of G. A. Macdonald)

lacerated hands and knees. So crossing one of these flows is a dreary, difficult and painful job. No wonder the Polynesians call them *aa* flows – and go round the long way!

However unpleasant these flows are to scramble over when cold, it is very instructive to watch them when hot. As the lava cools, not only does the surface solidify, but the material at the sides does too. As soon as the flow becomes established, in fact, piles of solid lumps of lava build up at the sides of the flow, and help to confine it to its course. These marginal banks rapidly build up, and the lava soon finds itself channelled into a sort of self-made canal. Often, the initial rapid rate of flow decreases, and then the level of the lava in the canal drops, leaving the banks, or *levées* as they are called, standing up high and dry like walls. If the flow rate should increase for any reason, the lava may burst out over the *levées*, flooding out to form a new branch of the

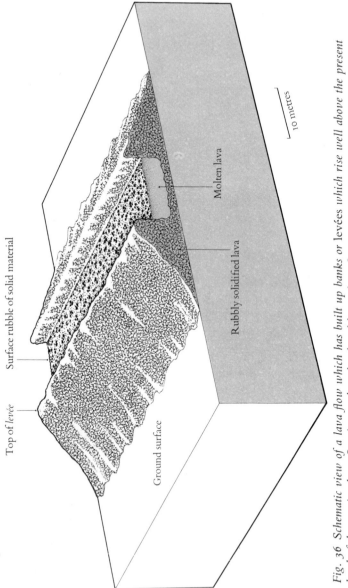

Top of *levée*

Surface rubble of solid material

Ground surface

Molten lava

Rubbly solidified lava

10 metres

Fig. 36 *Schematic view of a lava flow which has built up banks or levées which rise well above the present level of the moving lava. Levées are best developed by aa lava flows.*

20. *Well-developed lava* levées *on a lava which flowed down from the summit crater of Teide volcano in Tenerife. The* levées *are so regular that they look almost artificial.*

main flow, and this 'break out' will itself rapidly become established between *levées*.

Solid lumps of lava also pile up in front of the advancing nose of the lava. In the higher, hotter parts, the lava continually advances forward over this solid material, engulfing it and rolling it up like the tracks on a tank or caterpillar tractor. In the lower, colder parts, though, there is much more solid material on the surface, on the flanks and in front, and the lava can no longer simply advance over the top of the mass of its own rubble in front of it. The flow doesn't stop, though. From the outside, it may look like a static heap of boiler slag, but it's still very much alive, and mobile lava is still arriving deep within it and pushing forward. So the nose of the flow is unstable and there is a constant gentle clatter of small lava chunks falling forward. Every few minutes a large solid mass breaks off and topples forward in a cascade of loose, glowing material, and comes to rest a few feet from the main mass, leaving a fading, sullen red glowing scar to mark the place on the flow where it came from.

In this way, with one small rock fall following another, the flow continues to advance, very slowly, clanking and rattling forward like a shuffling slag heap. This movement, perhaps only a few metres per hour, continues until the supply dies away at source, and the nose of the flow gradually slows down and stops, still and silent. In a matter of hours the surface will be cold enough for geologists, sight-seers and small boys to swarm over it without harm, apart from singed boots and perhaps bottoms. Deeper down, though, the main mass cools down much more slowly, so that for weeks afterwards the core of the flow will be red hot, with the glow visible from time to time when small collapses take place. The rubble of solid chilled material overlying the hot core naturally tends to insulate it, and it does so very efficiently. There is even one report of a couple of Russian geologists hopping on to the bouldery surface of an *aa* flow on the slopes of the Klyu-chevskaya volcano in Kamchatka while it was still moving. They were carried along on their gently-moving conveyor belt at a speed of about one and a half kilometres an hour, while they made determinations of the viscosity of the lava beneath the rubbly crust, and eventually hopped off again, none the worse for wear.

## Features associated with basalt lava flows

A stream of lava is a long and complicated object and a great many things can happen to it, depending on its own physical condition and the sort of ground it is moving over. For example, a basalt flow which is moving over a dry, sandy surface is quite well-behaved and peaceful, but if the same flow were to advance on to an area of wet, boggy ground, or on to a snow-field, the water trapped beneath the lava may be heated up and turned into high-pressure steam. This steam sometimes blasts its way up to the surface through the lava, causing what is known as a *phreatic* explosion, so the advance of the lava is then anything but peaceful, and unwary spectators are sometimes injured by the explosions. Processes such as these produce a great range of minor surface structures and other curiosities, but unfortunately, there is only space here to mention one or two of them.

*Lava tunnels* result from the rapid cooling of the surface and side of a flow. If the flow is a big one, this usually means that the flow has an outer layer of rubbly fragments, an intermediate layer of solid, hard lava, and a core which is still molten.

This core of lava may continue to flow for a long while, but when the supply of fresh lava slows down at source, there will not be enough coming through to fill the whole volume of the core, so an empty space will be left, and this will form a long tube or tunnel running along the centre of the flow, sometimes for many kilometres. Such lava tunnels are quite common, and they can be most useful. At one time, there was one high up on Etna which

21. *Blasting a road cutting exposed this lava tunnel on Tenerife. The entrance is rather obscured by rubble; inside, it is very spacious.*

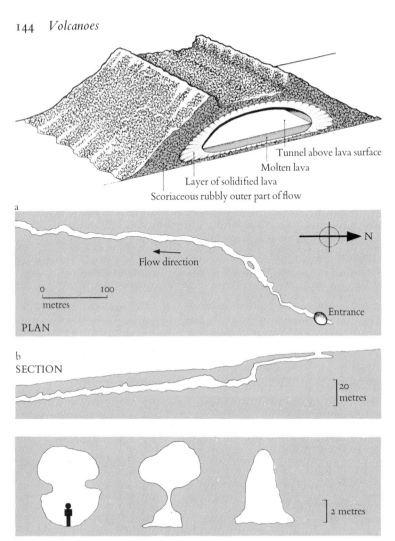

Tunnel above lava surface
Molten lava
Layer of solidified lava
Scoriaceous rubbly outer part of flow

a

Flow direction

N

0    100
metres

Entrance

PLAN

b
SECTION

20
metres

2 metres

*Fig. 37 A simplified sketch of a lava flow, to show how lava tunnels develop when a solid roof forms above a hot core of molten material, and subsequently the level of lava drops to leave an empty space.*

*Fig. 37a and b Plan section and cross-sections of lava tunnels in a 1,900-year-old basalt lava flow in Washington U.S.A.* (After R. Greeley and J. H. Hyde)

served as a convenient overnight refuge for geologists watching activity in the crater. It was at a height of nearly 3,000 metres and the air outside was well below freezing, but the lava tunnel was in an area of recent activity, and as a result it boasted beautiful under-floor heating. Near the entrance the temperature was comfortable, but further in it rose progressively until it was intolerable. Brewing up was easy – all that had to be done was to shift a few boulders to reach a hot spot lower down, and pop a billy-can of snow into the hole. All things have drawbacks, however, and the sulphurous fumes wafting down from the crater were distinctly smelly, and the occupants of the tunnel awoke in the morning with headaches and mouths that tasted like the bottom of a parrot's cage.

Lavas which are fluid enough to produce tunnels also produce a number of other oddities. Sometimes, in the middle of a flow, or else at the small mouths or *boccas* from which the flows emerge, gas venting from the lava flings small glowing gobbets of it short distances up into the air. These fall back to earth as soft, squishy pancakes which pile up closely round the vent, soon enclosing it in a kind of chimney or *hornito*. These hornitos, which are also known rather aptly as *driblet cones*, go on growing as long as there is both gas and lava to feed them, and they may reach a height of many metres. The rate of flow of gas blowing off through these vents is often surprisingly fast. It's sometimes possible to approach them closely enough to stick a device like an anemometer, or wind speed gauge, into the gas jet, and by doing this, supersonic speeds have been recorded. Unfortunately, though, the gas is often extremely hot, probably over 800°C, so the instrument that comes out of the jet is often only a sad relic of the instrument that went in. Sometimes it doesn't come out . . .

## Submarine basalt lava flows

It may seem self-evident that submarine lava flows should be different from those formed on land, and that their formation should be accompanied by violent interaction between sea water and hot lava. In some cases, where large *aa* lavas flow from land into the sea, this is true, and great quantities of steam are generated, while the lava is broken up into small glassy fragments which pile up in thick heaps at the front of the flow. A lava flow originating on land can advance considerable distances into the sea in this way, building up a kind of delta of fragmental material on to which the flow proper can advance.

Surprisingly, though, small *pahoehoe* lavas can pour into the sea with as little disturbance as cream poured into coffee, there is a little steam, but little else. This unexpected situation seems to arise because, when the molten lava enters the water, a layer of steam bubbles forms around it immediately, and this forms an effective insulating blanket, so that no violent interaction is possible.

The same is true of lava flows which are actually extruded under water. These are common enough, since, as has already been

22. *A good exposure of pillow lavas, which were originally erupted below water. The pillows characteristically sag downwards into the space between the pillows beneath, and they often have a concentric pattern of vesicles, as you can see in the two just to the right of the hammer.* (Institute of Geological Sciences photograph)

mentioned, a large proportion of the world's volcanoes are situated in or below the oceans. Unfortunately it is not easy – for obvious reasons – to study modern submarine lava flows in their proper environment. The most convenient way to study flows of this sort is to look at old examples which have been brought up above sea level by earth movements of one kind or another, and which have been subsequently cut through by erosion and exposed in clean, dry cliff sections. Their appearance in such an exposure is extremely distinctive. Instead of a single thick unit, like a land-based basalt, a submarine flow consists of a multitude of little packets of lava, commonly about one metre across, each with a fine-grained, glassy skin, and these packets are piled on top of one another, sometimes in thicknesses of hundreds of metres or more. These packets are properly called *pillows*, and the lavas *pillow lavas*. It is clear that the skin of each pillow must originally have been fairly flexible, since, as plate twenty-two shows, the base of each pillow characteristically sags into the gap between the ones below it.

For many years there was much debate about how pillow lavas formed. One idea was that they roll downslope from the submarine volcanic vent like plastic bags full of water, before piling up on top of one another; another was that they whizzed along the sea bed, supported by a cushion of collapsing steam bubbles; while a third suggested that 'pillows' aren't separate entities at all, but long, worm-like tubes whose thickness varies along their length. It also used to be thought that pillow lavas could form *only* at great depths below the surface.

In the last few years our understanding of pillow lavas has advanced dramatically, due almost entirely to some remarkable observations made by diver-geologists of pillow lavas actually in the process of formation in the sea off Hawaii. In some of the most outstanding film sequences of volcanic activity ever made, the divers were able to demonstrate to the world exactly how pillows are born. Their film shows the steep underwater flow front of a lava flow which was being erupted from a vent on Hawaii itself. The flow front appears as a mass of rounded pillows, disappearing into the blue haze of the Pacific, all appears to be motionless. Suddenly the camera picks out a rounded tongue of hot lava being extruded from the flow front; there is a brief flash of red, almost immediately extinguished, and a new pillow has been created. The flow advances in a manner similar to that of *pahoehoe* flows on dry land, and the pillows are budded off so quietly that the cameramen were able to swim up to within less than a metre of the swelling pillows. The only hazards, in fact, lay in the presence of pockets of scalding water, and in the possibility of a newly-formed pillow becoming detached from the steep flow front and rolling down on top of them.

Their unmistakable appearance, coupled with the fact that they always form under water, makes pillow lavas very useful in interpreting the volcanic history of geologically old rocks. Pillow lavas have been identified in some of the oldest rocks on earth, over 3,400 million years old, and in rocks of all ages up to the present. Wherever one finds pillow lavas in sequences of old rocks, one can be sure that they formed under water in the same way as their modern counterparts, and this, amongst other things, helps to establish the sites of ancient oceanic volcanoes and mid-ocean ridges.

## Andesite lava flows

Describing natural phenomena under separate headings always has the unwelcome implication that they can be considered as separate entities, each in its own water-tight compartment. There is no hard-and-fast difference between basalts and andesites; there is a broad transitional group of rocks between them, known as *basaltic andesites*, just as there is a similar transitional group between andesites and the next group of rocks to be described, the rhyolites. So the discussion of these three groups will necessarily be in general terms.

The first generalization that can be made is that andesite lavas are more viscous than basalt ones. This difference is *primarily* an effect of the composition of the lava, but to a certain extent it may also be the result of the high proportion of phenocrysts present in the lava. A typical basalt contains a few per cent of phenocryst minerals, but in an andesite phenocrysts may form as much as 50 per cent volume of the rock. Such lavas resemble raspberry jam that is half pips (or is it wood shavings they use?); they are not so much liquids as pasty mushes of solid material. In an andesite, the phenocrysts may be up to a centimetre across; the groundmass (or jam) is extremely fine-grained, and is often glassy, even in the centres of flows.

Basalts, because of their low viscosity, tend to form low, thin flows which spread out over large areas, and are rarely more than thirty metres thick. Andesites, by contrast, form massive flows which may be anything up to 500 metres thick. Some andesite lavas reach staggering proportions; the largest yet described, in northern Chile, has a volume of no less than twenty-four cubic kilometres! If this flow could be transported to North Wales, it would stand half as high as Snowdon; if it could be transported to Surrey, it would be half as high again as the highest hill, and, such is the attraction of all high objects from mountains to the cost of living, it would be an important landmark, regularly thronged in summer with picnickers and ramblers, and would feature on scores of postcards. Basalts can also form large volume flows, in some cases exceeding twenty-four cubic kilometres, but because they are so much thinner, they are not so conspicuous and don't attract attention. Another consequence of the greater viscosity of andesite lavas is that they flow more slowly. A basalt flow can advance over a kilometre of flat ground in a matter of hours; an andesite may take months. Similarly, andesite flows show none of the obvious surface features of 'liquid' lavas: *pahoehoe* flows never occur and all andesite flows have a rough bouldery surface. This is often not quite so unpleasant as an *aa* flow to move across; instead of loose angular cindery material, the surface consists of big, angular, smooth-sided blocks of solid lava, much more agreeable to touch and walk over. This kind of flow is called *block* lava.

The blocks are produced because andesite lavas are so viscous that they flow as plastic, rather than liquid, materials and consist of an outer chilled surface of solid rock with a steady progression towards increasing plasticity in the hotter, central parts of the flow. Because the outer layer is hard and brittle, any heaving or shifting of the more mobile material deeper down will cause it to break up, providing the clean, sharply-defined angular blocks which cover the surface of the flow. Sometimes quite large 'solid' blocks break off from the flow, with the same kind of clean fracture, and then, since they are still very hot, continue to flow slightly! This emphasizes the vital point that in geology a solid is only a solid if you think of it on a short enough time-scale. In many respects, rocks are like pitch, which flows like a liquid if it is left unsupported for long enough, for example on a steeply-sloping roof, but will also break suddenly along clean shiny fracture surfaces if it is given a sharp blow. It was mentioned in chapter one that the rocks making up the Earth's mantle show the same kind of behaviour – on a short time-scale, they are rigid ('solid') enough to transmit shock waves from earthquakes, but on a much longer time-scale, they can 'flow', and accommodate the convection movements which are believed to provide the driving mechanisms behind Plate Tectonics.

The viscous nature of andesite lavas has some interesting side-effects, especially in those which approach rhyolites in composition – that is, they contain more silica than an 'average' andesite. These rocks, called *dacites*, are often so viscous that they scarcely flow at all, and merely heave themselves sluggishly to the surface to form an irregularly flat-topped mound over the vent. These mounds are not really lava flows at all; they are the lava *domes* (sometimes also called *tholoids*) that were mentioned earlier in connection with the eruption of *nuées ardentes* and the destruction of St Pierre.

*Lava domes* form remarkably slowly. The dome of Santiaguito in Guatemala has been growing ever since 1922, and was still growing at the time of writing. In a case like this, it's clear that an extremely viscous, semi-solid lava is being slowly and continuously forced upwards through the vent; as it does so, it cools, and thus the dome grows effectively by the addition of material from within. In the case of Santiaguito, there is little evidence that the dome is actually growing at all – one can sit and watch it for hours without seeing anything more than a few wisps of steam from the top – and it's quite safe to scramble all over it. Material is continually arriving deep within the mass of dead-looking rock, however, and the pressure of this imperceptibly forces up spines of solid lava which rise in jagged battlements along the crest of the dome. It's impossible to see these spines growing, but easy to record their growth with a series of photographs taken from the same place over the course of a couple of months. So domes don't sound particularly exciting things. But as they continue to build up and up, with spines getting higher and higher, the time comes when large portions of the mass become mechanically unstable, and break away, collapsing in a clattering, roaring avalanche. Usually, these are ordinary 'cold' avalanches such as one finds on any mountain, but if the collapse is a big one and it exposes hot rock deep within the dome, a *nuée ardente* may be produced. So dome-watching is not so dull after all. Santiaguito, which was a complex of four distinct domes joined on to one another in a single elongate ridge, is rarely quiet for long, and one can literally hear it growing, because there is an almost continual rattle of small stones and rocks falling from the higher parts down on to the scree slopes below it. Even when the tholoid is shrouded in mist and invisible, as it often is in the afternoon, the dry clattering continues, with every now and then a much larger collapse taking place. These start off usually with a thin, gentle slithering sound of sliding boulders on the scree slope, which abruptly gives way to a much louder, roaring collapse as the main mass of rock falls away and hurtles downhill, and then afterwards minor falls continue intermittently for long periods. Sometimes a single boulder bounds and clatters down the scree pile, echoing loudly, sometimes a larger mass breaks away, sometimes the scree itself shifts and readjusts itself in a prolonged rattling clatter – a noise rather like the sea swashing back over pebbles.

Domes like Santiaguito often develop within the crater walls of an older volcano – Santiaguito itself is nested inside a large crater on the flanks of a volcano called Santa Maria. The crater was formed by a powerful eruption in 1902, the same year as the eruption of Mt Pelée. That eruption also involved the growth of a lava dome in the Étang Sec, and it was from this dome that the great spine of Mt Pelée was forced up. Such spines are a common feature of lava domes; in fact they are an almost predictable result of the squeezing of viscous lava into a pile of loose, broken rocks. The Mt Pelée spine was exceptional only for its extreme height – over 300 metres. In every other respect it was typical of its kind, and like most spines, it was short lived; as it cooled, it cracked and started to break up, while the heaving of fresh pulses of lava in the dome below rapidly caused what was left to collapse. Within a few months of reaching its greatest height, nothing remained of it but a heap of rubble.

Sometimes a mass of viscous lava gets intruded near the surface, but doesn't actually manage to break through; instead it forces up the surface of the ground on top, forming a considerable hill where there was no hill before. This has happened twice in the crater of the Usu volcano in Japan, the first time in 1910, the second in 1943. The first upheaval produced a hill which was called Sin-Zan, or 'Roof Mountain'; the second, logically enough, was called Showa Sin-Zan, or 'New Roof Mountain'. Showa Sin-Zan grew during the height of the Second World War, so that there were no official records of its growth, but a particularly astute village postmaster, Masao Mimatsu, kept a valuable pic-torial record of its progress by drawing a series of profile sketches on the paper covering of his window. This is what happened. After a long series of preliminary earthquakes, a circular area of ground began to rise slowly and steadily in January 1944; by April the area affected was three kilometres across, and had gone up fifteen metres; by June it had gone up fifty metres, and had taken the village of Fukaba and all its inhabitants with it. Some fairly violent explosive activity then followed, forcing the people of Fukaba to leave their homes, but still no new lava showed its head above ground. By October, the uplifted area was no less than 150 metres above its surroundings, but still no lava had broken through the cover of soil and rocks. Eventually, in November 1944, a plug of incandescent lava poked up through the middle of the elevated dome, and this gradually rose during the course of the next year until it was over a hundred metres above the top of the dome, and nearly 300 metres above normal ground level. The odd thing about this new lava plug is that it went straight up, like a piston in a cylinder, wearing on top a thick cap of mud and clay, which had originally been deposited in a crater lake and had formed the ground surface prior to all the upheaval. Apart from being baked hard by the heat of the lava, these sediments were quite undisturbed, and had been carried bodily as smoothly as if they had gone up in a lift.

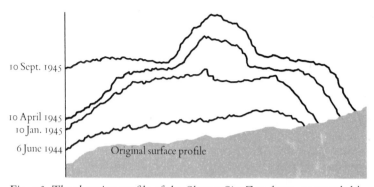

10 Sept. 1945

10 April 1945
10 Jan. 1945

6 June 1944    Original surface profile

*Fig. 38 The changing profile of the Showa-Sin Zan dome, as recorded by Masao Mimatsu on a piece of paper covering his window.*

## Rhyolite lava flows

Lavas become scarcer amongst rocks of more acid compositions and rhyolites are much less abundant than andesites. They are highly viscous, never flowing far from their source, and usually merely ooze up from the vent like toothpaste to pile up into short, thick flows and domes. Like dacite domes, rhyolite domes often form within the crater of a pre-existing volcano, but they may equally well pop up at the surface as isolated extrusions, not visibly related to any volcano.

Obsidian, it will be recalled, is the black volcanic glass with the composition of rhyolite. Although it is one of the most widely-known volcanic rocks, obsidian lava flows are rare. In Europe the only flows of any consequence occur on small volcanic islands in the Mediterranean, the most famous of all being those on the island of Lipari, which are thought to have been erupted about 1,400 years ago. Even better-known are a pair which were erupted about 1,000 years ago in Sisikyou County, California. These two formed a massive pile, hundreds of metres thick, which the Americans, in their inimitable way, call 'Glass Mountain'. A mountain of glass it certainly is. From the air it looks exactly as if someone had poured a couple of bucketsful of molten glass on to the surface, forming a puddle which slowly oozed away. The flows are covered with large, high wrinkles and ridges, concentric with the edges of the flow, where the stiff surface layer was crinkled up by the pressure of more material arriving from behind – rather like a *pahoehoe* surface on a basalt lava, but on a much bigger scale.

23. *Small flow folds pleat the flow banding of this obsidian lava flow on the island of Lipari, in the Mediterranean. Most obsidian lavas have a similar appearance and large masses of obsidian without flow banding or flow folds are unusual.*

Obsidian itself is splendid stuff. The best material is jet black, pure glass, free from bubbles or other imperfections. It shatters satisfyingly when hammered, and it does so in a characteristic way. There are any number of razor-sharp splinters and jagged, irregular surfaces, of course, but some fragments usually show what is called a *conchoidal* fracture: the surface is fairly smooth, but ridged with a number of concentric corrugations, centred on the point of impact of the hammer, and the effect produced is somewhat reminiscent of the appearance of the ridges on a cockle shell. Unlike most volcanic rocks, obsidian does not contain phenocrysts; it is, so to speak, all glassy groundmass. Glasses are not particularly stable materials, and in the course of time they devitrify, acquiring a micro-crystalline structure, and losing their glassy transparency.

In some cases, devitrification begins at centres scattered regularly throughout the whole mass, and this can produce very attractive effects. Some obsidians, such as those from the Yellowstone National Park, have white spots about a centimetre across scattered liberally throughout the black glass. This is called 'snowflake' obsidian, and is something of a collector's item.

In most glassy lavas, bands of devitrified glass and layers of frothy, bubbly glass are interleaved with layers of unaltered material. When this happens, one can see clearly displayed just the convulsions and contortions the lava goes through as it flows: the bands are tightly folded in tortuous patterns. These folded patterns are characteristic of flow in all kinds of media – one can see similar folds in glaciers, in some kinds of metamorphic rock which have been heated strongly, and whenever immiscible liquids become intermingled. The iridescent films of oil on top of puddles provide perhaps the best analogies. If such a puddle is stirred gently, the swirling, winding folds produced look exactly like those in obsidian lavas.

Few obsidian lavas consist of obsidian all the way through. In general the obsidian forms only on the outer skin of the lava, which is rapidly chilled, while the central parts of the flow, which remain hot for a long while, consist of rhyolite. Rhyolites are pale grey or buff-coloured rocks with a micro-crystalline structure and a rather distinctive sugary texture or 'feel'. Like obsidian, they usually have a well-developed banding running through them, which shows up the flow folds in the lava plainly. By no means all rhyolite lavas are associated with obsidian – the majority are not – and, as one goes further back through the geological record, obsidian becomes progressively more and more scarce, due to devitrification, and none at all is found in rocks more than a few million years old.

## A Plate Tectonic re-cap

Rather a lot has been said in this chapter about the minor details of lava flows. It's important, however, not to lose sight of the bigger issues. All the differences that have been discussed between basalts, andesites and rhyolites fundamentally reflect their differences in composition, and this in turn is a function of the geological environment in which the lavas occur. Basalts are the rocks which are formed at mid-ocean ridges, and which make up the entire oceanic crust. Some basalts do occur in continental areas, notably the basaltic flood plateaux mentioned in chapter three, but to see an eruption of basaltic lava taking place, one would have to fly (at short notice) to an oceanic island volcano, such as Iceland. On Iceland, one might, if one were lucky, also find small quantities of andesitic and rhyolitic rocks being erupted but they are scarce, since they can only be formed by skimming off silica-rich material from a large volume of basaltic magma, in the same way as cream is skimmed off the top of milk. Andesite lavas are characteristic of destructive plate margins, where the rocks of the oceanic crust are diving down beneath a continental plate. The Andes is obviously a good place to go looking for an eruption of an andesite lava, but one would be extremely lucky to find one, because although there are numerous 'active' volcanoes along the Andean chain, andesite eruptions are really rather rare events compared to basaltic ones. Destructive plate margins tend to produce a greater variety of lavas than constructive ones, and in some cases basaltic and andesitic rocks are found together. Although rhyolite lavas do not occur in large volumes anywhere in the world, they are much more characteristic of destructive plate margins than constructive ones. They are rare because, since they are so highly viscous, rhyolite magmas are involved in more explosive eruptions than either basalts or andesites, and therefore are usually erupted as pyroclastic rocks rather than lavas. Which brings us on nicely to a discussion of pyroclastic rocks themselves.

*Chapter 5*  Volcanic rocks – pyroclastic fall deposits

Pumice is much the best-known of all pyroclastic or 'fire-broken' rocks, but it is only one of many types which are ejected from volcanoes as solid, fragmentary material. This chapter will be concerned with the most straightforward kinds of pyroclastic deposits: those which are made up of fragments which have simply been shot up into the air and fallen back down again, so they are known as *pyroclastic fall* deposits. The following chapter will be devoted to an examination of the rocks produced by *nuées ardentes* and similar phenomena; these travel over the surface of the ground as *pyroclastic flows*, and are very different.

A shorter word for 'pyroclastic fall deposits' is *tephra*. Tephra comprises all the solid fragmental matter ejected by all types of volcano, and covers all rock compositions from basic to acid. The tephra in any one place may include a wide range of different-sized fragments and a simple set of terms is used to distinguish between these:

*Ashes* are particles less than four millimetres across.
*Lapilli* (Italian: 'little stones') are between four and thirty-two millimetres across.
*Bombs* and *blocks* are lumps bigger than thirty-two millimetres across.

Thus while newspaper accounts and other sources (including this one), often talk rather loosely about volcanic 'ashes' during an eruption, a vulcanologist properly restricts this term only to the smallest particles.

Tephra are often erupted extremely rapidly. During its 1947 eruption, the Icelandic volcano Hekla ejected ash at a rate estimated to be nearly 100,000 cubic metres per second during the first half hour, slowing down subsequently to a more modest 30,000 cubic metres per second. Rapid production of such large amounts of material clearly has profound effects on the land round the volcano. In the immediate vicinity of the vent, ashes and *lapilli* pile up to form a mantle many metres thick, which blankets the countryside like a dirty snow fall; like a snow fall too, the ash tends to smooth out the earlier irregularities of the ground surface, ultimately producing a landscape of soft, gently moulded hillocks and hollows. Such carpets of ash sometimes cover thousands of square kilometres, but they need not be particularly extensive to be damaging. The town of Heimaey in Iceland was buried under

24. *A pyroclastic fall deposit in the making. A steady rain of basaltic ash is pouring out of the eruption cloud above the volcano, and is accumulating beneath to form the new island of Surtsey. A similar fall of ash buried the town of Heimaey in 1973.* (Photo courtesy of S. Thorarinsson)

basaltic tephra in a matter of days after the commencement of the eruption of the volcano Helgafell in 1973. During the space of a few hours, a one-metre thickness of ash accumulated in some parts of the town which were only a few hundred metres away from the active vent and many house roofs collapsed under the weight. In other parts of the town, a kilometre or more from the vent, the ash fall was thinner and damage proportionally less.

Since there is such a wide difference between the least violent types of eruption (Hawaiian) and the most violent (Plinian), it is

25. *A house in Heimaey which was buried beneath several metres of basaltic ash during the 1973 eruption. Fortunately, the eruption ceased before the weight of ash caused the roof to fall in.* (Photo courtesy of S. Thorarinsson)

scarcely surprising that there is an equally wide difference between the kinds of pyroclastic rocks produced by each. Recent work has shown that the types of deposit produced by different kinds of eruption can be recognized by objective criteria such as the total volume of material erupted, the distance that it travels from the vent, the degree of fragmentation, and the range of particle sizes present at any point. The details of this analysis of pyroclastic deposits are rather complex, so only a few of the more interesting aspects will be described here.

## Hawaiian eruptions

One consequence of the extremely fluid nature of the lavas erupted in Hawaiian eruptions, especially those of the Hawaiian volcanoes themselves, is that they are sometimes so fluid that when 'fire fountains' are spraying lava upwards, some of the liquid sets solid into teardrop shapes, with bulbous ends and long-drawn-out tails. They are made of basaltic glass, so when they come to rest, they glisten blackly on the ground. The Hawaiian islanders have their own name for these glassy droplets; they call them *Pele's tears*, after the Hawaiian goddess of volcanoes, Pele. (Not to be confused with the volcano Pelée in the Caribbean.)* If a piece of ordinary glass is heated over a gas flame, it softens easily, and eventually the heated part will gather itself into a drop and fall to the ground. It doesn't detach itself completely, though; as it falls, it draws out behind it a thin, flexible thread of glass, which seems to stretch almost indefinitely. The same thing happens with Pele's tears; they draw off behind them a long hair-like tail of glass, which may be a metre or more long. If the hair should snap off from the tear, it may drift for many kilometres on the wind, falling slowly, and come to rest a long way down-wind

* It has been suggested that the term *achnelith* (Greek, 'spray stones') should be used to describe pyroclastic particles which originated from lavas so fluid that they owe their shape more to the effects of surface tension than any other cause.

from the vent. The finest of these thin threads of glass are extremely soft and flexible, and are a light golden brown in colour. Little wonder, then, that they are known as *Pele's hair*. There are even reports that this hair is gathered by the more discriminating kinds of birds to build their nests!

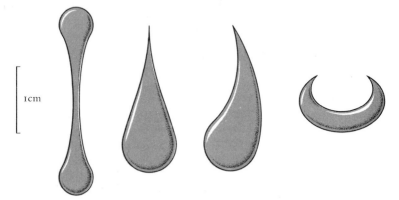

1cm

*Fig. 39 Some typical Pele's tears from Hawaii, showing the wide variety of possible shapes.*

When less fluid lavas are involved, which don't break up into droplets, large gobbets of the molten rock are flung up from the vent, spreading out into irregular plates which may break up in the air into smaller bits. As they trace their lazy parabolas back down to earth, these bits twist around slowly, over and over, until they hit the ground with a flop or a flump, splodging out to form round, flattish masses. When cool, these splodges look like the brown steaming splodges observed near cows on pastureland, so they are known as *cow-pats*. The individual cow-pats are often still very hot and plastic when they hit the ground, so that as they pile up one on top of each other, they spread out further, and weld together, forming a solid mass known as *spatter*. A *spatter cone* or *spatter ring* consisting exclusively of welded cow-pats often builds up around the vent. These spatter cones contain little, if any, fine-grained ashy material and are amongst the most characteristic products of Hawaiian eruptions.

26. *These large, irregularly-shaped lumps form part of a spatter ring. Some blocks are loose, but most were firmly welded together when they fell. Tenerife, Canary Islands.*

## Strombolian eruptions

The most abundant basaltic pyroclastic material is variously termed ash, clinker, cinders or slag, depending on local preference. These terms are all very descriptive, since the material which accumulates around a Strombolian vent does indeed look rather like boiler slag, but it is more correctly called *scoria*, and the cones which build up around the vent *scoria cones*. The scoria from a typical Strombolian eruption consists of loose, rubbly material, with a wide range in size of the constituent fragments, but with only a small proportion less than about one millimetre in size. The fragments themselves characteristically have a light, frothy texture, the lava being honeycombed with large numbers of gas bubbles or vesicles. Normally, basaltic scoria is a drab grey colour, but sometimes when it is fresh the surface may be beautifully iridescent, shining in peacock blue colours. Quite often, also, hot steam blasting through a scoria cone may oxidize or 'rust' the iron in the rock, giving the scoria a deep reddish-brown colour.

27. *A road-side section through a typical basaltic scoria cone. The regular layering, dipping to the left, shows clearly how the cone built up through successive pulses in the eruption, which deposited layers of different degrees of coarseness. Some large blocks or bombs are conspicuous.*

Scoria cones are themselves distinctive objects. They are rarely more than a couple of hundred metres high, and they are usually symmetrical, although they may be 'breached' on one side, where a lava flow has emerged. Their most characteristic feature, though, is that the angle of slope of the sides of the cone is *always* that of the 'angle of rest' for loose scoria, which means that *all* young scoria cones have side slopes of 33°, so they have this profile:

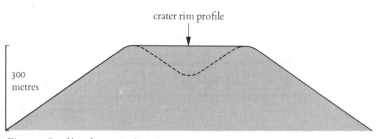

crater rim profile

300 metres

*Fig. 40 Profile of a typical scoria cone.*

Naturally this crisp geometrical profile becomes softened and less perceptible as scoria cones grow older and are subjected to the normal processes of erosion.

Many of the fragments which go to make up a scoria cone are individually big enough to be called 'blocks' or 'bombs', according to the simple size classification. But how does one differentiate between a block and a bomb? It has been suggested that a bomb be simply defined as an ejected block with a shape sufficiently interesting to attract attention. While this is not a particularly scientific definition, it is perfectly adequate, and the term 'bomb' is in common use in vulcanology, although this is perhaps unfortunate since it may suggest to the reader some unpleasant kind of projectile which explodes on impact. This is not the case. Volcanic bombs are just lumps of solid (or sometimes plastic) lava which are lobbed out of the vent, fall back to earth with a wallop, and that's all. The biggest bombs, though, land with a considerable wallop, and are quite as unpleasant to be standing beneath as any military weapon, and they can be a good deal larger. Cotopaxi in

Ecuador is reported to have lobbed a 200-ton bomb over fourteen kilometres, but this seems a little difficult to swallow. Macdonald, however, has described a well-documented case of an eight-ton bomb being hurled nearly one kilometre by an explosion in the crater of Halemaumau, Hawaii in 1924, and there are many other equally impressive accounts. Such large bombs are rather exceptional, though; most are well under a metre across, and don't travel more than a few tens of metres from the vent.

There are a number of different kinds of bomb, some of them known by a variety of colourful synonyms, but in many cases, there is a good deal of argument about exactly how they acquire their shape. Some are undoubtedly produced when ropy strands or shreds of sticky lava are flung up out of the vent, twisting and turning slightly in the air before falling back to earth; these are known as *rope* or *ribbon* bombs, and they may be as much as one metre long. When a bigger, more compact lump of lava is ejected, it commonly happens that the outermost skin of plastic lava tends to be pushed backwards towards the trailing edge of the bomb by the rush of air passing it. If the bomb also twists or spins at all, the skin gets drawn into a tail, forming a *spindle bomb*.

28. *The flanged, elliptical shape of this spindle bomb is quite unmistakable.*

Ribbon and spindle bombs both owe their shapes to events taking place within and above the volcanic vents, but other shaping processes also operate. Bombs made from plastic lavas tend to remain where they fall, but denser, more solid bombs sometimes bounce off the sides of the scoria cone at a glancing angle, and acquire a rapid spin. Once spinning, they are difficult to stop, and they flash down the slopes in a series of great leaps and bounds, making a loud whirring noise, and travel sometimes for hundreds of metres. In their headlong rush they naturally tend to get their corners knocked off at each bounce, so they end up as peculiarly smooth, rounded lumps, the smoothness being the result of mechanical abrasion. Such bombs often smash into other bigger, stationary boulders at the base of the cone, shattering into smithereens, but in doing so they leave their own mark on the boulder. Walking around the base of an active cone erupting these bombs is a bit like walking around a battlefield, with spent rounded *cannonball bombs* and shattered fragments of cannonballs lying around, and many big battered boulders exhibiting the bruises of a long volcanic siege. Every few minutes a fresh fusillade of whirring bombs hurtles downwards to smash into the debris below, compelling the observer to stop walking idly around and take cover.

## Surtseyan eruptions

In chapter three it was mentioned that the effect of getting large volumes of water mixed up in a volcanic eruption is to make it more violent. Not surprisingly, one result of this is that the pyroclastic material erupted in a Surtseyan eruption is much more highly fragmented than that in a similar basaltic eruption taking place on land, and this in turn means that the deposits produced contain a much greater proportion of very small particles than their Strombolian counterparts. This doesn't mean that there are *no* large fragments present; there are merely less of them. A second consequence of the more explosive nature of a Surtseyan eruption is that the pyroclastic material gets scattered much more widely. This means that a typical Surtseyan cone has a different profile from a Strombolian one. Put side by side, the differences are obvious:

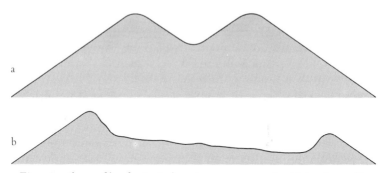

*Fig. 41a, the profile of a typical scoria cone compared with b, the profile of a Surtseyan ash ring. (b is in fact drawn from the Diamond Head ring on Hawaii.)*

These low, broad cones are called *ash rings*. They are quite un-mistakable, and are often very elegant indeed, especially when they are perfectly circular and symmetrical.

29. *An example from Ethiopia of a very beautiful, symmetrical Surtseyan ash-ring.* (Photo courtesy of H. Tazieff)

Ash rings are characteristic of submarine eruptions, but they are by no means confined to marine environments. They can be formed on land near the sea, in shallow lakes or indeed anywhere where it is possible for a large volume of water to find its way into the volcanic vent.

## Vulcanian eruptions

The deposits produced by Vulcanian eruptions are similar to those produced by Surtseyan eruptions, in that they too consist of highly-fragmented material, with a large proportion of it less than one millimetre in size. The principal difference between the two is that Vulcanian deposits consist of non-vesiculated material. Each fragment is a small, dense, angular piece of lava, quite unlike the frothy, vesiculated basaltic material that is characteristic of both Strombolian and Surtseyan deposits.

Probably the best known Vulcanian deposit is one produced by an eruption of Vulcano itself in the 1880s. This deposit mantles

30. *Part of the crater wall of Vulcano in the Mediterranean. The whitish rocks represent the original cone which existed prior to the last major eruption in the 1880s. The grey material overlying them is the pyroclastic rock ejected by the eruption.*

the flanks of the pre-existing cone, but is no more than a few metres thick at most. Littering the slopes of the volcano are thousands of large bombs ejected by the eruption, some of them over a metre in diameter. The most intriguing of these are *bread-crust bombs*, which are rounded or angular lumps with a smooth, glassy crust broken up by deep cracks and fissures which expose the frothy, vesicular core of the bomb, so that it looks rather like a well-baked crusty loaf. These bombs were produced when lumps of viscous, gas-rich lava were ejected from the vent; the outer surface of the lump chilled quickly, forming the glassy crust, but the inside remained hot, and the gas trapped within it continued to come out of solution and to expand, forming a spongy mass of vesicles. This internal expansion caused the outer skin to crack open, forming the diagnostic crusty-looking surface.

31. *A splendid example of a breadcrust bomb, ejected during the eruption of Vulcano in the 1880s.*

## Air-fall pumice deposits

The pumice deposits produced by Vesuvian (sub-Plinian) and
Plinian eruptions are much the most interesting of all pyroclastic
rocks, so they will be discussed in a little more detail. First, a word
about pumice itself. The pumice that we know from painful experience in the bathroom consists of material containing over 65
per cent of silica, and there is a general tendency to associate
pumice only with acid rocks such as rhyolites. Strictly speaking,
though, pumice is only a kind of highly vesicular glassy rock with
a low density, so low that many types will float on water, and it
may be anywhere between basalt and rhyolite in composition.
Pumice of basaltic composition, however, is rather rare, although
there are some rather peculiar varieties in the Hawaiian Islands.
Some of these are the lightest known rocks in the world, with
apparent densities of only 0·3. Surprisingly, these ultra-light
pumices sink in water, since there is so little basaltic material and
so much air space that all the air spaces are interconnected, and
water can fill the whole mass. Ordinary pumice, by contrast,
shows a wide range in density, depending upon the degree of
vesiculation that has taken place in the magma, but it is still
nothing more than a solidified rock froth. The vesicles are separated from one another by thin films of glass, so that air can be
trapped inside, enabling the pumice to float. Sometimes, when a
volcano erupts in the sea, massive carpets of floating pumice
accumulate on the sea around it and may drift a long way from it.
These have occasionally given rise to strange sea-farers' tales of
'floating islands'. These islands are rapidly broken up by wind
and waves, but the pumice fragments may be carried thousands
of kilometres, to be washed up on some distant coral strand. No
pumice will float indefinitely, though. After a period of months,
water finds its way into even the innermost air spaces, and the
pumice becomes waterlogged and finally sinks.

All air-fall pumice deposits originate in the same way – in
Vesuvian or Plinian gas-blast eruptions which throw up dense
clouds of ash tens of thousands of metres into the air. The violence

of the eruption and the lightness of the pumice fragments means that they will go higher, and stay air-borne longer than any other kind of pyroclastic material, and it is this that gives pumice deposits their unique properties.

Around the volcanic vent itself, a jumbled mass of highly-irregular pumice fragments, most of them very large, piles up to form a conical heap round the vent. Unlike a scoria cone though, a pumice cone is usually rather low and poorly defined, and sometimes does not even have a recognizable crater. In a Plinian eruption, it's usually impossible to pin down the site of the vent exactly, since it stands a high chance of being obliterated or destroyed by the eruption itself. Pumice deposits, in fact, are usually much better preserved and more informative when one sees them at points some way from the vent. As one goes away from the

*Fig. 42  The variation in thickness of the* A.D. 79 *Vesuvius ash deposit away from the volcano.*

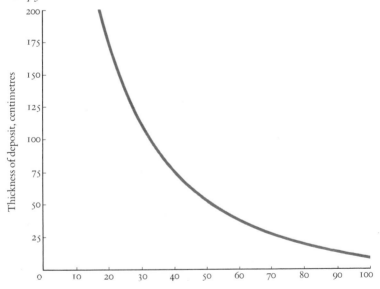

Distance from vent, kilometres

vent, two effects become apparent. First, the thickness of the deposit steadily diminishes; one which is ten metres thick close to the vent may be only twenty centimetres or so thick at twenty kilometres' distance. The thickness does not decrease linearly, but follows an exponential curve, with the thickness decreasing much more over the first kilometre than the second, and so on:
Second, and also predictably, the average size of the fragments present at any one point also decreases with distance from the vent.

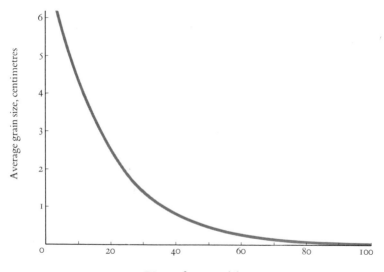

Distance from vent, kilometres

*Fig. 43 The variation in average size of the largest fragments in the A.D. 79 Vesuvius ash deposit away from the volcano.*

Perhaps the most interesting property of all, though, is that the range of sizes present at any one point in an air-fall pumice deposit is rather restricted, so that the fragments tend to be all more or less the same size, or to put it formally, the deposit is said to be *well-sorted*. This point can best be illustrated with a couple of size-frequency graphs:

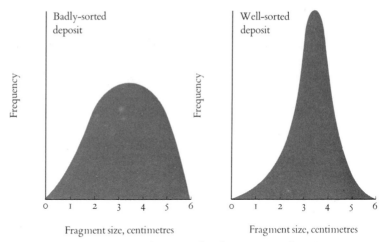

*Fig. 44 Comparison in size-frequency distribution curves for a badly-sorted deposit, left, and a well-sorted one, right.*

A badly-sorted deposit gives a low, broad curve, whereas a well-sorted deposit, which has exactly the same range of fragment sizes, gives a single very well-defined peak. This kind of peaked size-frequency distribution is thoroughly typical of air-fall pumice deposits, so how does it come about?

It's all to do with what happens to the fragments of pumice while they are in mid-air, suspended in the ash cloud above the volcano. Within the cloud itself, violent currents are at play, sweeping round and round in tight convulsive cells, just as in a thundercloud. These currents keep all the ash thoroughly mixed up, but inevitably, as the ash cloud drifts away down-wind, the heavier particles tend to fall out, leaving the finer ones behind them. This doesn't contradict Galileo's famous observations on the speeds of falling bodies; the pumice fragments are so light that their aerodynamic properties rather than their weight control their rate of fall. The larger particles, naturally, fall out nearer the vent; the smaller ones fall more slowly and are dispersed by the wind. The finest material may be carried for tens of kilometres down-wind, and some of it may even stay suspended for many months, eventually falling back to earth on the other side of the globe. The process is a bit like winnowing, the old method of using the wind to separate wheat from chaff, except that in the case of pyroclastic material there is no simple division into light material (husks) and heavy (grain) but a continuous gradation in sizes (and therefore weight) of particles from fine to coarse. So it is a wind-winnowing process that is responsible for the well-sorted distribution of grain sizes that is characteristic of air-fall deposits. The same process operates *throughout* the size spectrum. This latter is quite an important point, because although it may not be immediately obvious, a deposit which consists only of large particles can be just as well-sorted as one which consists only of small ones.

A case which illustrates some of these features well is the ash

*Fig. 45 This map shows the progressive drift of the ash cloud from Quizapu, with the dotted lines marking the dates at which the first falls of ash were recorded.*

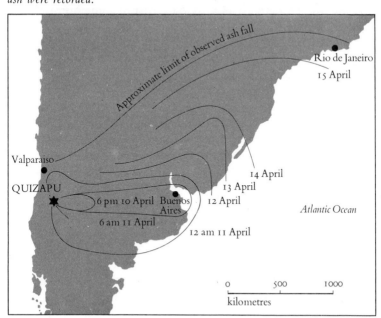

erupted by the Chilean volcano Quizapu, during a Plinian eruption in 1932. The ash cloud reached over 15,000 metres in height and was carried by the prevailing winds to the north-east, into Argentina. Ash began to fall on Buenos Aires seventeen hours after the eruption had started on Quizapu, 1,120 kilometres away. The ash-fall was thick enough to darken the sky, and about half a centimetre accumulated on the ground. A few days later, ash from the same eruption had reached Rio de Janeiro, 2,960 kilometres away, but here the fall was very scanty indeed – not thick enough to form a measurable deposit – and consisted only of the finest, dust-like particles. The ash cloud drifted at somewhere between twenty-five and sixty kilometres per hour, and it covered in all more than two million square kilometres of the South American continent.

## Isopach maps

Because they have been an important part of some historic eruptions, a few pumice deposits are well-documented, but surprisingly few have been studied closely from a geological viewpoint. This situation is changing, though, and some interesting things are now being done with pumice deposits. One of the simplest and most informative things to do is to measure the thickness of the pumice deposit at as many places as possible, plot these thicknesses on a map, and then draw lines on the map, rather like contour lines, linking points of equal ash thickness, say ten metres, five metres, one metre and so on. These lines look a bit like the isobars on a weather map, but the lines are *isopachs*, and the map an *isopach map*. (Bear in mind that pachydermal = thick skinned.) These maps are useful in a number of ways. It's immediately obvious how the thickness of the deposit varies away from the vent, and it's also possible to work out fairly rapidly the total volume of ash erupted. Less important, these maps show up clearly the direction of the wind at the time of the eruption, since the isopachs are all elongated down-wind. (To digress for a moment, it's a curious fact that most isopach maps for pumice deposits reveal winds blowing generally in an easterly direction; the ash deposits are all concentrated to the east of the volcano. Partly, this may be due to the fact that outside the tropics atmospheric circulation is from west to east, due to Coriolis forces, the forces which result from the effect of the Earth's rotation on moving bodies.)

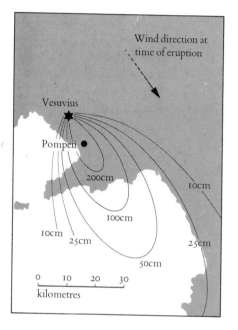

*Fig. 46 The isopach map for the* A.D. 79 *Vesuvius eruption. (After G. P. L. Walker et al.)*

In areas where there are a number of pumice deposits present, all of them looking much the same, it's clearly a difficult job to tell them apart and, more important, to recognize the same individual deposits in separate localities which may be many kilometres apart. Much slow and painstaking geological detective work is needed to make correlations such as these, but the results can be very valuable. The use of successive pumice or ash deposits in building up a history of the eruptive activity in an area is known as *tephrachronology*, and this is increasingly being used to add precision to the study of the history of volcanic areas. Not only does tephrachronology enable a far-flung ash to be uniquely identified, but if the ash can be independently dated at any single locality by isotopic methods, then it provides a firm foundation on which to build the history of a volcano.

32. *A simple problem in tephrachronology. Here, an air-fall pumice deposit (white) is sandwiched between two sets of basaltic scoria (dark), and there is obviously no difficulty in distinguishing between the three units.*

On the academic side, detailed tephrachronology makes it possible to study patterns in the behaviour of volcanoes – the magma erupted from one volcano may become steadily more acid, or it may show cyclical changes, or it may even vary consistently during each eruption, starting off fairly basic and ending up at the close of the eruption much more acid. Evidence of this sort can provide clues to the history and origin of the magmas themselves, and of the processes which are acting deep below the volcano.

Turning briefly to Plate Tectonics, studies of pyroclastic deposits can contribute much useful information. It is easy enough to measure the volumes of lava flows, but it is only by constructing isopach maps that the volume of pyroclastic material erupted can be estimated, and this is particularly important in volcanoes at destructive plate margins, where the mass of magma represented by pyroclastic rocks sometimes far outweighs that represented by lavas. This is a point that has been commonly overlooked in the past, even by geologists, since there is a general tendency to assume that the only rocks worth bothering about are 'hard' rocks, which can be hit with a hammer!

The ratio of the proportions of lavas and pyroclastic rocks in any area is of some intrinsic interest, but the *total* rate at which new pyroclastic rocks and lavas are erupted at destructive plate margins is of more fundamental significance. Although oceanic crust is consumed at destructive plate margins at very nearly the same rate at which it is being produced at constructive plate margins, a small proportion of the oceanic plate – perhaps only a few per cent – is involved in the generation of andesite magmas at destructive plate margins, and contributes to the volcanic rocks being erupted at the surface. The effect of this is that there is a slow but steady conversion of oceanic crustal material into continental crust, and therefore a steady net increase in the volume of continental crust. It's been estimated that this might be of the order of one cubic kilometre per year. This in turn means that over the course of geological time, the continents have been, and are, getting steadily bigger ... don't worry, though, the extra real-estate coming on to the market won't make mortgages any easier to get!

# Chapter 6   Volcanic rocks – pyroclastic flows

Many readers will have noticed that very fine powders such as flour and cement sometimes behave rather oddly, and some will recall an old television advertisement for a brand of flour that was 'so fine it flows'. If a shovelful of cement is dropped on the floor, it will hit the ground with a *flumph*, spreading out widely with 'rays' shooting off in all directions, and the whole heap will look as though it is smoking, with a thin haze of cement dust wafting around it. The cement behaves like this because in falling, a small volume of air gets trapped beneath the main mass as it hits the ground, and the particles in the cement are fine enough to get dispersed by the blast of the trapped air as it escapes, some of the powder spraying out in radial rays. This chapter will be concerned with how pyroclastic rocks behave in somewhat similar conditions, but it will also involve examination of some completely non-volcanic phenomena, such as ordinary rock avalanches, and even a chemical engineering process, since these can tell us a good deal about how pyroclastic flows are formed. We'll start, though, with things which are rather a long way from any of these, but which are probably the simplest of all to appreciate; mudflows.

## Mudflows

At approximately 9.15 on the morning of Friday 21 October 1966, about 140,000 cubic metres of coal-mining waste collapsed abruptly from the colliery tip-heaps built up on the sides of the valley above the Welsh village of Aberfan. A black tongue of coal dust, shale and water flowed down the valley slopes into the village, engulfing successively two farm cottages, a canal, a railway embankment, a school and eighteen houses before it finally came to rest. A total of 144 men, women and children were killed, 114 of them inside the Pantglas Junior School. This singularly distressing event demonstrated how easily large volumes of fragmental, rocky material can flow, and flow rapidly, when there is enough water present to 'lubricate' the mass. That was exactly what happened at Aberfan; the tip-heaps were thoroughly sodden after heavy rain, and were also supposed to have been built up over a surface stream. This was not in itself dangerous, but the tips had also been built up so high above the solid rock of the hill side that they were mechanically unstable, and a great mass of the waste material slumped away, turning as it did so from a solid-looking pile to a slurry of rock and water. The TV and press coverage described plainly what the flow was like, and it is useful to recall these accounts, because this flow was identical in many important aspects to the mudflows which occur on volcanoes.

*33. A very small mudflow which was formed in 1969 after heavy rainfall on a volcano in Chile. Some mudflows, like this one, build up banks or levées which channel the flow, so in this respect they resemble lavas.*

Such mudflows are not uncommon – they are all too common on some volcanoes – but they are not widely known, since they tend to get lost in vague press descriptions of 'eruptions'. Mudflows on volcanoes need not necessarily be linked to eruptions at all. In tropical areas with heavy seasonal rainfall, such as Indonesia and the Philippines, the volcanic ash that accumulates on the slopes of active volcanoes may become saturated during the monsoon; a lot of it will be washed away by ordinary erosion processes, but some will rush down the flanks in Aberfan-like flows. The speed at which the flow travels will depend on many things, such as the steepness of the slope, the viscosity of the sludge and the nature of the channel it flows down, but it can be very fast indeed, of the order of ninety kilometres per hour. Rapidly-moving flows such as these are obviously the most dangerous, but slower ones are even more common, and no matter how fast they flow, the deposits laid down by them are similar.

34. *This vertical section through a large mudflow shows clearly the chaotic homogeneous mixture of large and small fragments which is characteristic of pyroclastic flows.*

The characteristic feature of mudflow deposits, and of all pyro-clastic flow deposits, is that they are *unsorted*; they contain a mixture of fragments of all sizes, from the finest grains of mud to, in ex-treme cases, boulders as big as houses. There is no trace of bedding or layering; the flow is homogeneous from top to bottom, and generally from one end to the other. Normally, a volcanic mud-flow will consist mainly of volcanic ash and lava fragments from the slopes of the volcano, but it's also possible that it will pick up all sorts of other rubbish *en route* – soils, boulders of non-volcanic rock, tree-trunks, dustbins and even motor cars.

It's easy enough to identify the deposits left by a mudflow when there were eye witness observations of its happening, but what about older deposits? The bouldery nature of the deposit is a guide, but unfortunately it's a feature that is common to several other kinds of geological formation – the debris laid down by glaciers (boulder clay) is a good example. The best indication is the overall shape of the deposit. Mudflows generally have well-defined snouts or *flow fronts* where the flow came to a halt, and the snouts often show up as prominent features, especially on aerial photographs. Less often, the surface of the deposit has pat-terns of concentric ridges on it, produced by the faster-moving rear parts of the flow piling up into the front, rather like a viscous lava flow.

Volcanic eruptions may trigger off mudflows both indirectly and directly. A major Plinian eruption, ejecting ash high into the atmosphere, may propagate a torrential rainstorm in the right conditions, since the ash particles act as nuclei or seeds, round which water collects to form raindrops, and the rainstorms that result may initiate the kind of 'cold' mudflows that have just been mentioned. Much more unpleasant mudflows result when an eruption blasts up through a crater lake, expelling the water and a good deal of volcanic debris at the same time. The lake water may be boiling hot, so that the mudflow which rushes down the gullies round the volcano is a lethal mixture of scalding water, mud and boulders, a combination much more deadly even than that which poured into Aberfan. It was a hot flow of this kind which swept over the Usine Guérin, a few days before the St Pierre disaster.

Indonesia is a country which has suffered dreadfully from volcanic mudflows, and the Indonesian word for them, *lahars*, is often used by vulcanologists to describe them. Kelut volcano on Java is particularly notorious for its mudflows, and for the numerous attempts that have been made to prevent them. The problem with Kelut is that it has a deep crater lake, which has been blown out by many eruptions, only to reform again later. After a particularly disastrous episode in 1919 when 5,000 people were killed by *lahars*, the Dutch Colonial authorities decided it was time to take action. What they did was to dig a series of horizontal tunnels through the wall of the crater, to drain off as much as possible of the lake water. They succeeded in lowering the level of the lake by about fifty metres; and for nearly thirty years the mudflow peril seemed to have been averted. In 1951, though, another major eruption took place, which did *not* cause any mudflows, but *did* ruin the drainage system, and also deepened the crater considerably, so that the crater lake became deeper than ever. Only seven people were killed by this eruption, but unhappily two of them were officials from the local vulcanological observatory who had come to check up on the volcano, but were caught out by an unexpected blast while they were actually inside one of the drainage tunnels. Subsequently, it proved impossible to repair the tunnels damaged by the eruption, and a rather ineffectual attempt was made to drain the crater lake by a single tunnel, through which it was hoped all the trapped water would escape by seepage. The newly-deepened crater lake was estimated in 1964 to contain forty million cubic metres of water, and it presented an obvious danger. Two Indonesian scientists published a paper pointing out the inadequacies of the seepage drainage system, and the necessity of digging a completely new set of tunnels. They forecast a new eruption within five years; it came in 1966, only two years after their prediction, and because their warnings had been ignored, many hundreds of people were killed by mudflows. After this eruption, new drainage tunnels were dug . . .

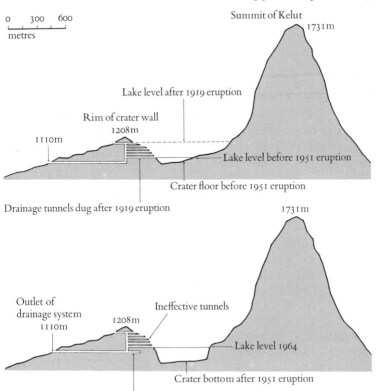

*Fig. 47 The Kelut crater lake and the tunnels which were excavated to drain it. The top diagram illustrates the situation before the 1951 eruption, the lower one the situation before the 1966 eruption. (After Zen and Hadikussumo)*

Although they are not particularly uncommon, there are few important historical mudflows. Probably the most significant was the one which smothered Herculaneum in A.D. 79, but even that wasn't particularly big as mudflows go. The largest known are rather old. One of the biggest is the Osceola mudflow in the State of Washington, U.S.A. which originated on the Mt Rainier vol-

cano. It flowed along the White River valley, and eventually
spread out over 300 square kilometres. That happened about 5,000
years ago, but Mt Rainier is known to have produced about fifty-
five major mudflows in the last 10,000 years, and the area covered
by the Osceola mudflow is now thickly-populated. One can only
hope that there will be ample warning of any future mudflows
from Mt Rainier . . . In recent years, the mudflow which has
achieved most notoriety was that which caused the Tangiwai
disaster in New Zealand in 1953. A small eruption of the volcano
Ruapehu caused a breach in the walls of the summit crater which
contained a crater lake. The water in the crater gushed out,
lowering the lake level by nearly ten metres and the sudden flood
generated a mudflow which swept down the flanks of the volcano.
The mudflow was not particularly large, but it was big enough to
destroy a railway bridge across a valley low down on the slopes
of Ruapehu. A passenger train attempted to cross the bridge before anything could be done to stop it, and there was a large
number of fatalities when the train crashed into the valley.

## Avalanches, hot and cold

In a mudflow, the mud and rock debris travels mixed up with a
comparable volume of water, so it's not too difficult to visualize
how it can flow for long distances. But dry rock avalanches can
also travel remarkably far, and it's not so obvious how they do so.
(Bear in mind in reading these pages that snow avalanches are not
included under this heading, although they have some similar
properties, and are certainly cold.) The mechanism operating in a
'cold' non-volcanic rock avalanche is of first importance in understanding the origin of some of the most enigmatic volcanic
phenomena, such as *nuées ardentes*, so we will begin by examining
a well-documented example of an entirely non-volcanic avalanche, so that later we will be able to differentiate between purely
volcanic effects, and those that are common to all moving masses
of debris.

In 1903, the small coal-mining town of Frank in the Rocky

Mountains was overwhelmed by a major rock avalanche. One half of the town was wiped out, with severe loss of life, but there were also many survivors who were able to provide first-hand accounts of the event. What happened was this. The town is situated in the valley of the Crow's Nest pass in the Rockies, with mountains rising on either side of it. Long-continued coal-mining in the area had made some of the rocks on the valley sides unstable, and it is likely that the shock from a sudden mining subsidence triggered off the avalanche. A mass of limestone about 150 metres thick fell away from the face of Turtle mountain, about 640 metres above the valley floor, and the whole mass crashed down the slopes of the valley side, rushed across the flat floor of the valley for four kilometres, *and climbed about 140 metres up on the other side of the valley*! Afterwards, it was found that about two and a half square kilometres of the valley floor were covered with rock debris to an average depth of twenty metres. What is particularly informative about this avalanche is that although all the evidence showed that it must have travelled at about 160 kilometres per hour, a lot of the material in it had been transported without being knocked about much, so that moss and soil were found still clinging to some boulders, along with completely undamaged tree-trunks. Press reports also spoke of domestic equipment, houses and even people being carried for tens of metres without damage.

The survivors of the avalanche reported that it was accompanied by a violent blast of air, and this, coupled with the evidence of lack of abrasion within it, gives us a clue to what happened. The debris could not have travelled so far horizontally, nor climbed at all vertically, simply as a result of falling under the influence of gravity; because a falling mass of 'ordinary' rock would lose most of its momentum as it crashed into the ground. The mass as a whole must somehow have preserved its momentum in translation from a vertical descent to horizontal travel, and so it must have behaved like a 'viscous fluid', as one contemporary account put it. This is where we return to the flour that is 'so fine it flows' and to the cement. The flour flows so easily because it contains a large proportion of air mixed up with it. A falling mass of rock, just like a shovelful of cement, will trap a large volume of air within and beneath it as it falls, and it is this air, escaping under pressure, which 'buoys up' the lumps of rock, thereby enabling them to travel long distances.

If this seems hard to swallow, consider what happens in the chemical engineering industry. One of the techniques used in the industry is known as *fluidization* and it is the same kind of process that operates in nature. Industrial chemists use fluidization to make solid, particulate materials behave like fluids, since this helps their alchemy in many ways. What they do is to pile up their material in a dry, granular form in a special apparatus, and then blow a stream of gas up through it. At first, there is not much to see, but as the gas flow is increased, the particles begin to shiver slightly, then to dance around and finally the whole mass of particles appears to be boiling, with all of them in a state of constant turbulent movement. In this state, a light object such as a cork or a plastic duck will bob around on the surface of the powder (lecturers in chemical engineering love to use a plastic duck), and if it's pushed under with a finger, it will pop up immediately, just as it would in the bath at home. The dry powder is behaving like a liquid, and is said to be in a *fluidized* condition, and in this condition the dynamic mixture of gas and particles has a lower density than the original powder. It's important to realize that the particles don't actually 'float' on the gas stream, like ping-pong balls at a fair-ground shooting gallery; they remain in intermittent contact with one another, and only *part* of their weight is taken by the gas stream. If the *whole* weight were taken, then they would rapidly get blown clean out of the apparatus!

In a dry rock avalanche, then, the separate bits and pieces are partially supported by the trapped air rushing up through the collapsing mass, and this 'fluidizes' the moving mass, giving it a lower density and enabling it to travel much further than an unfluidized mass. Since the disaster at Frank, many other rock falls have occurred, and these all lend support to the fluidization concept. In particular, survivors of many of them consistently describe a powerful air blast preceding the arrival of the avalanche. In what was perhaps the worst single natural disaster of the century, the Peruvian earthquake of 1970, a great mass of ice and rock on the face of Mt Huascaran (6,665 metres high) was dislodged by the tremor, and crashed down the face of the mountain, falling free for nearly 1,000 metres. This avalanche travelled over twenty kilometres, at a speed estimated at 480 kilometres per hour, killing many thousands of people in the towns and villages along the valley below the mountain. Some observers reported that the air blast that preceded the avalanche was responsible for extensive damage even before the main mass of debris arrived. One estimate put the volume of this debris at forty million cubic metres, but in some places it is clear that this enormous mass must have been supported on a cushion of air, because near the foot of Huascaran, quite delicate glacial surface ridges and even some vegetation survived, directly in the path of the avalanche.

Now let's get back to volcanoes. Many volcanoes are high mountains, and therefore are just as prone to 'cold' avalanches as any other mountain – perhaps even more prone, since an earthquake or the tremors produced by a small eruption could initiate the collapse of an unstable part of the volcanic pile. Such avalanches clearly don't differ significantly from ones like the Frank or Peruvian cases. Much more significant are the so called *hot avalanches*, since these lead on in a natural progression to two other kinds of pyroclastic flow; *nuées ardentes*, which have already been mentioned several times, and ignimbrites, which have not.

Hot avalanches occur when a mass of newly-formed hot lava begins to break up. In the simplest case, a normal basaltic lava flowing down a volcano may encounter a slope too steep for it to flow down smoothly; the front part of it tends to break up and cascade down the steep slope in a shower of glowing fragments. Where slightly more viscous lavas are involved, the lava may gather itself into balls, which roll along in the flow getting bigger and bigger, like snowballs, and these may sometimes detach themselves completely from the lava flow and roll away ahead of it. They are known as *accretionary lava balls* and they are best-developed on steepish slopes such as one finds on the higher slopes of a volcanic cone. Much larger avalanches take place when more viscous lavas find themselves flowing down steep slopes, or even when a growing lava dome gets too big for itself, becomes mechanically unstable, and bits of it begin to break away. In both these cases, the lavas are usually extremely viscous andesites or dacites, but they are virtually gas-free, so there is no explosive activity; the collapse is purely a mechanical one. This differentiates them from *nuées ardentes*, which are usually triggered off by explosive eruptions.

Apart from the fact that they are composed of hot, possibly incandescent material, 'hot' avalanches behave very much like 'cold' ones, and they travel comparable distances. Some of the best known 'hot' avalanche deposits occur on the high volcanoes of the Andes of northern Chile. For example, a thick mass of andesite lavas has been building up over the last few thousand years on the 6,000 metres high San Pedro volcano, near the border between Chile and Bolivia. The andesite pile had become so high and steep that when the last lavas were erupted they oozed only a little way before finding themselves overhanging a steep slope, which falls away in a long gentle sweep through 2,000 metres vertically towards the distant valley of the River Loa. As each successive flow was pushed out on to the steep slope, the front end of it reached a point of instability, and broke off, sending a great mass of glowing lava crashing down the slope. As more and more lava extruded, the process was repeated, so the lower flanks of the volcano are covered with a carpet of avalanche debris, in which many of the successive collapses can be identified. None of these avalanches were observed, unfortunately, since they all occurred in prehistoric times, but the deposits they left have been little affected by erosion.

Each flow is bounded by a well-defined snout and edges, which may be several metres high. (Like mudflows, there is no gradual petering out, the deposit stops abruptly.) The surface is always strewn with boulders, sometimes arranged in long linear trains, and some of them so large that they look like small craggy castles. Some of the boulders have features which demonstrate conclusively that the avalanche was hot when it occurred; they are broken up by sets of polygonal fracture planes into prismatic segments. These fractured blocks are often called 'hot blocks', and

35. *The steep lava dome of St Pedro volcano in northern Chile. The low cliffs are the avalanche scars left when sections of andesite lavas collapsed to form 'hot avalanche' deposits, parts of which can be seen in the foreground.*

their very distinctive pattern of fractures is the result of the rapid chilling of the blocks after they were deposited by the avalanche; it could not possibly be duplicated in a 'cold' avalanche.

## *Nuées ardentes*

It is not very easy to draw a hard and fast line between hot avalanches and *nuées ardentes*. Several different kinds of *nuée* have been described, and what would be termed a hot avalanche by one vulcanologist might be called a *nuée* by another. Broadly speaking, though, *nuées* tend to be associated with more violently-explosive activity than hot avalanches. Much the most famous *nuée* of all was that from Mt Pelée which destroyed St Pierre in

1902, but a great deal has been learned about them since. In particular, another major eruption of Mt Pelée which started in 1929 provided a unique opportunity to study *nuées* at first hand, and, so to speak, in their ancestral home.

At this point, an intriguing character arrives on the scene. He is Frank Perret, an electrical engineer who had worked with Edison in America on early electrical equipment. In 1902, he suffered a major breakdown in health, and when he heard the news of what had happened to St Pierre, he decided to make a complete change and to devote the rest of his life to the study of volcanoes. He spent much of the next thirty years observing volcanic eruptions anywhere in the world he could – in Italy, Japan, Hawaii, Tenerife and elsewhere. When he heard the news of the 1929 eruption of Mt Pelée, he was in near-by Puerto Rico, but he immediately dropped everything and rushed to Martinique, equipped with only what he stood up in, plus a home-made earth contact microphone (to detect tremors) and a 'folding pocket Kodak'. He installed himself initially on the roof of a hotel which commanded a good view of the volcano and later on built himself a small observatory much closer to it. He spent much of the next three years in this observatory watching the eruption, and was able to see hundreds of *nuées ardentes* at close quarters. Almost too close, for on one occasion he was engulfed in the cloud of dust and ash from a small *nuée*. Fortunately, though, he survived unscathed, and his observations have provided a basis for much of the later work on *nuées*.

The *nuées* of both the 1902 and 1929 eruptions were all pretty similar, and all were associated with the growth of lava domes on the highest part of the volcano. You may recall that during the 1902 eruption a lava dome grew on the site of the Étang Sec on Mt Pelée. Fresh explosive activity in this same dome produced some of the most violent of the 1929 *nuées*, but over the course of months the old dome was largely demolished, or 'eviscerated' in Perret's graphic terms, by the successive explosions. As the eruption continued, a new dome grew, and this eventually stood higher than the old. As it grew, the *nuées* became less violent, and the last ones of the eruption appear to have originated in the collapse of parts of the new dome, so that they were in effect hot avalanches rather than *nuées* proper. Almost all the *nuées* that Perret saw were initiated by powerful explosions, either directed upwards or laterally, and he considered that all the fragmentary ejected material was itself highly gas-charged, and that gas was continually escaping in large volumes from the solid material during the passage of the *nuée*. It was to this continuous discharge of gas that Perret attributed the peculiar flowing properties of *nuées*. Some impression of what the *nuées* Perret observed were actually like can be gained from this description, in his own words:

The first thing seen but rarely heard except in the more highly-explosive early outbursts is a more or less obliquely advancing mass, expanding at a rate so rapid that it should, seemingly, fill the entire heavens in a moment or two, but suddenly the cloud ceases its swift upward expansion, spreading out horizontally, or even downwards on the mountain slope, and at the same time developing upward in cauliflower convolutions of dust and ash. These convolutions grow out of a flowing mass of incandescent material advancing with an indescribably curious rolling and puffing movement which at the immediate front takes the form of forward-springing jets, suggesting charging lions.

36. *One of Frank Perret's classic photographs of* nuées ardentes *erupted during the 1929–32 eruption of Mt Pelée. This one was taken on 7 January 1930, four minutes after the first emission. The advancing front of the* nuée *is on the lower left, the wall of cloud in the upper right is noticeably more diffuse.* (Photo courtesy of the Carnegie Institute of Washington)

This description, vivid though it is, can only be a faint shadow of what the original was like. It's quite easy, though, to make a realistic model, by stirring up the water in a deep, clear pond with steeply-sloping muddy sides. The most obvious thing that will happen is that turbulent clouds of sediment will come rolling upwards, probably obscuring the view, but with a bit of luck, some tightly-convoluted clouds of sediment will be seen rolling off in long trains directly down-slope, hugging the bottom, and with opaque curtains of sediment-laden clouds rising above them. This model is obviously non-volcanic (although it is in fact an exact model of another geological phenomenon, known as a *turbidity current*), but the principles are the same, and the appearance almost identical. Full-scale *nuées*, of course, travel in air rather than water, and they travel very fast, at speeds comparable with those of ordinary avalanches, perhaps as fast as a hundred kilometres per hour. We now know that to behave in this fashion the material within a *nuée* must be in a fluidized state. Perret himself realized this clearly, although fluidization as such had not then been applied to geology:

... the horizontal movement ... is due to an avalanche of a dense mass of hot, highly gas-charged and constantly gas-emitting fragmental lava ... extraordinarily mobile and practically frictionless because each particle is separated from its neighbour by a cushion of compressed gas. For this reason too its onward rush is almost noiseless.

The silence of the *nuée* is somewhat unexpected, since one instinctively expects any powerfully-destructive force to be accompanied by immense noise. This eerie quiet must be due to a variety of effects. First, the only area in which noise can be generated is in the extreme base of the flow, where solid matter is being battered around; the upper parts of the *nuée* being nothing but a turbulent cloud of ash and gas. Secondly, any noise that *is* produced will be effectively blanketed by the envelope of compressed gas in the lower part of the *nuée*. The difference between the base of the *nuée* and the cloud above it must be emphasized. The towering wall of cloud that rises above the rolling front of the *nuée* may be several kilometres high, and is much the most conspicuous part of the whole affair, but concealed at the base, and responsible for it all, is the main avalanche of fast-moving incandescent debris, consisting of everything from the finest ash to boulders several metres across.

Most of the Mt Pelée *nuées* flashed down the same valley on the mountain, the valley of the Rivière Blanche, and in the highest part of the valley the gouging, scouring action of the successive *nuées* stripped the sides of the valley of vegetation right down to the bare rock, and even that was abraded and grooved. Lower down the valley, where the *nuées* were running out of energy, material was deposited and accumulated to a considerable thickness. Many of the *nuées* actually reached the sea, and a small delta was built up at the mouth of the valley by the material carried down by them. Rather surprisingly, the *nuée ardente* deposits themselves have never been described in detail, but it seems from the contemporary accounts which exist that they were closely similar to those of hot avalanches, right down to the presence of prismatic-jointed 'hot blocks'.

37. *The dacite dome that grew on Mt Pelée during the 1929–32 eruption. The remains of the old 1902 dome are visible to the left of the new dome.* (Photo courtesy of the Carnegie Institute of Washington)

Although the nature of the deposits is of great importance to vulcanologists, the conditions prevailing within the *nuée* itself are probably of more immediate interest. Most of the destructive eruptions that have been discussed so far have involved the production of large volumes of ash – Pompeii, it will be recalled, was buried under three metres of the stuff. Now it's an interesting fact that the *nuée* which wiped out St Pierre deposited only a few centimetres of ash in the town itself, so it's immediately clear that the *nuée* must have been of relatively low density. The extensive damage it did was purely a result of the force of the 'tornadic blast' of the *nuée*, and not due to the weight of ashes. The evidence for the force of the blast is abundant; walls up to a metre thick were demolished, and many of the bodies found in the ruins were completely naked, having been stripped of their clothes by the blast, just as victims of bomb blasts sometimes are.

It was suggested in chapter two that the almost total mortality in St Pierre was the result of the victims inhaling the searing hot gas of the *nuée*. In some of the buildings which had *not* been burned by the subsequent fires, pieces of glassware were found which had been softened by the heat of the gas, suggesting a temperature of 600–700°C, so it's scarcely surprising that there were so few survivors. But what about the composition of the gas? Could it have been poisonous? It seems unlikely that this could have caused many deaths, since the whole episode lasted only a few minutes, and the volcanic gases which might have been present in the *nuée*, principally sulphur dioxide, are more suffocating than poisonous. Any choking, irritating gas could only have aggravated the situation, though, by causing the victims to inhale even more deeply than they might have done otherwise. Some of the survivors of the St Pierre and Morne Rouge *nuées* did specifically mention the presence of sulphurous fumes as well as steam in the *nuée*, but Perret, on the occasion when he was enveloped by a small *nuée*, reported that even with his 'trained sense of smell', he was confident that there was not a trace of hydrogen sulphide or sulphur dioxide. He *did* experience a 'burning of the air passages', so he almost certainly experienced in a mild form the effect that killed so many people in St Pierre. He was lucky to escape so lightly.

## The 1968 eruption of Mt Mayon

Mt Mayon is in the Philippines and is widely regarded as the most perfectly symmetrical volcanic cone in the world; it rises in un-broken smooth curves from sea level to 2,462 metres. The con-cave slopes steepen steadily upwards towards the summit crater, which is only 200 metres in diameter. Mayon has had a long his-tory of destructive eruptions; the first recorded one was in 1616, and since that date there have been a total of about forty others which have been responsible for the deaths of more than 1,500 people. The 1968 eruption provided one of the few opportunities in recent decades for geologists to study the formation of *nuées* at first hand.

The eruption began on 20 April, when a reddish glow was ob-served in the summit crater. On 21 April a small eruption cloud was seen, and a series of explosions ensued during the next few

38. *Mt Mayon in a tranquil mood.* (U.S. Geological Survey photo by courtesy of G. A. Macdonald)

days. The largest of these hurled blocks up to 600 metres in the air and produced vertical eruption columns which rapidly climbed as high as ten kilometres into the air. From the base of these vertical columns *nuées ardentes* emerged and swept down the flanks of the volcano, following the deep ravines and gullies. Fortunately, two American geologists, J. G. Moore and W. G. Melson, were on hand at the time, and were able both to fly over the volcano while eruptions were in progress, and also to examine on the ground the deposits left by the *nuées ardentes*. Here is how they described the appearance of the *nuées* by night:

Formation of the *nuées ardentes* was clearly seen during the night of 1–2 May under favourable cloud conditions. Explosions occurred every few minutes, hurling incandescent blocks and finer ejecta as high as 600 metres above the summit. This material fell back and produced a glowing collar on the surface around the summit crater. As this material flowed down the slope, it produced a rapidly-moving pinkish mass with bright moving particles speckling its surface. From a distance of twelve kilometres, these glowing blocks could be clearly seen through binoculars; many of them must have been several tens of metres across. Commonly the downward-moving blocks changed direction abruptly and simultaneously divided into several brighter particles, apparently as a result of bouncing or striking ravine walls, breaking into smaller pieces, and exposing the hotter brighter interiors. The downward-flowing blocks rapidly cooled and faded in colour, but incandescence could commonly be seen at an elevation of 1,000 metres down from the summit. .However, the continuous mantle of glowing material generally divided about 500 metres from the summit, and glowing material was confined to narrow tongues, probably in ravines below that elevation.

During the day, no incandescence was visible, and the *nuées* appeared as rapidly-moving tongue-shaped light-grey clouds, which expanded outwards and upwards, and became darker grey in colour, forming ultimately great cauliflower cloud-masses which often became so big that they obscured the whole volcano. Only about five minutes elapsed from the time of the first emission of the *nuée* until it disappeared into a disorganized mass of expanding cloud.

39. *Mt Mayon during the eruption of 1968. The cone of the volcano is almost completely obscured by dense clouds of dust and ash, but beneath the main vertical eruption column the tightly-convoluted dust clouds from radial* nuées ardentes *are visible on the lower left.* (Photo courtesy of W. G. Melson, Smithsonian Institute)

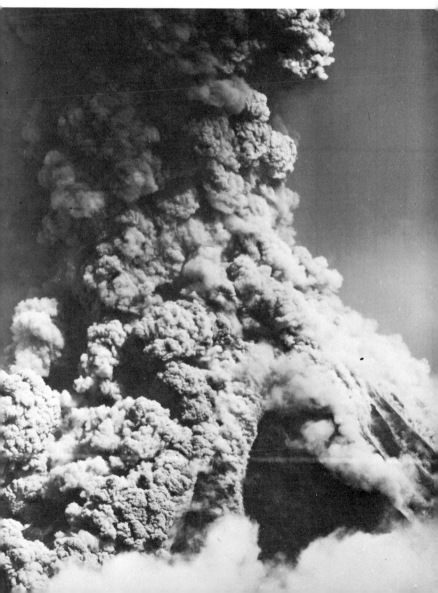

From their visual observations of the *nuées*, Moore and Melson concluded that they were the result of avalanching of material which was initially ejected from the crater vertically upwards, but then fell back to earth. This differentiates these *nuées* from the St Pierre kind, which were produced by explosions taking place in a growing lava dome. Moore and Melson's work on the ground after the eruption also throws some fascinating light on the physical conditions prevailing within the Mayon *nuées*, and their mechanisms of transport.

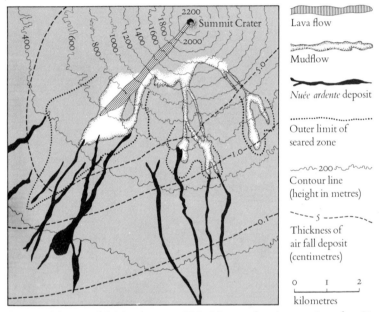

*Fig. 48 Moore and Melson's map of Mt Mayon after the eruption of 1968.*

The deposits left by the *nuées* were particularly informative. They were often several metres thick, had well-defined flow fronts (like the Chilean hot avalanches) and consisted entirely of loose masses of ash and blocks of all sizes. (One block twenty-five metres across was found low down on the flanks of the volcano.) Many of the blocks were still hot when they were examined in the field, and

many of them also had a characteristic 'breadcrust' textured surface, which indicated that the lava which gave rise to them was
rich in gas, and that the blocks had been puffed up after their
eruption from the vent. The extremely fragile condition of some
of the blocks also suggested that, since they were found intact, the
expansion and bread-crust cracking must have taken place very
late in the period of flow, possibly even *after* the *nuée* had come to
rest. The fact that gas is exsolved from the fragments within a
moving *nuée* lends support to Perret's suggestion that it is this gas
which gives *nuées* their great mobility.

Surrounding each *nuée* deposit was a clearly-defined 'seared
zone' which ranged from a few metres in width to over two
kilometres. On the outer parts of these zones plant leaves were
shrivelled and browned; on the inner parts all the vegetation
facing towards the crater was charred and many trees were completely stripped of foliage on the same side.

All the animals in the seared zone were killed outright. A
farmer, unfortunately caught within one zone, died shortly afterwards as a result of severe burns; before dying in hospital he is
reported to have said that he was caught in 'a blast of hot gas'.
It's clear that he shared the same kind of fate as the unfortunate
inhabitants of St Pierre. As in St Pierre, also, it appears that each
*nuée* from Mayon was preceded by a 'tornadic blast' of cold air
and some estimates suggest that this may have had a speed of
about 200 kilometres per hour. Estimates of the speed of the *nuées*
themselves are rather variable, but one which was recorded on
film appeared to be travelling at something between fifty and a
hundred kilometres per hour. Finally, it's worth noting that the
immense clouds of dust rising from the *nuées* appear to have triggered off torrential rainstorms which fell within minutes of the
passage of the *nuées*. The rain water from these in turn swept away
the loose ash from the slopes of the volcano to form destructive
mudflows which extended down many kilometres below the
lowest points reached by the *nuées* themselves. These mudflows
caused a great deal of damage to roads, a railway line, pipelines,
and extensive areas of farmland.

## Ignimbrites

If lavas, ashes and *nuées ardentes* are the conventional weapons in the volcanic arsenal, then ignimbrites are the nuclear deterrents. Ignimbrites are a group of rocks which are believed to be formed in much the same way as those deposited by a *nuée ardente* (the name 'ignimbrite' is itself a compound of two Latin words meaning something like 'fire cloud rock'), but they are both much more important in geological terms, and much less well understood than *nuées*. They occur in large quantities all over the world and dominate substantial parts of the landscape in countries such as Mexico and New Zealand, but they have only been recognized as a distinct group of rocks since 1935. Partly, this obscurity is because no ignimbrite eruption has ever been observed, and partly because an 'ignimbrite' can be anything from a loose, sandy ash to a solid, glassy rock, like obsidian. Little wonder, then, that the links between these extremes were not recognized for many years, until the mechanism of their origin began to be understood, at least in part. Ignimbrites also have the distinction of being the most potentially dangerous of all volcanic phenomena. Single ignimbrite flows often extend over fifteen kilometres, and a few are more than 150 kilometres long. Some of the largest, in Nevada, are reported to cover 18,000 square kilometres, and it has been estimated that in the San Juan mountains of Colorado, there were originally some 20,000 cubic kilometres of ignimbrite, made up of hundreds of individual flows. Any one of these colossal flows may have been erupted in a matter of hours or days, so it is difficult to imagine quite how catastrophic such an eruption would be if it were to occur at the present time in an inhabited area.

It's perhaps fortunate, then, that ignimbrite eruptions are rather rare events. The only one known to have occurred in historic times was in 1912, in a remote part of Alaska. Although no one observed this eruption directly, the area involved has subsequently been examined minutely, and a great deal has been learned from these studies about what ignimbrites are, and how they are formed.

Mount Katmai, the volcano involved, is located on the horn-like peninsula which leads off westwards from the mainland of Alaska into the Aleutian Islands. Up until 1912, it had been a well-behaved volcano, eroding away slowly into a genteel old age. On 2 June 1912, seismic tremors were felt by the thinly-scattered population of the area, but these were largely ignored, just as most of the premonitory shocks before an eruption are. The shocks continued, however, and increased in severity, becoming alarming on 4 and 5 June. On 5 June, ash clouds were observed for the first time and it was plain that an eruption was under way. On 6 June the eruption reached its climax, with a fully-developed Plinian ash cloud showering ashes over a huge area. Approximately two metres of ash eventually accumulated at Kaflia Bay, about fifty-six kilometres from the volcano, and a few centimetres at Kodiak, 160 kilometres away. A native of Kaflia Bay, Ivan Orloff, wrote a letter to his wife on 9 June in which he conveyed in simple unaffected language a clear impression of the nightmarish quality of the ash fall:

> We are waiting death at any moment. A mountain has burst near here. We are covered with ashes, in some places ten feet and six feet deep. All this began June 6. Night and day we light lanterns. We cannot see the daylight. We have no water, the rivers are just ashes mixed with water. Here are darkness and hell, thunder and noise. I do not know whether it is day or night. The earth is trembling, it lightens [sic] every minute. It is terrible. We are praying.

During 6 June two stupendous explosions were heard, the sound carrying nearly 1,600 kilometres, and on the following day a third great explosion reverberated around Alaska. After these climactic blasts, the activity gradually declined and all became quiet once more. At the time, that was all that was known of the eruption: that three major explosions had occurred, presumably on Katmai volcano, and that a huge quantity of ash had fallen. No one had seen or experienced anything more than this, so no one had the slightest idea of what had actually been happening to the volcano itself.

The scientific world at the time was aware that this had been a particularly big eruption but, perhaps because everyone was still overawed by the Krakatoa eruption of thirty years before, it was not until 1916 that a scientific expedition sponsored by the National Geographic Society of America was sent to investigate the circumstances. The first object of the expedition, naturally, was to examine Mt Katmai itself. A wonderful surprise awaited them.

The original 2,300-metres-high volcano had been lowered by fully 300 metres and in place of the original cone there now gleamed a turquoise blue lake, filling a deep roughly-circular crater five kilometres across and 800 metres deep. This lake was steaming gently round the edges, and the water was hot, heated by volcanic steam. A small island, formed by a small cinder cone, rose up above the surface of the water. This was not the only discovery they made. To the north-west of the volcano, there had been a valley along which the Ukak river flowed. To the amazement of the expedition, they found that this valley had been transformed into a flat plain, four kilometres across at its widest, from which countless numbers of jets of steam were playing. As Robert Griggs, leader of the expedition put it: 'It was as though all the steam engines of the world, assembled together, had popped their safety valves at once, and were letting off steam in concert.' Suitably enough, he named this the 'Valley of Ten Thousand Smokes' and a wonderful spectacle it must have been. Sadly, though, the steam jets died away after a few years, and now the valley is quite still. But what had caused this remarkable transformation?

Griggs's party found that for a length of about twenty-two kilometres the original Ukak valley had been filled with loose, sandy ash material, which they described as a 'sand flow'. They inferred that the 'sand' must have been incandescent at the time of its eruption, and that the thousands of steam vents were produced by the vaporizing of water trapped in the sand and gravel

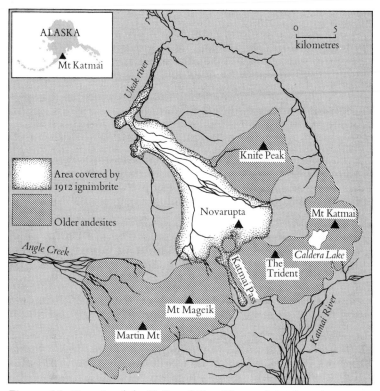

*Fig. 49 Mt Katmai and the Valley of Ten Thousand Smokes, showing the extent of the 1912 ignimbrite.* (After G. H. Curtiss)

of the river bed beneath the cooling mass. The party spent some time camped in their valley, and found good use for the steam – they cooked their meals over the escaping jets. (This was not such a good idea as it sounds, since the steam turned out to contain a high proportion of acid, so they were in effect spraying their saucepans, kettles and billy cans with an acid aerosol. This rapidly led to corrosion, and holes appeared in some of their pans.)

Since Griggs's expedition in 1916, several others have visited the area, and the sequence of events of the 1912 eruption has been more or less unravelled. The great Plinian eruption which showered ash over Kodiak and the area around it is not now thought to have involved the Katmai volcano solely, but also a series of vents eight kilometres west of it. These vents were a series of longitudinal fissures running across the head of the Ukak valley, and it was from them that the 'sand flow' – or ignimbrite as it would now be called – was ejected. Recent work has shown that the old Ukak valley was filled to an average depth of about thirty metres and that the volume of the ignimbrite was not less than *ten cubic kilometres*! This whole mass must have been expelled in a space of about twenty hours during the climax of the eruption, at a rate of something like 500 million cubic metres per hour. After the emission of the ignimbrite, activity quietened down, and a small dome of viscous lava piled up over the largest of the vents. This dome was named Novarupta, suitably enough, and it seems to have represented a last waning gasp in the eruption. There has been no activity since.

But how did Mt Katmai come to be demolished? It's thought that at the time of the eruption a large volume of molten rock may have existed in a magma chamber beneath the volcano, and that this was connected by some kind of subterranean volcanic plumbing with the vents around Novarupta, eight kilometres away, so that most of the material that was actually erupted at these vents was derived from beneath Katmai. The sudden, almost instantaneous escape of all this magma left the supra-structure of the volcano unsupported, so it collapsed bodily into the space left by the disappearing magma, forming the huge new crater, now filled by the lake. Significant though it may be from a historic point of view, the Katmai ignimbrite is only the most recent of many millions of older ignimbrites. The problem that it poses is this: is this one eruption typical of all the earlier ones, and if not, why not? We'll consider this from two points of view: first, the rocks themselves, and second, the overall geological associations of ignimbrites.

Ignimbrites are composed mostly of pumice fragments, that is, small lumps of frothy rock identical with those of an ordinary air-fall pumice deposit. They may also contain a large proportion of bits of solid lava, loose crystals and odd bits and pieces picked up somewhere along their way. Since they are composed of material identical with that of an ordinary air-fall deposit, ignimbrites must have originated from the same kind of magma. What then is the difference in the way they are erupted? Now, as was explained earlier, a Plinian eruption is the result of the explosive de-gassing of a viscous magma. As the magma approaches the surface, the pressure on it decreases, the gas expands, and a

*Fig. 50 The contrast between a Plinian eruption and an ignimbrite-producing one.*

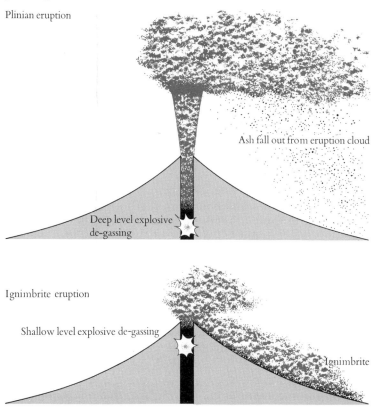

Plinian eruption

Ash fall out from eruption cloud

Deep level explosive de-gassing

Ignimbrite eruption

Shallow level explosive de-gassing

Ignimbrite

violently self-accelerating process takes place, blasting the fragmented magma up out of the vent. The basic difference between
a Plinian eruption and an ignimbrite-producing eruption seems to
be the site at which the de-gassing takes place. In the Plinian case,
it must occur deep down in the throat of the volcano, so that the
pumice is blasted upwards like shot from a gun, whereas when
ignimbrites are erupted, the de-gassing takes place near the surface, so that the whole mass froths out sideways rather than upwards.

There is clearly no hard and fast boundary between these two
extremes, and most ignimbrite eruptions appear to have been
preceded by a Plinian blast of air-fall pumice. It has been suggested
that the two types of eruption form a natural sequence, with the
violent Plinian phase representing the first explosive de-gassing of a
new magma, while the ignimbrite phase represents a later stage
when the magma has become depleted in gas. The situation as a
whole is rather like shaking up an open bottle of beer with your
thumb over the top. If you shake it vigorously, the carbon dioxide
gas in it comes out of solution, and pressure builds up in the neck
of the bottle. If you don't press hard enough with your thumb, it
will be blown off, and a spray of beer will squirt out high in the
air, probably showering most of the people in the room. This is
the Plinian stage of the eruption. After this first spray, particularly
if it's beer that normally has a good head on it, it will continue de-
gassing rapidly, and beery foam will climb up out of the bottle
and run down the neck. That's the ignimbrite. With a good long
shake and some practice, almost the whole bottle can be erupted
in one go, but don't try it; it's a waste of good beer!

So an ignimbrite can be likened to a sort of continually-
expanding rock froth which floods out of a vent. The fragments
of pumice which make up the magmatic component of the
ignimbrite are themselves solid, but the copious volumes of gas
that are continually exsolved from the pumice fragments mobilize
the whole into a cloud of low density and viscosity, which travels
over the ground surface at high speed and spreads over a great
area. So the mechanism of travel is like that of a *nuée ardente*, except that in some *nuées* the gas that cushions the flow may be air

entrapped by the onrushing mass of debris, while in an ignimbrite the gas is derived from within the flow itself. It is for this reason that ignimbrites can travel for tens of kilometres over flat or gently-sloping surfaces; most *nuées ardentes* rarely extend further than the slopes of the volcano. Ignimbrites therefore are even better examples of fluidization processes at work than *nuées*, and there is plenty of evidence for this in the rocks themselves; they are totally unsorted, with fragments of all shapes and sizes jumbled up in a complete hodge-podge, through having been constantly stirred up by the turbulence within the flow.

The fact that the ignimbrites are made up of pumice fragments, and that they are erupted while intensely hot has some interesting implications. The Katmai ignimbrite had the texture of dry, loose sand, and many of the ignimbrites around the world are similar – they are soft enough to be scooped up with a spoon. In such cases, all the particles are disaggregated: there is no tendency for them to stick to one another. But pumice fragments are made of frothy volcanic glass, and glass softens easily when heated. So if the particles making up the ignimbrite were still hot when the flow

40. *A quarry exposure of an ignimbrite sheet in Tenerife. The fine-grained base of the sheet is visible level with the geologists' heads; above that the ignimbrite is homogeneous. The black holes that are visible are interpreted as moulds of tree trunks which were swept up by the flow and subsequently vaporized.*

came to rest, they would be soft and the edges of adjacent particles would tend to stick together where they touched, so that the whole mass would become *partly welded*. If the temperature were higher, or if it stayed hot for longer, the welding process would be carried further, so that ultimately the whole thing would become one solid glassy mass, like obsidian. Many such glassy ignimbrites have in fact been confused in the past with glassy lava flows.

Welded ignimbrites are rare compared with unwelded ones, and only a few ignimbrites are welded right through from top to bottom. In most ignimbrites, in fact, there are a number of well-defined layers with different properties. The lowermost layer of all is rarely welded, since it is cooled by contact with the ground beneath. Above this basal layer there may be a number of different zones showing different degrees of welding, but the degree of welding decreases steadily upwards, so that the topmost parts of the flow are generally completely unwelded. Although one of the characteristic features of pyroclastic flows is their chaotic, unsorted nature, there is often a tendency for the low–density pumice fragments to congregate in the upper parts of ignimbrite flows, and for the denser fragments of solid rock to be concentrated in the lower parts.

41. *The black streaks in this ignimbrite are* fiamme *of flattened glassy pumice fragments. The texture is quite unmistakable.* (Photo courtesy of I. G. Gass)

Ignimbrites typically form extensive flat sheets which range in thickness from a few centimetres to tens of metres. In a thick sheet there is clearly a heavy load on the bottom layers, so if these parts are hot and plastic, they may get squeezed out, become much denser, and acquire a very distinctive texture. The largest lumps of pumice (which are commonly many centimetres across) all get squashed out into thin, pancake-like discs. These, seen in cross-section on a broken piece of ignimbrite, look a little like candle flames, and are known by their Italian name of *fiamme*. The same kind of texture can be seen even on a microscopic scale, with tiny glass shards flattened and moulded over one another, and all of them streaked out in the same direction. This texture is peculiar to ignimbrite; it cannot be produced in any other rocks, so it's a valuable criterion for identifying old ignimbrites, even those which have been buried beneath tens of millions of years' accumulation of sediments or have been folded and deformed by successive mountain-building episodes. It's one line of evidence that demonstrates that exactly the same kind of volcanic activity that we know today was going on on the Earth in the dim and distant past, even before life itself had become established. It's known, for example, that extensive ignimbrite volcanism was

42. *A small part of an ignimbrite plateau in northern Chile. Three separate ignimbrites can be seen as white bands in the wall of the quebrada. One of them can be traced for over one hundred kilometres upstream.*

going on in North Wales, Shropshire and the Lake District at intervals between 400 and 700 million years ago. It has even been shown recently that Norfolk, a county well-known for the beauty of its flat, wind-swept pasturelands and quiet waterways, was many hundreds of millions of years ago also covered by ignimbrite sheets, though one would never suspect this from the surface geology. Core specimens recovered from a deep bore-hole going down thousands of metres revealed exactly the same kind of *fiamme* as those in ignimbrites only a few hundreds of years old.

## Geological relationships of ignimbrites

The Katmai ignimbrite was intimately linked with the formation of a major crater or *caldera* (a caldera is strictly a crater greater than one kilometre in diameter). But are ignimbrites *always* related to calderas? The relationship is certainly a very common one. In Japan, for example, ignimbrites are sometimes called 'Aso lavas', since they are so prominent around the Aso caldera, and as one looks around the rest of the world, the same relationship crops up time and again. Not all ignimbrites are associated with calderas, though, but wherever they are found, the same train of events seems to have happened. First, there is a stage of upwarping or tumescence when intrusion of large masses of magma arches up the ground surface over a wide area. This weakens the rocks stretched over the arch, fissures open, and ignimbrite foams out. This creates a void beneath the arch, which then collapses. Think about what happens to a frozen chicken pie when it is cooked. Usually, the pastry wells up splendidly initially, and then, perhaps because the gravy inside overboils, a fissure opens, and rich brown ignimbrite spreads itself over the floor of the oven. When the pie comes out of the oven, it still looks splendid, but as soon as it begins to cool, the pastry collapses downwards, leaving a sad-looking relic. This kind of process can either produce calderas, if it is centred at one point, or long linear features known grandly as 'volcano-tectonic depressions'. The Taupo basin of North Island, New Zealand is one of these. It is about ninety kilometres long by thirty kilometres broad, and contains some of New Zealand's biggest volcanoes. The whole of the central part of North Island is in fact a broad, slightly-eroded ignimbrite plateau built up of many hundreds of individual ignimbrites, with a volume totalling 7,500 cubic kilometres.

## World distribution of pyroclastic flows

One can't really make any useful generalizations about where in the world volcanic mudflows are most likely to occur, not from geological considerations anyway. Their distribution is governed mainly by climate, and they are clearly likely to be more common in areas of heavy rainfall than in arid ones. Hot avalanches, *nuées ardentes* and ignimbrites are somewhat easier to deal with, since they are characteristically associated with relatively viscous magmas of andesitic or even rhyolitic composition, and are therefore much more likely to turn up at destructive plate margins than at constructive margins, where fluid basalt lavas predominate.

*Nuées ardentes* are not confined to Mt Pelée and the Caribbean plate margin, although a great deal of space in this book has been devoted to them. They occur in many other geologically similar environments, and in particular on volcanoes round the circum-Pacific 'Ring of Fire'. Apart from the 1968 eruption of Mt Mayon in the Philippines, *nuées* were produced during the eruption of Hibokhibok volcano, also in the Philippines in 1951. These were responsible for the deaths of 500 people. In the same year (1951 was a bad year for *nuées*) 3,000 people were killed by *nuées* erupted from Mt Lamington volcano in Papua, New Guinea. Fortunately, there have not been any such disastrous *nuée* eruptions since then – there were few casualties on Mayon, since the areas at risk were evacuated early on.

Since the vast majority of ignimbrites are of rhyolitic composition, they too are most characteristic of destructive plate margins, and should, in theory at least, be scarce on mid-ocean volcanoes. Ignimbrites are in fact almost absent from most major oceanic volcanic areas such as Iceland and Hawaii, but by one of nature's quirks they *are* abundant on some oceanic islands such as the Azores and the Canary Islands. Strangely enough, ignimbrites are also abundant along the East African Rift System, and form substantial components of some of the major mid-plate volcanoes in Africa, such as Tibesti and Jebel Marra. There are some remarkable similarities between these mid-plate volcanoes and some oceanic islands such as the Canaries, but at present, geologists have little idea why there should be such similarities between volcanoes in such different environments. Plate Tectonics, it seems, does not provide all the answers. Or not yet, anyway.

*Chapter 7*    Volcanic landscape forms

Volcanic landforms are different from all others in one vital respect. Most of the scenery we see around us is the result of a one-
way process of erosion by wind, water and ice, whose ultimate
effect is to reduce even the mightiest mountain range to a flat
plain. Volcanic landforms, however, are the end result of *two*
opposing forces, constructive and destructive. *Constructive processes* which build up volcanoes clearly operate only during their
active lives. This may be extremely short – a matter of days or
weeks – or very long, with activity continuing intermittently
over thousands or even millions of years. The *rate* of construction
may be equally varied. In the last chapter it was mentioned that
the 'sand flow' in the Valley of Ten Thousand Smokes in Alaska
was erupted at the staggering rate of 500 million cubic metres per
hour. Most of us, though, wouldn't think of an ignimbrite (the
'sand flow') as a typical volcanic landform. A more familiar
example of rapid construction is Paricutin in Mexico. This 'ordinary' scoria cone volcano was born in a small field belonging to a
Mexican farmer on 20 February 1943. After one year of activity
it was 325 metres high, and when it finally simmered into silence
in 1952 it was 410 metres high. In its nine years of activity about
2,000 million cubic metres of ash and lavas were erupted. Stromboli, on the other hand, has been in a state of continuous mild
activity for centuries, but is still only 931 metres high.

Two kinds of destructive forces work in the opposite direction,
tending to destroy the structures a volcano has built up. First,
there are the ordinary processes of *erosion*, which will have started
their work on the volcano long before it stops growing, before

even the lava has cooled. The rate at which erosion proceeds is governed by climatic conditions – a volcano in an area of heavy tropical rainfall and rampant vegetation will be much more rapidly attacked than one in a cold, arid desert. Second, *explosive activity* may take place, either as part of an eruption, or as an isolated event, and can accomplish in a few moments what it would take millions of years for erosion to do. Since most large volcanoes have very long lives, during their lifetime they may go through several phases of construction, erosion and explosion, and sometimes erosion may be proceeding in one part of a volcano while construction is going on simultaneously in another.

## Constructive processes

### Basalt plateaux

Two factors influence the shape that a volcano adopts: they are the mechanism of the eruption, and the nature of the volcanic raw material, the magma. These are also the factors which dictate the differences between the major types of eruption, so it is scarcely surprising that different kinds of eruption produce different land-

*Fig. 51 The area covered by the basalt lavas of the Deccan plain.*

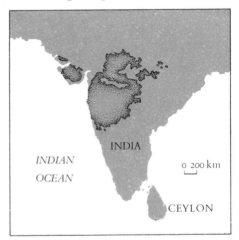

forms. When basalts are erupted through fissures, they may do so in huge quantities, forming flood basalts (chapter three).

These voluminous flows pile up one on top of another, drowning earlier hills and valleys, and eventually form uncannily flat basalt plateaux, which stretch from horizon to horizon. The Columbia River plateau in North America is the best-known example, but it is not the biggest. The whole of north-western India – the Deccan Plain – is underlain by basalt lavas, which now cover some 250,000 square kilometres. The immense basalt plain is probably itself only an erosional remnant of a more extensive one which may have covered twice the area.

The Drakensberg mountains in South Africa are also the remnants of a basalt plateau, one which has been deeply dissected by rivers, so that the individual flows can be seen plainly in the sides of cliffs and gorges. Some of the flows were probably erupted immediately after one another, but others must have been separated by long intervals, because layers of gravel and soil are found sandwiched between them, showing that there was time for some

*43. Basalt lavas total nearly 1,000 metres in thickness in this deeply-dissected basalt plateau in Natal, South Africa. Each flow is very nearly horizontal, and so was the original plateau, as the flat tops to the mountains clearly show.* (Photo from *Understanding the Earth* courtesy of Artemis Press)

erosion to take place between eruptions. When deeply dissected by erosion, thick piles of basalt lavas give rise to a characteristic sort of 'stepped' topography. Erosion eats its way rapidly along the soft scoriaceous upper parts of the lava flows, and along the soil or gravel layers between flows, but the lower part of the flow is solid rock, and much more resistant. The hard lavas therefore tend to form cliff-like 'risers', while the softer upper parts form flat 'treads', and, when repeated throughout the thickness of a lava pile, a complete staircase is produced. This easily-recognizable feature of basalt plateaux once led to their being called collectively 'traps', after an old Swedish word for a staircase, and geologists customarily talk still about the 'Deccan traps'.

Although each individual flow in one of these lava piles probably spread out rapidly, the pile as a whole would undoubtedly have taken a long time to accumulate, probably many millions of years. The volume of lava poured out on to the Earth's surface in eruptions like these is almost unimaginable. In the Parana basalts of Uruguay and Brazil, a sequence of basalts some 3,000 metres in thickness is present, and the volume may be in the order of 800,000 cubic kilometres. The many thousands of individual flows involved range in thickness from five to a hundred metres. Most of the great basalt plateaux in the world are located in areas where rifting occurred prior to continental drift. This means that the erosional remnants of basalt plateaux that turn up in many widely-separated parts of the world are closely related. In figure fifty-two it's clear that the Brazilian basalts were once united with some in South West Africa, before the Atlantic Ocean opened and separated them by thousands of kilometres, and similarly the basalts of the Drakensberg mountains are believed once to have formed part of the same plateau as those on the coast of Antarctica.

Britain, too, has her share of plateau basalts. Northern Ireland, Skye, Mull, Rhum and many of the small islands in the Inner Hebrides contain remnants of an old, rather complex plateau, which about sixty million years ago covered much of the area north of the Irish and west of the Scottish coasts which is now below the sea, and which was once united with similar remnants in the Faroe Islands, Jan Mayen, Iceland and Greenland. This ancient plateau, now highly fragmented and dispersed by sea-floor spreading, has been called the 'Thulean plateau'.

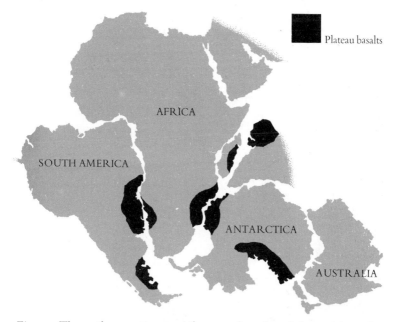

Plateau basalts

*Fig. 52 The southern continents as they may have been before continental drift.*

Incidentally, two of Britain's best known landmarks, the Giant's Causeway in Antrim, and Fingal's Cave on the island of Staffa both originated when the Thulean plateau was being formed. Both are famous for the elegance of the hundreds upon hundreds of hexagonal columns which stand out in the cliffs and on the shore. These hexagonal columns (or strictly polygonal, because four-, five-, seven- and eight-sided shapes also occur) are examples of *columnar jointing*, produced by the slow cooling and shrinking of a thick basalt lava. In some ways, columnar jointing is similar to the polygonal cracks that develop in the mud of a puddle that has been dried up and baked by the sun, except that in a lava, the cracks are not confined to a shallow surface layer,

44. *Some of the myriads of elegant basalt columns that make up the Giant's Causeway in Antrim, Northern Ireland. Most, but not all, are hexagonal.* (Institute of Geological Sciences photograph)

but may extend vertically throughout the entire thickness of the flow, dividing it up into pillars or columns.

### Shield volcanoes

When basalt lavas are erupted through a single central Hawaiian-style vent, a broad, convex swelling volcano is produced, usually with a relatively small sunken crater or caldera on the crest of the swelling. These are known as *shield* volcanoes, and there are several splendid examples in the Hawaiian islands themselves, although the name was first given to Icelandic ones. Shield volcanoes, like basalt plateaux, are built up of thousands of individual lava flows, none of them very thick, and since the lavas are of low viscosity, the slopes of the shield are rather gentle, usually between two and ten degrees. This gentle slope, however, does not prevent shield volcanoes from becoming high mountains. Mauna Kea and Mauna Loa in Hawaii both reach over 4,000 metres above sea level, and if one takes into account the part of them that is below sea level, they are the highest mountains on Earth, over 9,000 metres high.

2 km   Mauna Loa

] 2 km

*Fig. 53 Profile of Mauna Loa, one of the biggest Hawaiian shield volcanoes.*

Fortunately, volcanism in the Hawaiian islands is extremely active and has been closely observed over the last hundred years, so there are good records of how shield volcanoes are built up. Over a period of a hundred years (up until 1950), there were thirty-four recorded eruptions of Mauna Loa, adding on average thirty million cubic metres of basalt per year to the already huge bulk of the volcano. Many of these eruptions followed a fairly similar pattern. A typical one is that of 1940. This started when a series of small fissures five kilometres long opened up on the summit of Mauna Loa, running right across the impossibly-named summit caldera Mokuaweoweo. Fire fountains played almost all the way along the length of the fissure and rivers of lava poured from them, some flooding into the caldera, the rest streaming away down the outer slopes of the volcano. Activity gradually concentrated on one small area near the centre of the caldera, where, at the height of the eruption, lava was sprayed 200 metres into the air, and thread-like wafts of Pele's hair began to drift down on observers round the caldera. Most of the lava was emitted during the first few hours of the eruption, and it formed a lake in the caldera six metres deep. During the five months that the eruption lasted, a total of about 600,000 cubic metres of lava were emitted. This eruption demonstrated three important features of shield volcanoes. First, although they are basically 'central' vent volcanoes, fissure eruptions play a vital part in their growth. These fissures are usually radially arranged around the summit. Second, much of the lava emitted during an eruption emerges from fissures on the flanks of the volcano, rather than from the summit crater. Third, although fire fountains are a common and spectacular part of an eruption, the pyroclastic material they eject contributes little to the total volume of new basalt erupted. By far the largest proportion of the erupted material comes up as basalt flows, and it is this that gives shield volcanoes their characteristic shapes. The eruptions that build up shield volcanoes clearly have much in common with those that give rise to basalt plateaux, and some vulcanologists now believe that basalt plateaux consist of groups of shield volcanoes with extremely gentle slopes.

## Conical volcanoes

Conical volcanoes are everybody's idea of what a volcano should look like. The association between the mental concept of a volcano and the image of an elegant, symmetrical cone is so strong that cones of this sort are used universally as symbols to represent volcanoes in publications of all kinds from comics to learned academic journals. The strength of this association is somewhat unfortunate, since it tends to create the impression that sym-

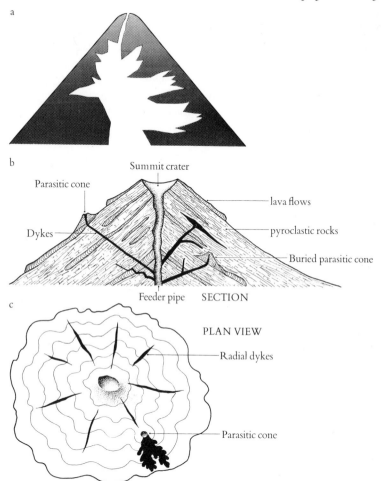

Fig. 54a *A rather bad example of the kind that often appears in schoolbooks, purporting to show the internal structure of a conical volcano.*

Fig. 54b *A rather better version of the same thing. Small parasitic cones on the flanks of the volcano are often buried by lavas and pyroclastics from later eruptions.*

Fig. 54c *The same volcano in plan, when erosion has exposed some of the radial dykes which fed parasitic cones on the flanks.*

metrical volcanoes are the standard form of volcano. This is far from the truth. Cones with pleasing profiles like that of Mt Fuji are by no means rare; Fuego in Guatemala, Mayon in the Philippines, Popocatepetl in Mexico, El Misti in Peru, and Egmont in New Zealand, to name but a few, are equally beautiful. These however, are merely fine examples of a much bigger group of volcanoes, known as *strato volcanoes*, or better, *composite volcanoes*. It is volcanoes of this kind that most of us have seen at one time or another illustrated in school textbooks, neatly sectioned down the middle, so that the highly unconvincing works are displayed.

Examples of the simplest kind of conical volcano are the scoria cones described on p. 165. These are often elegantly symmetrical, but they differ from composite conical volcanoes in that they are much smaller – they rarely exceed a couple of hundred metres in height – and, more important, they are *monogenetic*, that is, they are produced by a once-and-for-all eruption. Composite cones are composite in two senses. First, they are built up by many eruptions taking place over a long period, so the shape of the cone is controlled by both constructive and destructive elements. As it grows, it builds into itself the smooth curves resulting from erosion of the growing cone. Second, the great conical composite volcanoes are usually built up by andesite magmas which are more viscous than basalt and give rise to more explosive eruptions, and hence a greater proportion of pyroclastic material is erupted along with the lavas, and the cone is built up of interleaved layers of lava flows and pyroclastics. Some purely basaltic composite volcanoes do exist, but generally, because of their need for a viscous magma and lots of pyroclastics, andesitic ones are more common, and, as a consequence, conical volcanoes are more abundant along the circum-Pacific belt than elsewhere.

Conical volcanoes owe their beauty to their smooth, symmetrical profiles. A very few, such as Mayon in the Philippines really are perfectly symmetrical, so that a horizontal section across them at any level would be circular. But this symmetry owes itself only to chance, in that all the eruptions of the volcano have

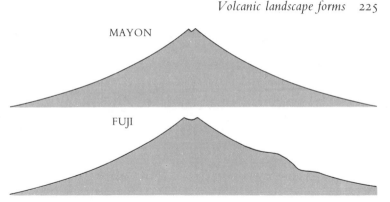

*Fig. 55 Profiles of Mayon and Fuji. The symmetry of Fuji is spoiled by a lump on one side.*

taken place from the same central vent. There is no reason why this should always be so, and successive eruptions on any given volcano may occur at different sites scattered round the highest point. This is why so many apparently perfect cones, like some

45. *A fairly viscous, partly glassy lava flow which spread out over the floor of the Las Cañadas caldera in Tenerife. The flow has a steep, high, well-defined flow front. In the foreground are the levées of another lava flow, with a typical aa surface.*

women, only stand inspection from a distance – if one looks closer, blemishes appear. Even Mt Fuji has a lump on its northern side, so it's always photographed from the south.

At each new site of activity, a parasitic cone is built up, so that ultimately the volcano as a whole may consist of a large massif with many hundreds of individual vents scattered round it, but the whole structure still preserves a broad overall identity. Etna displays this arrangement well. For a long while it has had two summit craters at roughly the same level, both active, but throughout its history new vents have been opening up round its flanks, and new parasitic cones have been built up, usually above a radial fissure. As in Hawaii, most of the recently erupted lava comes from these vents rather than directly from the summit crater.

## Destructive processes

*Explosive activity and crater formation*

One always associates explosions with craters, but unfortunately, the term 'crater' is applied to any hole-shaped depression produced by any kind of explosion. Basically, there are three kinds of crater that one may encounter in this world, volcanic craters, meteorite impact craters and bomb craters, ideally in that order. (But the human race being what it is, bomb craters are more abundant than meteorite craters.) Craters formed by single short-lived events tend to have similar features, whatever their cause; they are usually broad and shallow, with a low upraised lip. As we shall see, a few volcanic craters are of this form. Only a few though; there is a wide variety of different types, which can be grouped under three rather artificial heads; those formed by *eruption*, by *explosion* and by *subsidence*.

ERUPTION CRATERS

*Eruption* craters are simply the holes at the top of a volcanic cone where all the action happens. In general, they are funnel-shaped depressions which owe their existence as much to the accumulation of material round the vent as to the explosive ejection of it – as the cone gets progressively higher, so does the base of the crater. The crater within a typical Strombolian scoria cone is the result of comparatively long periods of spasmodic eruption, rather than single bangs, but often it may be enlarged, and its walls steepened, by major blasts. When activity ceases, the crater rapidly becomes partially filled by loose debris falling into it from the walls, but once it has reached a condition of equilibrium, its outline, although softening slightly, will remain unchanged for a long time. Many such craters, now overgrown and weather-beaten, are still recognizable in the scoria cones of the Auvergne area of Central France, an area which somehow seems an improbable site for recent volcanic activity. The last eruption there was a few thousand years ago.

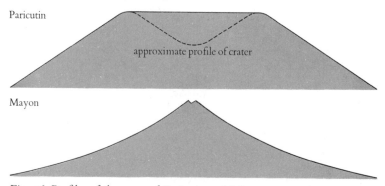

Paricutin

approximate profile of crater

Mayon

*Fig. 56 Profiles of the cones of Paricutin and Mayon, not to the same scales.*

Figure fifty-six illustrates a typical young scoria cone, that of Paricutin in Mexico, which grew to a height of about 300 metres in 1944. The outer slopes of the cone are strikingly regular, sloping uniformly at an angle of 33° to the horizontal; the side-slopes of the crater within are similar since in both cases the slopes are governed by the angle of rest for loose scoria. Notice how big the crater is compared with the size of the cone. Alongside the profile of Paricutin is one of 2,400 metres high Mt Mayon for comparison. The flanks of Mayon gradually increase in steepness upwards, reaching a maximum of 35° near the summit; the summit crater is remarkably small, only about 200 metres in diameter.

## EXPLOSION CRATERS

The simplest kinds of these need not directly involve volcanic material at all, but they usually occur in areas where there has been some volcanic activity. They are produced when surface water percolating downwards through ordinary (non-volcanic) rocks comes into contact with hot magma, and is converted explosively into steam; the resulting (phreatic) explosion blasts up to the surface, blowing out a large hole in the ground.

Craters of this kind are usually simple, circular depressions surrounded by low rims of ejected debris. The walls are steep sided initially, but are quickly worn away to gentler slopes, and since they are, by definition, holes in the ground rather than structures

46. *The Malha explosion crater in the Darfur Province of the Sudan. The original land surface was just above the white rocks exposed in the walls of the crater; the grey material above this is all ejected debris. The lake at the bottom of the crater is fed by a series of small fresh-water streams; they are vital to the people of the region, since they are the only source of water for hundreds of square miles.*

built up above it, they are almost invariably filled with water. The splendidly circular little lakes in the Eifel area of Germany, which are only a kilometre or so across but are optimistically known as *maare* are examples of this kind of crater. Because the German examples are so well known, the name *maar* is used all over the world for similar features. Some of these are very interesting indeed. One in the western Sudan is about a kilometre across and a hundred metres deep. It was blasted through this thickness of sandstone, and there is a well-preserved rim of ejected debris round the crater. Strangely, however, there is little sign of the sandstone in this debris, which consists mostly of boulders of granite and gneiss, derived from rocks *below* the sandstone! Since it is located in an arid desert area, the original shape of the *maar* is well-preserved. It has at present a flat bottom, making it look rather like a soup bowl, and giving it a superficial similarity to that most famous of all meteorite craters, the Meteorite Crater in Arizona, U.S.A. The flat bottom of the Sudanese crater, however, is a secondary feature, resulting from the accumulation of debris within the crater.

47. *Meteorite Crater, Arizona, 1,300 metres wide and 180 metres deep. Although quite similar to the Malha crater, there is very much less ejected material round its rim.* (Photo from *Understanding the Earth* courtesy of Artemis Press)

The simplest kind of *maar* has a rim of ejected material which consists only of non-volcanic material, but there is a continuous gradation between craters of this type, and others where the ejecta are almost entirely volcanic. These we have encountered before; they are the ash rings produced by Surtseyan eruptions. Such eruptions, of course, are the result of the interaction of large amounts of water with a basaltic magma, and the main difference between a *maar*-forming eruption and an ash-ring-forming one is that in a *maar* little volcanic material actually manages to find its way to the surface; the explosive activity is triggered off deep below the surface. It is probable that many *maars* are the surface expression of another kind of geological structure – *diatremes*. Diatremes are vertical pipes or necks drilled through the solid rock, which are filled with a peculiar mixture of angular rock fragments of all sorts and conditions. Some may be lumps torn off from the sides of the pipe; some may be from rocks much higher up, some from much lower down, and some may be of obviously volcanic origin. Since they are entirely subterranean structures, it's difficult for a geologist to study diatremes and necessarily he has to work with old ones, which have been exposed in rocks brought to the surface by uplift and erosion. In such cases, he can only see a small part of the diatreme, but if he's lucky he may be able to show that it extends a long way vertically, and opens out from a narrow pipe to a carrot-shape near the surface, and that its natural expression at the surface would be a *maar*-like crater.

The best way to study the changes in shape of a diatreme with depth, though, is to drill a mine shaft vertically down through it and run off horizontal drives at various levels, so that it can be accurately mapped out in three dimensions. At Kimberley in South Africa a hugely expensive mine has been devoted to just this, but this diatreme is different from most in that it contains an interesting number of gem quality diamonds. The diamonds actually occur in *kimberlite* which is a rock composed of mixed fragments of everything from coal to rocks like peridotite derived, it is believed, directly from the mantle. It is in these mantle rocks, formed at high pressures and temperatures, that the diamonds originated. The width of the pipe at present surface level is 300 metres and at the deepest part of the mine it is only thirty metres, but it is considered that the *maar* which it once fed was at least 500 metres across. It was the erosion and subsequent re-deposition of the diamantiferous rocks in the upper part of this diatreme and others like it that gave rise to the rich alluvial diamond fields of South Africa.

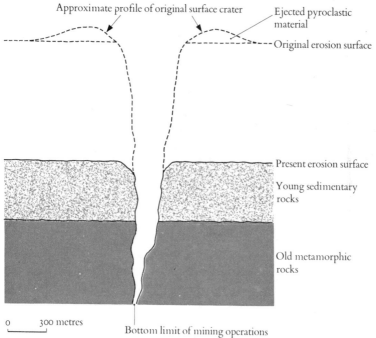

*Fig. 57 The Kimberley diamond pipe diatreme as it is today (solid lines) and as it may have been originally (dotted lines).*

CRATERS FORMED BY SUBSIDENCE

It's not easy to be sure of the extent of the part played by subsidence in the formation of some craters, but it may be a factor in the formation of craters ranging in size from a few metres to many kilometres. The biggest are formed by a rather complex series of

48. *El Viejo, a small crater which may have been formed largely by collapse or subsidence. The crater is less than one kilometre in diameter, and has very little pyroclastic material on its flanks.*

processes; these are the *calderas*, which were touched on in talking about ignimbrites. Nominally, a caldera is supposed to be greater than one kilometre in diameter, but Americans often use one mile as the lower limit. Smaller ones are usually known as *pit craters* or *collapse craters*. Pit craters are almost proverbial holes-in-the-ground, because they are commonly vertical-sided, and have no raised rims whatever, so that in flat country one would have to walk right up to the edge of the crater to know that it was there at all. These craters form by subsidence, when a large volume of magma underlying them is drained off, perhaps to be erupted elsewhere. This leaves the original roof of the magma chamber unsupported, so it falls in. Often the collapse is haphazard, but sometimes the whole mass slides downward, sinking along circular fractures just like a piston sliding down in a cylinder. An

Hawaiian vulcanologist, Gordon MacDonald, was lucky enough to see a small pit crater, Lua Nii on Hawaii, actually forming:

The initial breakthrough ... was marked by a dull explosion and projection of a small dark cloud of ash a few hundred feet into the air. The amount of ash thrown out was, however, less than 1 per cent of the volume of the hole, which was clearly the result of the sinking in of the older rocks, rather than the explosion. The explosion can have represented only the final disruption of the roof over a hole already formed or forming by the sinking of underlying rocks.*

A caldera is a different kettle of fish. (This is a painful pun. *Caldera* is Spanish for kettle.) They are usually circular in outline, with flat bottoms and steep to precipitous walls. Many of them are very large – the largest known at the moment is La Garita in Colorado, about twenty-eight kilometres across – and their size is in itself a matter of considerable interest, because calderas are amongst the few terrestrial features big enough to stand comparison with lunar craters. Originally it was thought that calderas were formed simply by colossal Krakatoa-like explosions blasting off the upper parts of a volcano. The more detailed work of recent times has suggested that this may not be the case, and that calderas may be formed in part by subsidence. This conclusion was arrived at by working out a sort of balance sheet for the volcano; finding out how much material was actually 'missing' from the ancestral shape of the volcano, how much of the volcano was spread out over the surrounding countryside in the form of pyroclastic deposits, and what was the 'empty' volume represented by the present caldera.

The classic example of this kind of geological accountancy was applied by the doyen of vulcanology, Howel Williams, to the Crater Lake in Oregon, U.S.A. This beautifully circular lake is nine kilometres wide, and occupies a caldera whose base is up to 600 metres below lake level, while the surrounding walls reach up to 600 metres above it. A small volcanic cone forming Wizard

* G. A. Macdonald, *Volcanoes*. This quotation and that on page 313 by permission of the author and Prentice-Hall Inc., New Jersey, 1972.

Island occupies one corner of the lake. Williams's work showed that the present caldera occupies the site of an old major volcanic cone, which he estimated to have been about 3,600 metres high. He called this ancestral volcano Mt Mazama and showed that it had been heavily glaciated during the Ice Age, since the remains of valleys filled with glacial debris can be seen, cut off abruptly by the walls of the present caldera. About 6,000 years ago a series of stupendous explosions occurred, showering pumice and ash over a wide area, some of it reaching as far as Alberta in Canada. This was a major Plinian eruption, like the one which occurred in similar circumstances at Katmai in 1912. After the explosive activity a series of ignimbrite flows were erupted, probably from fissures on the flanks of the cone. While these ignimbrite eruptions were going on, the main mass of the mountain

*Fig. 58 Stages in the formation of a caldera. The volume of the ejected material is much less than that of the 'missing' material and the difference may be represented by the subsidence of material below the floor of the caldera.*

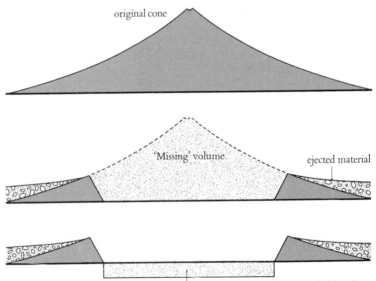

original cone

'Missing' volume

ejected material

volume represented by subsidence of caldera floor

foundered, collapsing downwards to form the present caldera.

Now comes the really interesting bit. Careful mapping of the area round Crater Lake shows that a total of about forty cubic kilometres of material, air-fall ash and ignimbrite were erupted from the volcano. That's a lot of rock, but the interesting thing is that the volume of the 'missing' parts of the original conical volcano is much bigger, about sixty cubic kilometres, so even if all the erupted material were put back into the caldera, it would not be enough to rebuild the original volcano! The odd twenty cubic kilometres or so can only be accounted for by the movement of magma somewhere *beneath* the Earth's surface, causing the caldera floor to subside bodily. No one knows where this dis-

49. *The Deriba caldera in the western Sudan. There are two small lakes within the caldera, one of them occupying the crater of a small younger cone. Subsidence may have played a part in the formation of this caldera, but a very large volume of pyroclastic material was ejected, and this can be seen in the foreground, exposed in the steep walls of the maze of gullies which have been cut into the soft, easily-eroded material.* (Photo courtesy of the Survey Department, Republic of the Sudan)

appearing magma went, but MacDonald has suggested that the draining away of the magma could have propagated the eruption. Withdrawal of some magma would reduce pressure on what was left in the magma chamber (just like pulling the handle on a bicycle pump), which would then cause the magma to vesiculate, frothing up and erupting at the surface. (Remember what happens when you let the pressure out of a bottle of beer.) This of course would reduce the volume of magma beneath the volcano still further, and collapse would follow.

Recently it has been suggested that this argument may not be valid, since refinements in the study of pyroclastic rocks have led to the suggestion that a large volume of very fine ash may be dispersed over areas far distant from the volcano – remember that ash from Mt Mazama reached as far as Alberta – and that this material, whose thickness at any one point would be negligible, might make up the 'missing' material in the caldera. If this is the case, then there is no need to invoke subsidence as a major factor in caldera subsidence.

## Erosion

Erosional processes may seem slow and boring compared with the spectacular activity of a volcano, but they do act over vastly greater periods of time than any eruption, and are therefore overwhelmingly important as landscape shapers. And, as we have seen, volcanoes are liable to impressive collapses and avalanches, not always related to eruptions, so there are a few dramatic moments in the otherwise quiet, unhurried grinding down of volcanoes. Before getting down to details, a couple of reminders. First, an active volcano is a dynamic system; it will *always* be under attack by erosion, but periodically it will retaliate with fresh eruptions. Second, while everyone is familiar with the standard agents of erosion, water, wind and ice, it's easy to forget that all these may be active on the same volcano at the same time, since major volcanoes rise up through many climatic zones. Chimborazo in Eucador, for example, is built up from a base level at about 3,300 metres above sea level to 6,262 metres. The lowest part of it is thickly forested and is deeply dissected by many streams running in steep-walled gullies, but the upper part is heavily glaciated. So different erosional forms occur at different levels.

At the beginning of the chapter, it was emphasized that erosion will get to work on an erupting volcano even before the new lavas have cooled. So it may be surprising to learn that scoria cones like Paricutin are scarcely affected by even the heaviest rainfall! Erosion by water is largely the result of surface streams flowing downhill, getting bigger and deeper as they do so, washing the finer particles down with them. The bigger the stream and the faster it flows, the more material it can carry away. But a scoria cone, built up of loose ash, is so porous that the rain falling on it simply soaks straight into it, so that surface streams can't form, and erosion can't get under way. Many of the old scoria cones in Hawaii are still in good condition, although they get about 5,000 millimetres of rain per year. No cone can escape indefinitely, though, and after a time atmospheric weathering will break down some of the smaller particles physically and chemically, producing impermeable clays, which will effectively seal off the cone and allow streams to develop. Once streams are well established, the rate of erosion is increased, and deep gullies can be cut remarkably quickly. On a large composite cone, gullies are almost always present, and these naturally radiate from it, like spokes on a wheel. It's not difficult to see examples of this kind of gullying; many of the tip-heaps in industrial and mining areas show it well. As a gully deepens, it acquires a typical, sharp v-shaped profile, and as erosion continues on the volcano, the space between gullies decreases until eventually adjacent gullies are separated only by a sharp ridge. In this state the weathered cone looks rather like a partly-opened umbrella, and the pattern of alternating v-shaped ridges and gullies is known as *parasol ribbing*.

Once gullies are well-established on a cone, material is progressively washed out from the middle slopes, where the streams are flowing fastest, and deposited again towards the bottom as the streams run out on to flatter ground, and loose their impetus. In depositing their loads, they build up fans of debris all round the volcano, and it is these that are primarily responsible for the

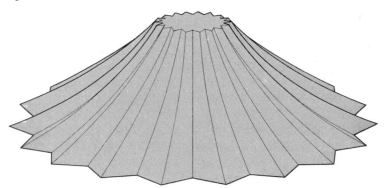

*Fig. 59 'Parasol' ribbing on a volcanic cone.*

elegant, sweeping shape we know so well. With the passage of time, this shape disappears, as streams bite their way deeper down into the heart of the volcano. Usually, a few 'master' gullies develop, cutting the old cone into triangular sectors. Ultimately even these disappear, and all that remains is a low, swelling hill, not very different from any other hill. The time required for this slow process of attrition to convert the original cone to a barely recognizable hill is dictated by variables such as the climatic conditions and the size of the volcano, but research in New Zealand suggests that it takes about fifteen to twenty million years, although in arid areas it is likely to take much longer, perhaps of the order of a few tens of millions of years.

Not all volcanoes are cones, and the sort of sequence that has been described will not fit every volcanic landform. It's not possible to discuss all the possible ways in which volcanic landscapes evolve, but there are some general trends, since each type of volcanic structure tends to weather away to produce its own characteristic forms.

EROSION OF PYROCLASTIC ROCKS

The first effects on the landscape of an air-fall deposit from a Plinian eruption are straightforward – the ash smooths out the earlier topography as it accumulates, filling every crack and crevice. But this doesn't last long. Because the ash is soft and loose, it is easily eroded, so directly the first rains set in it will be carved up, the original smooth appearance will be washed away, and complex systems of gullies established. The streams running through the gullies cut down vertically through the ash amazingly rapidly, and the result after a few decades or so, is a highly distinctive topography, consisting of an apparently flat plain, cut through by a ramifying *dendritic* maze of narrow vertical-sided wadis, canyons, *quebradas*, gulches or gorges, depending on where you happen to be. In one such area in the Sudan, a river has cut down through about a hundred metres of air-fall pumice (figure sixty); and has cut an extremely narrow wadi for itself, but some of its tributaries are merely narrow slits, less than a metre wide and perhaps fifteen or so deep. In places they are so constricted that it is scarcely possible to walk along them.

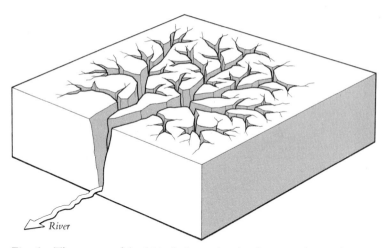

*Fig. 60 The pattern of dendritic drainage that develops in soft pyroclastic rocks. (Cf. Plate 49)*

Intensive gullying of this kind is common in soft rocks of all kinds (it can occur remarkably quickly as a direct result of human carelessness in clearing vegetation or overgrazing) and it is produced by heavy seasonal rainfalls in areas which are dry for most of the year. It is known as 'badland' topography, a descriptive name coming from the cowboy states of the U.S.A. Some rather startling shapes can be produced by erosion of pyroclastic rocks in 'badland' areas. In New Mexico, conical hills resembling wigwams are produced by deep gullying in soft ash; the wigwams are the result of the interweaving of the complex pattern of gullies, so that a tall cone of ash is left where two branches of a gully close in on one another again.

Unwelded ignimbrites, since they are composed of loose, pumiceous material identical with that of an air-fall deposit also give rise to 'badland topography' on erosion, but partly-welded

*Fig. 61 'Wigwams' may develop where two gullies intersect.*

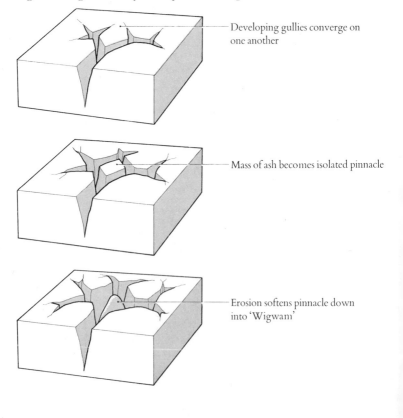

Developing gullies converge on one another

Mass of ash becomes isolated pinnacle

Erosion softens pinnacle down into 'Wigwam'

ignimbrites produce some different features. In many ways a pile of ignimbrite sheets is like a pile of basalt lavas – both form extensive plateaux composed of hundreds of separate flows. Probably the most extensive ignimbrite plateau is one in the Central Andes, which covers 150,000 square kilometres of north Chile, southern Peru and parts of Bolivia. Streams draining off the snowy tops of the many conical andesite volcanoes have knifed their way down through the ignimbrite, sometimes reaching the harder basement rocks underneath and cutting vertical-walled canyons hundreds of metres deep. Often, on the edges of the plateau, erosion has left flat-topped islands of ignimbrite rearing high above the plain, their walls as steep and forbidding as castle ramparts. If this kind of scenery sounds familiar, think about some of the Westerns you have watched. Though not always formed of ignimbrite, much of the scenery of the arid parts of the U.S.A. is similar, with 'stepped' valley sides, and flat-topped, steep sided *mesas* and *buttes*. Producers of Westerns use this rugged kind of landscape almost routinely to provide 'authentic' atmosphere for their almost routine creations.

Ignimbrite sheets characteristically develop sets of vertical joints similar in some ways to the hexagonal columnar jointing that develops in basalt lavas, like that in the Giant's Causeway. In ignimbrites, columns as such are not often developed, but the presence of vertical joints helps to explain why ignimbrites so often form vertical cliffs. (Funnily enough, few natural cliffs are anything like vertical.) Since the horizontal sheet is broken up by vertical joints, it is inevitable that on erosion the outermost part of the cliff will break away cleanly, leaving a smooth vertical surface behind. This feature is so characteristic of ignimbrites that it is often possible to spot an outcrop of ignimbrite from ten kilometres or more away. With the eye of faith, of course.

## NECKS AND DYKES

Some very distinctive structures may remain even after a volcano has been deeply eroded. The necks or feeder pipes of central-type volcanoes may form massive pillars of rock more resistant than the piles of lavas and pyroclastic rocks which make up the bulk of the volcano, and so are often preserved after the rest of the volcano has been worn away. Those oddly-situated churches in the Auvergne area of France, which often appear on travel posters, are perched up on volcanic necks which now stick up as steep spikes of rock. There are other, much older, examples in Britain. The Carboniferous Period, the period about 350 million years ago when all the great coal deposits of Europe were laid down, was also a period of great volcanic activity in Britain, especially in the area now known as the Midland Valley of Scotland. These volcanoes of course suffered erosion in their own time, and were ultimately buried under younger sediments. Now, however, erosion has worked its way back down to them and laid them bare once more, and the old volcanic necks can still be traced, poking up out above the surrounding sediments. By far the best known of these is a famous Scottish landmark, Arthur's Seat, near Edinburgh. This was the site of a large Carboniferous volcano, and the forms of many of the original lava flows can still be picked out clearly, as well as the old necks.

In the United States, of course, there are bigger and better examples. Some of these really are spectacular. Ship Rock, in the New Mexico desert, jags up in vertical-sided pinnacles 430 metres high, rising above a flat, featureless desert. Some dykes radiating out from the centre are also preserved, standing up starkly like walls in the desert. This beautiful piece of natural sculpture owes its soaring, perpendicular architecture to a well-developed series of vertical joints in the old, breccia-filled volcanic neck, and this feature is common to many other prominent necks all round the world.

The dykes round Ship Rock stand up as walls because they are more resistant to erosion than the rocks around them. (Remember that the English word 'dyke' itself originally meant a wall. The dykes in Holland keep the water out.) The opposite can also happen, though, when dykes are less resistant than the rocks they cut, such as hard, metamorphic *gneisses*. In the north-west Highlands of Scotland are some famous gneisses – they are the oldest rocks in Britain – and these are cut by a multitude of dykes associated with the Hebridean volcanic centres mentioned earlier. Each of these dykes can be traced for miles across the gneiss country as parallel-sided depressions often with steep walls, until they are displaced by faults.

## Atolls and atom bombs

To end this chapter, let's turn to something completely different, and cool off by dealing briefly with coral reefs and coral atolls. The sparkling blue waters, white beaches and coconut palms of these idyllic islands may seem a far cry from volcanic landscapes, but there is an interesting link between volcanoes and coral atolls. The growth of coral is well-known, and easily understood – we can see for ourselves the coral polyps at their work, and walk over the immense reefs they have built up. The problem is, though, that the reef-building polyps can only live in shallow water, less than thirty metres deep. Now the Pacific Ocean is on the whole immensely deeper than that, reaching 10,000 metres in places, yet parts of it are speckled with thousands of tiny islands and reefs, as well as some larger islands, so one is forced to ask: what is all the coral growing *on*, and how did it get established in the first place? This problem has bothered scientists for a long while, yet it was Charles Darwin, way back in the nineteenth century who suggested one of the most convincing hypotheses. (This was only one result of his five year's scientific marathon in the *Beagle*.) Darwin's idea was that the reefs and atolls first grew on the fringes of volcanic islands, and that as time passed, these volcanoes gradually subsided below the sea, while the coral polyps went on busily working, building up their reefs at such a rate that they could keep up with the rate of subsidence, and thus keep their heads not above, but just below water.

This was a remarkably sound idea, although it may seem odd initially, especially since Darwin was working at a time when there was little data on the nature of the Pacific Ocean floor, or of the deep structure of the atolls. We now know that the floor of the Pacific is dotted with hundreds of *guyots*, or sea mounts, flat-topped mounds that rise thousands of feet above the sea floor.

These were volcanic islands, once above sea level, which subsequently sank, acquiring their planed-off flat tops as a result of rapid erosion at sea level. Some further support for Darwin's hypothesis comes from a rather odd quarter. Before letting off a hydrogen bomb on Eniwetok atoll, American scientists drilled holes deep into it, to establish what lay beneath the surface. Basaltic rock was encountered after drilling through 1,200 metres of coral and shallow-water limestone, showing that the atoll was built up on an old volcanic mountain which rose three kilometres above the sea floor. Most of the atolls and guyots in the Pacific are

*Fig. 62 A simplified illustration of how coral atolls may develop when a volcanic island sinks below the sea.*

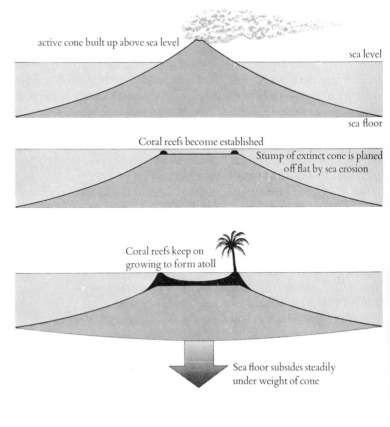

active cone built up above sea level

sea level

sea floor

Coral reefs become established

Stump of extinct cone is planed off flat by sea erosion

Coral reefs keep on growing to form atoll

Sea floor subsides steadily under weight of cone

crowded into the south-west corner, so it has been suggested that the colossal subsidence required to produce a 1,200 metre thickness of coral must have been the result of a large-scale subsidence of that part of the Pacific Ocean floor as a whole.

# Chapter 8    Some side-effects

A volcanic eruption does not take place in an environmental vacuum. It may have a variety of side-effects, most of them unpleasant. Some are predictable, others are less so; some are confined only to the immediate vicinity of the volcano, others are perceptible all over the world. In this chapter we will examine a few of the more important side-effects, such as volcanic pollution, the links between volcanic activity, earthquakes and tidal waves, and the effects of volcanic activity on world climate. This will take us in a progression from rather obvious, short-term effects to less obvious, highly contentious ones which may be far more profound.

## Subglacial eruptions

These are something of a vulcanological oddity, and are not common at the present day. In the past, though, when great expanses of both northern and southern hemispheres were covered by the glaciers of the last Ice Age, they were probably more frequent. Modern eruptions of this kind are known only from Iceland, which has four separate ice caps or *jökulls*, the largest of which is the Vatnajökull, and the eruptions are known from the Icelandic as *hlaups* (bursts) or *jökullhlaups* (glacierbursts). A *hlaup* is a colossal deluge of icy cold water, a far cry from the fierce heat of the eruption itself, but an important side-effect none the less.

When a volcano beneath an ice-cap erupts, large amounts of ice

*Fig. 63 The major ice caps or* jökulls *in Iceland, and the site of the Grimsvötn volcano.*

above it melt. It's possible that there may not be enough heat to melt through the entire thickness of the ice-cap, but even if there isn't, the ice-sheet over the volcano may collapse, forming an immense hole, and the water melted by the eruption will be ponded up in this natural ice-bounded dam. Normally, ice-caps are drained by one or more sizeable rivers emerging from their sides. In a *hlaup* the ice-dammed water bursts through the ice-cap, hacking a channel which may be well over a kilometre wide for itself and the melt water gushes out in a torrent, inundating the outwash plain beneath the glacier. The sheer volume of water involved is difficult to conceive, and no over-used adjectives can sufficiently convey an impression of it. Figures can help, though. The Amazon has an estimated flow of something like 200,000 cubic metres per second. In the 1934 eruption of the Grimsvötn volcano, beneath the Vatnajökull, the flow of melt water estimated to be produced by the melting of sixteen cubic kilometres of ice averaged 100,000 cubic metres per second over a two-day period. In the Katla eruption of 1918, the flow rate of melt water

was estimated to be not less than 400,000 cubic metres per second!
The energy of such huge volumes of water is considerable, and
they are capable of carrying millions of tons of mud, sand, rocks
and boulders down from their source and depositing them far
away – a boulder about 400 cubic metres in size was carried fourteen kilometres by the Katla *hlaup* of 1918. The whole coastline
of south-eastern Iceland has been modified by the deposits left
behind by these volcano-propagated floods, but fortunately,
since the area is thinly-populated, little damage has been done to
human life or property.

## Volcanic pollution

There's a good deal of thoroughly justifiable worry these days
about the effects of pollution on The Environment, with concern
ranging from the presence of D.D.T. in Antarctic bird species to
the disruption of the ozone layer in the atmosphere by supersonic
airliners. One of the most serious problems is the atmospheric
pollution caused by the continuous emission into the air of the
exhaust gases from millions of individual sources – motor car engines, power stations, brick kilns, steel works and so on. These are
all the direct results of human agencies, and it's often forgotten
that a volcano can be a *natural* source of a similar kind of pollution
while it is active, on a much bigger scale than even the biggest
and dirtiest power station. It's often forgotten, too, that eruptions
are not always short, sharp and nasty-while-they-last. Some drag
on for many years, blighting the countryside and the lives of the
people near by for decades.

One of the worst cases on record happened nearly 200 years
ago – the 1783 eruption of the Laki fissure in Iceland, which was
mentioned earlier as a classic example of a basaltic fissure eruption.
The eruption proper started on 8 June 1783, but for several days
before that a pungent bluish haze had been seen hanging over the
area. Fluid basalt lavas flooded out of the fissure for a period of
two months, spreading out over tens of square kilometres and
filling the Skaftar and Hverfisfljot river valleys to depths of well

over a hundred metres. Large volumes of sulphurous fumes were emitted throughout the eruption, and since they were denser than air, they tended to form a ground-hugging layer extending many kilometres down-wind from the fissure. A heavy fall of ash also rained down on the countryside. 10,000 people, about one fifth of Iceland's population in the eighteenth century, died as a result of the eruption. Of these, a small number were killed directly by the advancing lavas, but most died a lingering death as a result of the environmental damage done by the eruption. The rolling clouds of choking fumes were unpleasant, but it was the ash-fall that had the most disastrous effects. It destroyed growing crops and carpeted grazing lands, so that cattle either died of starvation, or were forced to eat ash-covered grass, and many died as a result – 190,000 sheep, 28,000 horses and 11,500 cattle are reported to have died. Because Iceland was so inaccessible in the eighteenth century, the loss of such a large proportion of her livestock produced a severe famine and most of the human deaths took place long after the eruption, the result of starvation and deprivation.

Iceland suffered again in a similar, but much milder way when Hekla erupted in 1947–8. An ash-cloud which reached a height of 27,000 metres was erupted during the first hours of the eruption, and a heavy ash-fall ensued. An area of 600 square kilometres of countryside was covered to a depth of over five centimetres, and only fifty-one hours after the eruption started, falling ash was recorded at Helsinki, 3,000 kilometres distant. The eruption continued at a more subdued level for just over a year, with an estimated total volume of one cubic kilometre of material being erupted. Livestock again suffered badly. Many of the affected animals were diagnosed as having died of fluorine poisoning, a rather unexpected discovery since fluorine is normally a very minor constituent of basaltic magmas. However, this finding is significant, since it may suggest why so many cattle died during the 1783 eruption – they too may have been the victims of fluorine poisoning. A less immediate, but still serious consequence of the ash-fall was that many of the cattle that grazed on the ash-covered grass suffered from severely abraded teeth; this impaired their feeding and consequently their health.

For a long time after the 1947 eruption had ceased, its effects were unpleasantly perceptible – even the ground water in the area became so hard as a result of all the dissolved material in it that it was barely drinkable, and it would not give a lather with soap. Animals continued to die for some time, since minor escapes of gases, particularly carbon dioxide, led to the accumulation of 'pools' of the dense gases in low-lying hollows and pockets, especially during windless periods. Animals straying into these pools suffocated, since carbon dioxide is colourless and odourless and they had no inkling of danger. Some of the worst pockets of gas were drained by digging ditches from them to channel off the heavy gases, which flowed away downslope.

Many other eruptions have caused problems like those of the Icelandic volcanoes – several thousand cattle died through eating ash-covered vegetation during the Paricutin eruption in Mexico, for example, but few volcanoes have been so unpleasantly trouble-some as Masaya in Nicaragua. Masaya is a large and complex volcano, which is known to have been intermittently active since the earliest days of European colonization of Central America, but its eruptions have on the whole been unspectacular. One small pit crater, however, known as the Santiago crater, has been a chronic source of trouble. Periodically, very small eruptions have taken place in this crater, and subsequently, large volumes of sulphurous fumes were emitted from it, presumably seeping steadily from a cooling mass of magma somewhere below the surface. The gases escaped quietly and there were no ash-clouds or other evidence of eruptive activity; the crater merely seems to have acted as a sort of chimney, from which sulphurous fumes poured continuously. Emission of the fumes continued for a long period after each of the successive minor eruptions, and was particularly severe between 1924 and 1927 and between 1946 and 1953.

Unfortunately, the volcano is situated in the middle of a rich coffee-growing region, and during the 1946 eruption fumes from the crater, wafted away by the wind, caused havoc to the coffee crop. Nearest the crater, where gas concentrations were highest, the leaves of the coffee plants withered and fell off within a few days of the eruption starting. Farther away the effects took longer to become established, with the leaves first of all becoming blotchy yellow and sickly-looking. Even on the coast of Nicaragua the effects were perceptible, with the vegetation acquiring the seedy, dejected look of plants in the vicinity of a large industrial city. The economic loss to Nicaragua was considerable. The fumes drifting down from the crater laid waste a broad swathe through the coffee plantations, rendering more than 130 square kilometres unproductive. Between 1946 and 1951 nearly six million coffee trees were affected. In addition to this, the acidic fumes also caused extensive damage to metal installations on the plantations, severely corroding barbed wire fences, telephone wires, corrugated iron roofs and the like. Total losses were estimated at over three million pounds, a severe blow to Nicaragua, a small and poor country, heavily dependent on her coffee crops.

Many different schemes have been proposed to combat the creeping fumes. During the 1924–7 crisis, two resourceful German engineers made a start on a funnel-like device which would enable them to draw off the fumes from the crater, pipe them downhill to a processing plant, and turn them into sulphuric acid. This scheme, of course, had the added attraction of turning an economic crisis into an economic success. Ironically, however, when installing their apparatus, the engineers did some blasting within the crater, which initiated a hundred-metre subsidence of the crater floor, and this effectively sealed off the fume supply, and put paid to their schemes.

## The links between volcanoes, earthquakes and tsunamis

Early on in this book, it was mentioned that mid-ocean ridges and oceanic continental plate margins were not only the sites of volcanic activity, but also of earthquakes. When the distribution of volcanoes and earthquake centres is plotted on the same world map, the two patterns that result look virtually coincident. This might seem to suggest that volcanoes and earthquakes are intimately linked; indeed they are, but only because they share a common origin in the movements of crustal plates. Major earthquakes only rarely give rise to identifiable volcanic eruptions – there are less than a dozen known cases. Volcanic eruptions, on the other hand, often produce seismic tremors, sometimes considerable ones, and these tremors can be used both to predict and monitor the course of an eruption.

Let's consider first what happened during the Krakatoa eruption of 1883. The explosions that took place then were far larger than any nuclear blast that has occurred to date, and they produced shock waves which would have been detectable on seismometers anywhere in the world, had they existed at that time. Although the air blast from the explosions rattled windows hundreds of kilometres away, there were no particularly severe seismic shocks on the neighbouring islands. But a series of *tsunamis* or seismic 'tidal' waves were initiated by the explosions, and these proved to be the most disastrous results of the eruption, since they ravaged the shores of Java and Sumatra, and drowned 36,380 people. These *tsunamis* were some of the largest ever recorded, and the havoc they caused is difficult to imagine. Death and disaster were so widespread that the contemporary investigators found it difficult to piece together exactly the sequence of events. The official Royal Society report on the eruption put it rather well:

> The times of arrival of the waves at different places on the shores of the Strait (of Sunda) are but vaguely noted, and this is especially the case with the great wave after 10 o'clock on the twenty-seventh (of August). Terror and dismay reigned everywhere, and darkness settled over the land. At Anjer . . . where this wave must have come, no one was left to see it, the few survivors having fled to the hills.

The 'great wave' referred to was the largest in a long series. It was estimated to have had a height of fifteen metres at the shore line, and where it washed up on to the land, its momentum carried it even higher. At Telok Betong, the sea reached to within two metres of the top of the hill on which the Dutch Governor's residence stood, twenty-four metres above ordinary sea level. In places, where the wave washed up into constricted channels and straits, it rose even higher, at times reaching over thirty metres.

Naturally, where the country was low-lying, the wave swept headlong inland, spreading devastation as it went. Near Telok Betong, a man-of-war, the *Berouw* was carried nearly three kilometres inland, and left stranded high and dry ten metres above sea level. Lighthouses were swept away and other landmarks obliterated along much of the length of the great marine highway between Java and Sumatra (figure twenty-one). Although most of the damage was confined to the Sunda Straits, the *tsunamis* did not stop there. In Ceylon, they were still big enough to produce visible effects, leaving small boats in the harbour temporarily stranded and then refloating them, while at the Cape of Good Hope they were easily measurable with tide-gauges. Very faint traces were also recorded in the Bay of Biscay, 17,255 kilometres from Krakatoa!

Despite the fact that the Krakatoa *tsunamis* are the most lethal on record (discounting those that might have followed the great eruption of Santorin in 1470 B.C.), little is known about what part the eruption played in setting them off, since, although the *topographic* changes brought about by the eruption are well-known, the *geological* mechanisms that were involved are only poorly understood. None the less it is clear that the *tsunamis* were only side-effects of the volcanic activity. Let's turn now to a different case; a modern, well-documented example of a major earthquake, which produced both a devastating *tsunami* and a volcanic eruption as side-effects. The earthquake responsible was the Chilean earthquake of 1960; it was one of the most powerful of the century, and, as the geophysicists put it, it 'set the world ringing', meaning that it set the entire Earth in vibration, like a vast spherical gong. The 'ringing' continued for two weeks – but of course, it was not audible, the vibrations were only detectable on seismometers. The sequence of events started at six o'clock on the morning of Saturday 21 May, when a substantial tremor rocked a large area of south central Chile. There was some damage, but this tremor was nothing special for Chile, a country that has learned to live with earthquakes. This first shock was followed by a long series of minor *aftershocks*, which continued until just before three o'clock on Sunday afternoon, when another shock, larger than the first, occurred.

Damage was extensive, and many people ran in fear from their houses into the streets. They were the lucky ones, for half an hour later, while many of them were still outside, a *third* major shock struck, this one twenty times more powerful than the first. The shaking lasted for a full three minutes, and caused widespread damage and numerous casualties – many buildings which had been weakened and damaged by the earlier shocks simply collapsed bodily.

Earthquakes are the result of movements along faults; fractures in the Earth's crust along which sudden jerk-like slips sometimes take place to ease the immense stresses that build up where the crust is being deformed, especially at plate margins. It's commonly thought that an earthquake produces gaping fissures in the ground, which swallow up the unfortunate victims, and then close forever, entombing them. In fact, though, there is only one known instance of this actually happening – almost all earthquake victims are killed by collapsing buildings. Usually what happens is that the fault movements produce small, closed rents in the surface soil, along which both horizontal and vertical movements may be detected. For example, a fault cutting across a railway line may produce a horizontal offset of the two ends of the line, as well as creating a difference in level between them. Careful surveying after an earthquake will often reveal exactly how a fault has moved: the famous San Francisco earthquake of 1906 was the result of a horizontal movement of about five metres along the San Andreas fault. Now the fault which was responsible for the Chilean earthquake appears to have lain almost entirely in the sea, running closely parallel to the coast of Chile. Surveys of the areas affected by the earthquake showed no signs of obvious rents or fissures, but there were some drastic changes of level, with an area of at least 390 square kilometres around the town of Valdivia being permanently flooded as a result of subsidence. Prior to the earthquake, Valdivia was a river port; after it became a sea port, the subsidence having brought the sea right on to its doorstep.

So much for the earthquake itself. But what about its side-effects? Shortly after the main shock had passed, while many of the inhabitants of the coastal towns were still outside their houses, in a rather distressed state, they noticed that the sea was retreating

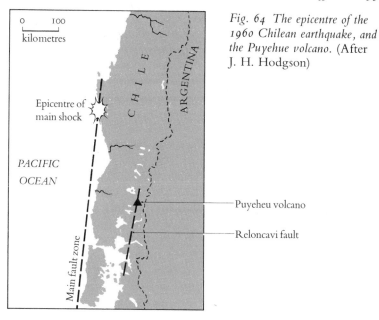

*Fig. 64 The epicentre of the 1960 Chilean earthquake, and the Puyehue volcano.* (After J. H. Hodgson)

rapidly, leaving their moored boats high and dry, and receding well beyond the normal low tide mark. The watching Chileans knew what was happening. They had seen it before, knew what to expect, and so were able to take some precautions. About a quarter of an hour after the recession had started, the first *tsunami* came washing back: a wave about six metres high, which crashed its way inland carrying away houses, cattle, cars and anything that stood in its way, reaching in some places nearly three kilometres inland. This was only the first of a series of waves which continued all afternoon, and it was not the worst – in many places the third and fourth were the highest.

*Tsunamis* behave like any other waves – just like the waves set up when a pebble is thrown into a pool of water. This means that they have a regular wavelength, and once initiated, will move outwards from the source in a regular train of crests and troughs. The ocean, in fact, behaves like a large pond, except that the time, or *period*, between successive *tsunami* crests may be as much as half an hour, while that for ripples on a pond is seconds or less. Since *tsunamis* are regular waveforms, it is possible to predict how fast they will travel, and therefore the time when they can be expected to arrive at different points away from the source. The velocity of any water wave (in pond or ocean) is given by the formula:

$$v = \sqrt{gD}$$

where v is the velocity, g is the acceleration due to gravity and D is the depth of the water concerned. So it was possible to predict accurately the time when the *tsunamis* propagated in Chile would arrive at other points around the Pacific. The earthquake struck at 18.56 on the Sunday (Greenwich Mean Time). By 22.04 reports of the effects of the *tsunamis* in Chile had reached Hawaii, and a warning was issued by the authorities that the people living round the coasts of the island could expect trouble. A few hours later, the arrival time of the *tsunamis* had been calculated and published. At 9.58 the following day, fifteen hours and two minutes after the earthquake, they arrived in Hawaii, within a minute of the predicted time. In most parts of the island, the waves were quite small, but at the town of Hilo they were particularly high. The third wave was the highest, reaching ten metres, and it swept well inland causing sixty-two deaths and extensive damage. Those killed had chosen to ignore the warnings given, perhaps because the *tsunamis* which had followed earlier warnings had proved insignificant. The arrival time of the *tsunamis* in Japan had also been accurately predicted: twenty-two hours after the earthquake they arrived. 180 people were killed. The deaths in Japan are more easily understood than those in Hawaii; Japan is nearly twice as far from Chile as Hawaii (17,055 kilometres) and no one could have expected the *tsunamis* to be so severe at this distance, but hopefully no one will take this kind of warning lightly again.

Forty-eight hours after the main earthquake, and long after the last ripples of the *tsunamis* had died away, Chile experienced a second side-effect of the 'quake – the volcano Puyehue began to erupt. Puyehue had previously been dormant since 1905, and although it did not react until two days later, it seems certain that it was triggered off by the earthquake. Not directly, though. It looks more likely that movement on the submarine fault, which produced the main earthquake, set off movement along a second, smaller fault, the Reloncavi fault, which runs parallel to the coast, about a hundred kilometres inland, and passes very close to Puyehue. So the volcanic eruption was very much a secondary effect. Nonetheless, it was quite substantial. It started with an explosive phase, sending a cloud of ash and steam 6,000 metres into the air, and subsequently continued less dramatically for several weeks, with new lava being erupted relatively quietly from a long fissure on the flanks of the volcano.

Chile is a country containing many hundreds of volcanoes, twenty-five of them 'active', but of all these it was only Puyehue that erupted. There were many reports from up and down the length of Chile of dormant volcanoes showing signs of re-awakening such as strong emissions of fumarolic steam, but although many of them must have received a severe shaking, none came to life. This emphasizes clearly that earthquakes and volcanoes have little in common with one another; the Puyehue eruption was something of an oddity. There is one other group of events, however, that is worth mentioning. Earlier on, it was remarked that the historic eruption of Mt Pelée in 1902 was preceded *on the previous day* by an almost equally large eruption of La Soufrière on Saint Vincent, an adjacent island in the Caribbean. The Mt Pelée eruption continued for many months subsequently, and it is significant that during this period there was an episode of unprecedented activity amongst the volcanoes of Central America, with a particularly big eruption of Santa Maria in Guatemala. Now the simultaneous eruption of different volcanoes is most unusual, and although it is probably unwise to speculate on events so widely scattered, it is possible that these eruptions were all triggered by the *same* major events, taking place somewhere deep down under the Caribbean.

## Volcanoes, the atmosphere and world climate

This is one of the most hotly-debated side-effects of volcanism. There's no doubt, though, that a major eruption can have profound effects on the upper atmosphere as a whole, not just in the immediate vicinity of the volcano. Much the best example of this is our faithful old stand-by, the Krakatoa eruption of 1883, but similar, if less dramatic results, have been observed after several more recent major eruptions such as that of Agung volcano, Bali, in 1963. The effects of the Krakatoa eruption were so widespread and dramatic that a separate section was devoted to their description in the Royal Society report on the eruption. This section, impressively entitled 'On the unusual optical phenomena of the atmosphere, 1883–6, including twilight effects, coronal appearances, sky haze, coloured suns and moons, etc.', ran to 312 pages, much longer than the account of the eruption itself. Its authors were no less impressive: the Honourable F. A. Rollo Russell and Mr E. Douglas Archibald.

Briefly, what happened was this. The eruption, and in particular the culminating explosions, ejected enormous volumes of ash into the air, perhaps as much as eighty kilometres high. Locally the effect of this was a heavy ash fall-out and stygian darkness as the ash-cloud blotted out the sun. But although the heavier ash particles quickly showered down, the finer ones remained airborne much longer and were wafted away westwards from the site of the volcano by the upper atmosphere winds. The eruption, remember, took place on 26 and 27 August. During the afternoon of 27 August, the haze produced by the dust cloud was observed in Ceylon; by 28 August it had reached Natal in South Africa, and by 30 August it was over the Atlantic, continuing its westward drift, spreading and being diluted the whole while. By 2 September it had reached the west coast of South America; by 4 September it was south of Hawaii in the Pacific, and on 9 September it was approaching the East Indies, having been carried *right round the world* by the prevailing winds. The spreading haze did not stop there, though, it continued to be wafted westwards,

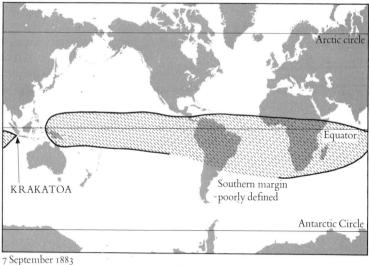

7 September 1883

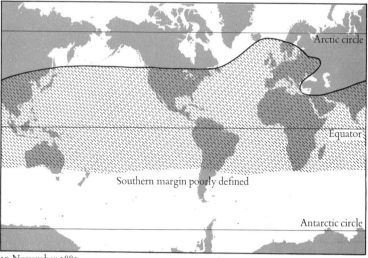

30 November 1883

Fig. 65 *Two maps from the Royal Society report on the Krakatoa eruption, showing the westward drift of the ash cloud and its spread northwards.*

and in effect, made several trips round the world. Whereas, however, on its first trip it had been confined to a narrow belt, more or less restricted to the tropics, it subsequently became more and more dispersed, until its effects were visible over most of the world, with the possible exceptions of the polar regions.

The 'unusual optical phenomena' that the haze of fine dust produced were many and varied. The most memorable were the glorious fiery sunsets that were a frequent occurrence all over the world. They even found their way into a poem of Tennyson's:

> Had the fierce ashes of some fiery peak
> Been hurl'd so high they ranged about the globe?
> For day by day, thro' many a blood-red eve,
> In that four-hundredth summer after Christ,
> The wrathful sunset glared against a cross . . .
>
> *St Telemachus*

To be more prosaic, such sunsets were caused by the rays from the setting sun lighting up the myriads of tiny particles in the atmosphere, while the sun itself was low on the horizon, or even below it. It's perfectly normal for sunsets to be red; refraction of the sun's rays by the atmosphere tending to eliminate all but the red wavelengths. Sunsets only find their way on to postcards though, when there is something for the red light to 'set fire' to. Normally, it's only layers of clouds that are lit up from below with a golden glow, but the effect is heightened if there's a lot of dust or ash in the air, be it from industrial effluent, forest fires, or a volcano on the other side of the world.

The haze from Krakatoa also produced some rather more bizarre effects, with the sun and moon showing up in distinctly peculiar colours. The *Ceylon Observer* for 17 September 1883 carried the following account:

The sun for the last three days rises in a splendid green when visible; about 10° above the horizon. As he advances he assumes a beautiful blue, and as he comes further on looks a brilliant blue, resembling burning sulphur. When at about 45° (above the horizon) it is not possible to look at him with the naked eye, but even at the zenith, the light is blue, varying from a pale blue to a light blue later on, somewhat similar to moonlight, even at midday. Then, as he declines, the sun assumes the same changes, but vice versa. The moon, now visible in the afternoons, looks also tinged with blue after sunset, and as she descends assumes a very fiery colour 30° from the zenith.

It's perhaps worth emphasizing that this kind of phenomenon was visible all over the world. The Honourable F. A. Rollo Russell, himself, no less, made a note in his diary of what he saw from his home in Surrey, surely the last place that one would expect to look for evidence of volcanic activity:

9 November. Sun set in very slight haze bank of cirrus; remarkable whitey-greenish opalescence above sun at sunset. About fifteen minutes after sunset the sky in the WSW., from near the horizon up to about 45° was of a brilliant but delicate pink. Below this a very curious opalescent shining green and slightly greenish-white, the pink opalescence going off into bronze-yellow, and that to the green tint . . . The sight was altogether an extraordinary one . . .

And in Gluckstadt, Germany, Herr Dr A. Greber wrote more fulsomely of what he saw; and initially interpreted to be a display of the northern lights or *aurora borealis*:

The phenomenon was most fully developed here from 26 November to 1 December . . . The display of 29 November was the grandest and most manifold, and I give a description as exactly as possible of this one, and its overwhelming magnificence still presents itself to me as if it had been yesterday. When the sun had set about a quarter of an hour there was remarkably little red (or ordinary) after-glow, yet I had observed a remarkably yellow bow in the south, about 10° above the horizon . . . this arc rose pretty quickly, extended itself all over the east and up to and beyond the zenith. The sailors declared, 'Sir, that is the northern lights!' and I thought I had never seen northern lights in greater splendour. After about five minutes the light had faded, though not vanished, in the east and south, and the finest purple-red rose up in the SW.; one could imagine oneself in Fairyland. The SW. sky was bathed in an immense sea of light red and orange, and till more than one and a half hours after sunset the colouring of the sky was much more intense than it is half an hour after a very fine sunset in ordinary conditions.

Apart from these vividly-coloured sunsets, another quite different phenomenon was also to be seen – a large *corona* or halo encircling the sun. This closely resembled the halo that is often seen when the sun is shining through high, filmy cloud, and it was first reported by a Mr Bishop in Hawaii on 5 September. In his own words:

Permit me to call special attention to the very peculiar corona or halo extending to 20° to 30° from the sun, which has been visible every day with us, and all day, of whitish haze with pinkish tint, shading off into lilac or purple against the blue. I have seen no notice of this corona observed elsewhere. It is hardly a conspicuous object.

This phenomenon was subsequently observed all over the world during the next two or three years, and became known as 'Bishop's Rings', in recognition of the first observer. Although they look rather like the 'ordinary' halos around the sun and moon, Bishop's Rings have a different origin. Whereas the 'ordinary' halos are produced by the *refraction* of light through the myriads of tiny ice crystals making up high level clouds, Bishop's Rings are the result of *diffraction* by solid volcanic particles in the air. The difference between refraction and diffraction needn't concern us here (any book on physics will cover it), but the practical difference is that in ordinary halos the reddish (or pink) coloration appears on the *inside* of the ring (just as it is in a rainbow) whereas in a diffraction halo, it's on the *outside*. Look out for it next time there is a major eruption somewhere in the world.

A slight qualification here before leaving these optical phenomena. It's generally been thought that they were the result of suspended ash particles in the atmosphere. Recent work, however, has suggested that some of the visible effects lasted far too long for them *all* to have been due to ash – fall-out should have been complete within a few months. It's possible that the longest-lasting effects may have been due to chemical precipitation of sulphates on the tiny condensation nuclei that are always present in the atmosphere. The sulphates, of course, would have been derived from the copious volumes of sulphur dioxide carried up into the atmosphere during the eruption.

Now, while these various optical phenomena are worth describing in their own right, they are also of deeper significance. While most of the world was revelling in the gloriously-hued sunsets that followed the Krakatoa eruption, astronomers at the Montpelier observatory in the south of France were recording a rather more sinister effect. The radiant energy from the sun reaching their recording instruments at ground level dropped by about 20 per cent when the pall of dust first arrived over Europe, and their readings remained about 10 per cent below normal for many months.

This discovery sparked off a controversy, which has flared up intermittently ever since, on the extent to which volcanic eruptions can cause climatic variations. The notion that volcanic eruptions and climate may be linked, however, had existed for a long while prior to the Krakatoa eruption. Probably the first person to link a relatively short spell of bad weather with an eruption was the great American polymath, Benjamin Franklin. While serving in Paris in 1783 as the first diplomatic representative of the newly-formed United States of America he wrote:

During several of the summer months of the year 1783, when the effects of the Sun's rays to heat the Earth should have been the greatest, there existed a constant fog over all Europe and great part of North America. This fog was of a permanent nature; it was dry and the rays of the sun seemed to have little effect towards dissipating it, as they easily do a moist fog . . . Of course, their summer effect in heating the Earth was exceedingly diminished.

Hence, the surface was early frozen.

Hence, the first snows on it remained unmelted . . .

Hence, perhaps, the winter of 1783–4 was more severe than any that happened for many years.

1783, of course, was the year of the eruption of Laki in Iceland, the largest eruption of historic times in terms of the volume of material erupted. Franklin had only rather vague information about the eruption but he did ascribe the fog which hung over so much of Europe to 'the vast quantity of smoke, long continuing to issue during the summer from Hekla in Iceland . . .'

Since the days of Franklin, and particularly after the eruption of Krakatoa, many scientists have explored the relationships between eruptions and climatic modification. Most diligent of all was Professor H. H. Lamb, of the University of East Anglia in Britain, who made a meticulous compilation of all recorded eruptions from 1500 A.D. to the present day, and attempted to assess their importance in producing a 'dust veil'. From Lamb's work, it is clear that individual major eruptions can cause significant, but temporary, effects on world weather. Apart from Laki and Krakatoa, one of the best examples is the eruption of Tambora in Indonesia in 1815. Little is known about this eruption, but some reports have suggested that it was bigger even than Krakatoa, and may have ejected 100 cubic kilometres of ash into the atmosphere. There are records of remarkable sunsets and luminous twilights in London for six months after the eruption, and it has been suggested that these may have inspired some of the best works of one of Britain's greatest artists, J. M. W. Turner, the 'painter of light'. The year that followed has sometimes been called the 'year without a summer', and it certainly seems to have been thoroughly miserable. One report speaks of there being only three or four days without rain between May and October in Merionethshire (Wales) with consequent poor harvests and food shortages.

Some scientists have gone much further than this and suggested that volcanic activity may cause much more profound long-term effects on world climate. Harry Wexler, an American, suggested in 1952 that, overall, the world's climate has been warming up since the beginning of this century, and that this warming up is due to the absence of any really *big* eruptions this century, whereas the latter part of the nineteenth century was marked by several. (The great eruptions of Bezymianny in 1956 and Agung in 1963 occurred after Wexler's paper was published.)

Apart from Krakatoa, Wexler singled out the eruptions of Tarawera (New Zealand) in 1886, Bandai-San (Japan) in 1888, Bogoslof (Alaska) in 1890 and Awoe (Indonesia) in 1892, as particularly big eruptions which could have led to a cooling of the world climate during the last decades of the nineteenth century. Being a bold sort, he went on from there to suggest the possibility that the great glacial periods of the Earth's history were also the result of volcanic activity. They were initiated, he suggested, by a long period of sustained volcanic activity, which maintained a sufficiently dense haze of dust and ash in the atmosphere to reduce surface temperatures enough to change the whole climatic equilibrium, allowing the ice sheets to spread away from the poles.

This idea met with a good deal of opposition, principally because there was *no* evidence that major episodes of volcanic activity are directly linked with any of the several major glacial periods – the last one, of course, ended only some 10,000 years ago. However, the idea remained a possibility, and found some enthusiastic supporters. The amount of dust required to reduce solar radiation by 20 per cent over a period of 100,000 years is, according to some estimates, really rather small – it would form a layer only half a millimetre thick if it extended all over the world – and the Japanese geologist Budyko has postulated that only fifty to a hundred major eruptions per century would be needed to sustain solar radiation levels at about 20 per cent below normal, and that the rate at which eruptions were occurring at the end of the last century was probably comparable with that during the last Ice Age. Geological evidence suggests that Budyko may even have erred on the conservative side; volcanic activity may well have been even *more* intense during the Ice Age. For example, many of the great volcanoes in the Andes seem to have been constructed wholly within the last few million years, but few of them show much evidence of activity *after* the end of the Ice Age – which lasted in all about a million years.

The argument languished at this point for some years, due to lack of fresh evidence. In 1974 J. P. Kennett and R. C. Thunell reopened the discussion with a paper dealing with an initially rather unlikely area – the sea floor. The deep ocean basins may not seem at first sight to be the best places to look for records of volcanic activity, but in fact they are almost ideal. Dust particles drifting downwind from a major volcanic eruption will shower down a steady rain of ash particles, which settle through the water, and eventually accumulate on the sea floor. Once settled, there is little erosion to disturb them, and ashes from successive eruptions will be preserved in a simple layer-cake stratigraphy, sandwiched between layers of non-volcanic sediments, mainly muds and oozes.

Kennett and Thunell examined 320 sediment cores obtained by the Deep Sea Drilling Project from all over the world, and found ash horizons in eighty-four of them. When they plotted up the number of ash layers against the age of the sediments, they found that there was an obvious increase during the Quaternary period – roughly the last two million years. Thus there appears to have been a world-wide wave of volcanic activity during the Quaternary, and this coincides closely with the period of the Ice Age, since the widespread continental glaciations are thought to have commenced about two-and-a-half million years ago. On the face of it, then, it appears as though there may be a link between volcanism and glaciation. But even if this could be *proved* it would only make the problem more fascinating, because it has already been suggested that an ice age could *cause* volcanic activity! This isn't as daft as it sounds. During an ice age huge volumes of water are removed from the oceans and locked up in the form of ice in the polar regions. This lowers the level of the oceans, perhaps by as much as 100 metres, and this, it is argued, could upset the equilibrium of the ocean basins by 'unloading' them, and this could in turn trigger off movements deep within the Earth, sufficient to cause widespread volcanic activity. This is not a tongue-in-cheek argument – or not entirely anyway – since there are many who believe that a lot of earthquakes and some volcanic eruptions are triggered by tidal stresses of a similar magnitude to those caused by unloading the ocean basins.

The possibility that the great glaciers which once engulfed large parts of the world in their frigid grip were the progeny of volcanic eruptions is only one of many strange side-effects of volcanism. An American geologist P. R. Vogt came up with a suggestion in 1972 which was even more far-reaching in its implications. In considering volcanic activity in relation to modern ideas about Plate Tectonics, he suggested that there are likely to have been episodes in the Earth's history of particularly intense volcanism all over the world, separated by quieter intervals, and he produced evidence to show that over geological history, the rates of volcanic discharge in the area of Iceland have followed broadly similar trends to those of Hawaii, on the other side of the planet. Now the significance of this is that over the course of geological history there have been a number of clearly-defined episodes of large-scale faunal extinctions, when numbers of animal species have suddenly, and for no apparent reason, died out. Much the best known example of this is the dinosaurs. These reptiles were the predominant group of land animals throughout the whole Mesozoic period from about 225 million years ago to sixty million years ago. It's often said that dinosaurs 'ruled the Earth' during that long time. There were a great many different species of dinosaur, adapted to a great variety of different environments and life-styles, but abruptly, at the end of the Cretaceous period sixty million years ago, they all became extinct. Several other major animal groups such as the ammonites also became extinct at the same time, but this simultaneous mass extinction of many different animal species has never been satisfactorily explained.

Vogt's suggestion was that the periods of major extinction were also broadly coincident with episodes of intense world-wide volcanism, and that the animals involved were in effect poisoned by pollution from the volcanic eruptions. We know today that concentrations of heavy metal ions such as zinc and cadmium in industrial effluents can be extremely toxic to wildlife and also to man – the painful and lethal *itai-itai* disease which has affected people living in small areas of Japan is a direct result of cadmium contamination of foodstuffs. When a volcanic eruption takes place, depositing ash over large areas, there is no doubt that the concentrations of trace metals in the environment are disturbed, and if volcanism *were* world-wide, then its effects on plants and animals would indeed be profound. It's most unlikely that the dinosaurs became extinct simply as a result of eating food covered in volcanic ash; it is much more probable that the volcanic pollution may have subtly altered the whole ecological balance of the community of which the dinosaurs formed only a part. It is well known today that toxic chemicals such as D.D.T. accumulate in animals, and that when animals are involved in food chains, the concentrations of the toxic material increase further along the food chain. In Britain, many predatory bird species such as the Golden Eagle have been rendered more or less infertile due to the accumulation in them of toxic chemicals; it is remotely possible that the dinosaurs shared a similar fate, except that there was no Royal Society to protect them from the results of global volcanic activity.

So volcanic activity may have had severe effects on life on Earth. Paradoxically, though, some vulcanologists also believe that it may have been the primary source of *all* life. It's been shown in a number of recent experiments that some of the fundamental chemicals needed for life to evolve, such as the amino acids, can be formed from simple uncombined elements by the effects of high-voltage electric discharges through gases. The powerful electrostatic fields that develop within the columns of ash and dust erupted from volcanoes produce some of the most intense electrical storms known on Earth, and thus provide ideal sites for the synthesis of life's basic chemicals. It is possible, then, that the first steps towards the origin of life on this planet took place over 4,000 million years ago in the flickerings of lightning above active volcanoes, almost as soon as the crust had solidified from its primeval condition.

Although speculations about the origins of life are always interesting, looking forwards to the future is often more thought-provoking. It is clear that volcanoes can be serious agents of pollution at a local level, but it is more difficult to determine how significant the pollution from volcanic activity is compared with that from industrial sources. Until recently this problem was ignored, but now there is much concern about the quality of the atmosphere, and the effects of industrial activity on it. It is well known that the proportion of carbon dioxide in the atmosphere has increased substantially this century, and it has been shown that the fresh-water lakes of Sweden are already being turned slightly acid by the sulphur dioxide pollution which originates in the industrial areas of Europe many hundreds of kilometres further south. Clearly, it is necessary to distinguish between the separate contributions of volcanic and industrial activity to atmospheric pollution, before steps can be taken to combat the problem. Few data are available on this yet, but one study suggests that the annual rate of discharge of sulphur dioxide into the atmosphere by volcanoes is an order of magnitude less than that from all industrial sources.

It may seem, then, that volcanoes present no serious cause for concern, but this is not entirely true. The environmental effects produced by a single volcanic eruption, such as that of Krakatoa, could temporarily far outweigh those produced by human activity, but intense volcanic activity sustained over geologically significant lengths of time could produce incomparably more serious results. It is probably true to say, though, that any changes taking place over a few tens or hundreds of years, and any adverse consequences they may have, are much more likely to be the result of man's unintelligent use of his resources than of volcanic activity. Volcanic activity may in the course of geological time wipe out the human species; only man himself can ensure his own extinction in the course of a few generations.

# *Chapter 9*   Volcanoes as money-makers

In the western part of the Sudan, deep in the heart of Africa, is the volcanic massif of Jebel Marra, an isolated mid-plate volcano. In one of the small hill stations on this remote massif sacks full of small lumps of pumice are sold in the village market. Not for the fastidious Sudanese tribesmen to scrub themselves with, but for faithful Muslims to spread out on the ground in neat rectangular patches, about two metres long and one metre wide, and facing east. This provides them with an ever-ready prayer mat for use during their obligatory five-times-daily prayers, and saves them the trouble of spreading out an ordinary prayer mat each time. The pumice is soft to kneel on, since it comes in such small lumps, and it's not dusty, so that when the Muslim touches his forehead to the ground as part of his devotions, he doesn't get smudged with grime.

Trading in pumice for prayer mats is not the sort of thing that big interests will ever want to move into in a welter of take-over bids, but this example does bring home just how useful volcanic products can be for unlikely purposes in unlikely places. This chapter will be concerned with some of the more important ways in which volcanic activity is directly beneficial to man, and hopefully it will demonstrate that volcanoes are not exclusively agents of death and destruction, but rather benefactors who conceal their long-term contributions behind short-lived smoke screens. For the sake of simplicity, the useful products of volcanic activity can be grouped under three rather artificial headings: bulk materials, ores and power.

## Bulk materials

Bulk materials are those volcanic products which are useful *en masse*, without special processing. The most familiar and vital of these are the fertile soils derived directly from volcanic ashes and lavas. The *first* results of a heavy fall of ash are naturally un-welcome – all the crops over a distance of many kilometres from the volcano will be smothered and killed off. Most of the ash, however, is made of fine glassy particles and the glass is easily attacked and broken down by weathering to give a soil rich in elements such as potassium, which are essential for plant growth. This process of soil formation is particularly important in tropical countries such as Indonesia, where two main agricultural prob-lems exist. First, the density of population and the restricted area of agricultural land require a high level of productivity from the land, which therefore tends to get rapidly depleted in plant foods. Second, this deficiency is compounded by the natural process of weathering in tropical climates where the heavy seasonal rainfall tends to wash out or 'leach' most of the useful elements from the topsoil and re-deposit them deeper down, beyond the reach of most crops.

Maps of population density in Indonesia show that the greatest concentrations of people are in the areas of active volcanism, since the volcanoes help to overcome the twin problems of productivity and depletion. The soils in some of the most densely-populated areas are so fertile that two or even three crops can be raised every year. In Indonesia, rice is the principal crop, but in other parts of the world, other crops are equally dependent on volcanic soils. The coffee from Costa Rica and Guatemala, by reputation the best in the world, all come from *fincas* on the slopes of volcanoes where soil and climate are just right. Guatemalans also claim that their tea is the best in the world, rightly or wrongly, and that too is grown on volcanic soils.

Lava flows are more resistant to weathering than ashes, but they too yield in the end. Their constituent minerals (pyroxenes, olivines and feldspars) break down to form clay minerals and a variety of iron oxides, which form rich, brown soils in temperate climates. The clay minerals cause complications, though, because clayey soils are impervious to water – as any gardener will know – so water cannot percolate through to continue the process of weathering on the rocks beneath the soil. In tropical climates where leaching takes place, deep brick-red *laterite* soils are produced, which are not very fertile since they lack the 'useful' elements. In extreme cases, leaching goes so far that a *bauxite* is produced, containing about 50 per cent of aluminium oxide, 5 per cent silica, 15 per cent of iron oxide, 2 per cent of titanium oxide, about 18 per cent of water and little else. Since it contains so much aluminium, a bauxite may be useful as an aluminium ore, especially if plenty of cheap electrical power is available for the extraction process. By no means all bauxites are derived from lavas (they can form from virtually *any* rock) but the first ones to be discovered, near Baux, in the Var department of France, were derived from basalt flows which were erupted and weathered some sixty million years ago. There are also good volcanic bauxites in many other places such as Jamaica and Victoria, Australia.

Major Plinian eruptions lead to the accumulation of enormous volumes of pumice. This material is so useful that it is transported for long distances, mostly in crushed form, but also to a minor extent in the form of the shaped lumps that you can buy from chemist's shops. Its most important use, apart from mortifying the flesh in the bathroom, is in the manufacture of cement and, in finely-ground form, as a mild abrasive. In some places, it is even used for this purpose in toothpaste, but in most countries limestone is preferred. Wherever it occurs in large quantities, the local inhabitants find a number of ingenious uses for pumice. In the Canary Isles, it is quarried on a large scale in pits extending deep underground. The local farmers make use of it by spreading a thin layer of it all over the surface of their potato fields. The covering of pumice protects the soil beneath from the hot summer sun, thus preventing it from becoming baked hard, while at the same time the pumice is so porous that any rain that falls will be able to soak straight through to where it is needed.

In many parts of the Canary islands, ignimbrite sheets were

much used in the past to provide housing. The peasants simply hollowed out a few rooms in the rock, an easy job since many ignimbrites are soft enough to excavate with pick and shovel. These dwellings were clean and dry within, in contrast to the dank dampness of most caves, and they are so structurally sound that in a few places they are still lived in – it's very odd to see ordinary-looking doors and windows let into the side of a rock face!

In Peru, partially-welded ignimbrites are common and are known by the local name of *sillars*. Sillars are extremely important in the economy of the area, since they make such splendid building stones. The rock is light, but strong, and it can easily be sawn or broken up into convenient blocks. Almost all the important buildings in Arequipa, the second city of Peru, are built of pale, grey-coloured sillar, giving the city a pleasant distinctiveness. All over the world, wherever ignimbrites occur their strength and lightness ensure that they are sought out and used in the same way, but like most other building materials, ignimbrites are only useful if they can be quarried within a short distance of the site where they will be used, otherwise the cost of transportation becomes prohibitive.

In the vicinity of Naples, another city that is built largely of ignimbrite, there is a pyroclastic deposit known locally as *pozzolana*. The value of this material was known to the Romans, who discovered that by mixing it with lime they obtained a hydraulic cement; that is a cement that will set under water. The secret of making hydraulic cement was subsequently lost, but was rediscovered by the English engineer Smeaton when he was building the third Eddystone lighthouse. He used a mixture of equal parts of earthy limestone and a pyroclastic deposit very like *pozzolana*, obtained from the Eifel area of Germany. The value of materials like *pozzolana* in cement manufacture is that their glassy particles are unstable, combine easily with lime, and set hard without the use of heat.

Some thousands of years ago, the Lipari islands off Sicily were the centre of a flourishing trade in volcanic rocks, vital in its time, but now quite extinct. On the island of Lipari itself there are some

50. *An ignimbrite quarry. The vertical slots are left by a saw which cuts directly into the rock face, producing slabs and blocks of standard sizes.*

of the few good obsidian lava flows in Europe, and in prehistoric times the black glass from these flows was in demand all over Europe, since it made by far the best and sharpest tools that the early civilizations could get their hands on. It's difficult for us in the twentieth century to appreciate just how important obsidian was in those early days, but some authors have suggested that it was as vital then as steel is to us today – a commodity that we could not think of doing without. Since it was so highly-prized, obsidian became a major item in trade, and some of the earliest trade routes across Europe have been identified by studying the distribution of obsidian artifacts, and trying to spot from which of the few possible sources they came. Obsidian from the Lipari islands found its way over most of the Mediterranean parts of Europe, and it played an important part in setting up the early links between different cultures and thus helped the spread of civilization.

The obsidian trade was not confined to Europe. An extensive series of trade routes has been discovered in Central America, which operated between 1150 and 500 B.C., the period of the Olmec civilization. The importance of this trade is illustrated by the fact that at one site alone, San Lorenzo, in Mexico, no less than 7,747 different bits and pieces of obsidian have been discovered, and San Lorenzo is nearly 300 kilometres from the nearest source of supply. As many as eight *different* sources have in fact been identified, by making trace element chemical analyses of the obsidian (a sort of geological finger-printing process), and it is clear that the Olmecs were pretty choosey about their obsidian. Their favourite material came from a locality in Guatemala, over 800 kilometres as the crow flies from San Lorenzo, and a great deal further on foot or by canoe. The Central American trade did not stop with the Olmecs. Extensive obsidian trade routes were established during the period of the Classic Mayan civilization between the third and ninth centuries A.D. and obsidian was still in everyday use by the Aztecs in Tenochtitlan (Mexico City) when it was conquered by Hernando Cortez in 1519. Its most notorious use then was in the sacrificial knives with which the Aztec priests cut out the hearts of their living victims, but it was also used for less blood-thirsty purposes as well. Finely-ground obsidian was used as a medicament, and when spread on wounds or sores was supposed to heal them quickly.

Flat, polished slabs of obsidian were used as mirrors by artists in different kinds of inlay work. One of the most striking and bizarre exhibits in the famous Museum of Anthropology in Mexico City is an elaborate mask, made from a human skull, completely plated with small squares of obsidian, except for bands of turquoise around the forehead and mouth. The mask is supposed to represent the sorcerer god Tezcatlipoca, and the skull almost

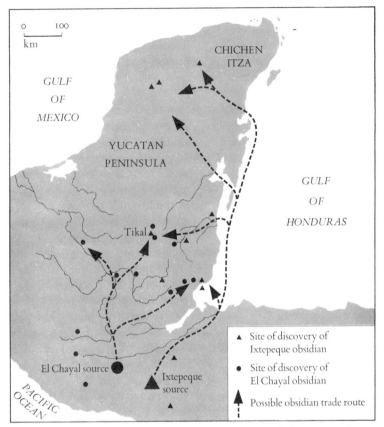

*Fig. 66 Two of the major sources of obsidian in Central America, and some of the places where specimens from these sources have been identified. (After N. Hammond)*

Within the figure:

0   100
km

CHICHEN ITZA

GULF
OF
MEXICO

YUCATAN
PENINSULA

GULF
OF
HONDURAS

Tikal

PACIFIC
OCEAN

El Chayal source

Ixtepeque
source

▲ Site of discovery of
   Ixtepeque obsidian
● Site of discovery of
   El Chayal obsidian
▲ Possible obsidian trade route

certainly came from a victim sacrificed to him. Sacrificed with an obsidian knife, of course.

There are countless other examples of obsidian being used in artistic work by different civilizations all over the world, its black glossy lustre making it a natural choice for jewellery, and it rates almost as a semi-precious stone. The craftsmen of Pharaonic Egypt knew and valued it – they probably obtained their supplies from the Lipari islands – and it turns up in some of their finest pieces of work. The sad, black eyes with which the young king Tutankhamen stares at us from his magnificent gold funerary mask are small pieces of obsidian, and it was also used in many of the other pieces of jewellery found in his tomb.

## Ores

In the good old days of mining, ore bodies produced by volcanic activity made a few miners rich beyond the wildest dreams of avarice, and a good many more hopelessly broke, but they are still a major source of many of the elements useful to man, such as gold, silver, copper and sulphur. For a long period before the twentieth century, in fact, almost *all* the world's gold and silver came from mines developed in volcanic rocks in the American parts of the circum-Pacific belt, and the gold 'rushes' that the discovery of these mines triggered off played a major part in the early development of both North and South America. At first sight, the average volcano looks anything but an economic prospect – it's just a heap of rather drab, barren lavas and pyroclastic rocks that any prospector worth his grubstake would ignore. Few young volcanoes are ever likely to be economically useful, but many old ones are just the opposite. Before describing how this comes about, though, three topics require discussion. These are fumaroles, hot springs, and the setting of volcanoes in the world.

### Fumaroles

For thousands of years after its last eruption, a volcano may simmer quietly, either blowing off a steady jet of steam which rises in a great white banner above it, or wafting out gentle warm breaths of damp, slightly smelly gas. In this state, the volcano is said to be in a *fumarolic* condition, and the steam vents are known as *fumaroles*. A close look at the ground immediately around a fumarole will usually reveal that the rocks have been highly altered, so that they are soft and crumbly, and they may be yellow with small crystals of sulphur. The sulphur in such cases is clearly deposited by the escaping steam, and if the steam were to be analysed, it would turn out to contain a good deal else beside sulphur. Typical fumarolic 'steam' consists of about 95 per cent water, 4 per cent carbon dioxide, small amounts of hydrogen sulphide, boric acid, ammonia, methane and hydrogen, and traces of other elements. Around some fumaroles it is possible to find small crystals of ore minerals such as magnetite and specularite (iron oxides), molybdenite (molybdenum sulphide), pyrite (iron sulphide), galena (lead sulphide), sphalerite (zinc sulphide) and a variety of copper sulphides, but these are rather rare. When a volcano which has been the site of fumarolic activity is eroded, its core is exposed, and then the extent of the changes which have taken place can be seen. The rocks of the core are heavily altered, and large volumes of sulphur are often present. Sometimes the alteration is so extensive that it is impossible to obtain an un-contaminated sample of the original rock, and it is obvious in such cases that large volumes of new material have percolated into the volcano.

## Hot springs

Hot springs are one of the most characteristic features of areas of recent volcanic activity, although they do also occur in other areas less abundantly. They range in temperature from merely tepid to boiling, and they can originate in two ways. They may be either derived directly from a body of magma deep below ground, or, more commonly, they may be 'ordinary' surface waters which have found their way underground and come into contact with hot rocks. Since the solubility of almost all substances is vastly greater in hot water than in cold, the water in hot springs is always rich in dissolved minerals. Some hot springs contain an almost bewildering range of elements. The famous Steamboat Springs in Nevada, U.S.A. contain silica, calcium, magnesium, strontium, sodium, potassium, lithium, chlorine, fluorine, bro-mine, iodine, boron and the carbonate sulphate and ammonium radicals. Such springs are often valued for their medicinal properties, but the water is almost undrinkable except by the most dedicated hypochondriacs. But although it may taste foul, the concentration of individual elements in mineral spring water is usually pretty low, and it might not seem that they could have any profound economic significance. A spring, however, flows night and day for thousands of years and in that time it can deliver a large tonnage of different elements to the surface from below, so that in the long term it may be an important mineralizing agent.

## *The world setting of volcanoes, and its economic relevance*

It is plain that large quantities of minerals are brought to the surface in volcanic areas by both fumaroles and hot springs. But where does all this mineral wealth come from? This is where the world setting of volcanoes becomes important. It has been emphasized that volcanoes are not randomly scattered around the world, but occur in well-defined belts along mid-ocean ridges and destructive plate margins. Ore bodies also are not randomly distributed, but the pattern is less obvious. If *all* the ore bodies in the world were plotted on a map, no coherent pattern would emerge, because ores occur in many different kinds of geological setting, and in rocks of all ages from over 2,000 million years to two million. If a more specific map were made, showing the distribution of ores of single elements occurring in ore bodies of particular ages, a much more coherent pattern would emerge. If, for example, all the gold deposits formed within the last sixty million years were plotted, they would turn out to be scattered in a well-defined belt all round the Pacific, closely paralleling the 'Ring of Fire' discussed in chapter one.

Copper is another particularly important example. Almost all the way up the west coast of the Americas, from Chile in the south to Alaska in the north, there is a narrow chain of copper deposits, known as *porphyry coppers*, which are associated with a group of intrusive rocks older than the present volcanic belt, but strictly parallel to it. These ore bodies are massive bodies of rather

Fig. 67 *The sites of known 'porphyry' copper ore bodies in the Americas. They very plainly follow the 'Ring of Fire'.*

homogeneous mineralized rock, containing 1 to 2 per cent copper, and the enormous open-pit mines developed in them include several of the world's biggest.

Now why should there be these concentrations of copper ore bodies along the Pacific plate margin? Plate Tectonics clearly has something to do with it. Since oceanic crust is continually being shoved under the continental margin, part of it gets stewed up into a molten condition, concentrating some of the metals which are normally present in the oceanic crust in small amounts, and this material eventually finds its way upwards, some of it to form, batholiths (chapter one) and some to be erupted at the surface as volcanic rocks. So if a piece of particularly copper-rich oceanic crust arrives at the plate margin from the mid-ocean ridge, it will give rise to a set of rocks in the continental crust which will have even greater concentrations of copper, and some of these will eventually be exposed at the surface as workable ore bodies. Now why the oceanic crust should happen to be rich in copper is quite another matter; it's more important for us to see how ore-rich rocks are related to volcanic activity.

It has already been mentioned that the development of volcanoes along destructive plate margins is associated with the intrusion of huge batholiths, the largest of them forming the batholiths of Peru and California. The present-day volcanoes round the circum-Pacific belt are probably sitting on top of similar large intrusions, which are not yet exposed by erosion. These huge batholiths cool extremely slowly and consequently, for a long while after their emplacement, hot gases and mineral-rich solutions percolate upwards from them, finding their way to the surface along paths opened up for them by the volcanic magmas, and eventually they soak their way up into the roots of the volcanoes at the surface. Hot metalliferous juices such as these are known as *hydrothermal solutions*. If the parent intrusive body was poor in ore minerals, then the hydrothermal solutions from it will also be poor, and the only minerals that result will be unimportant, unusable things like quartz and calcite (calcium carbonate). But if the intrusive rock was derived from a particularly metal-rich bit of oceanic crust, then not only will it have a high content of ore metals itself, but the hydrothermal solutions derived from it will tend to *concentrate* the ore metals, so that the ore bodies that are finally deposited in the volcanic rocks may have such a high proportion of useful metals that they are economically workable. It follows that any useful ore body is the final result of a long and complicated process of concentration, and it is really rather remarkable that it happens at all – the *average* content of copper in the continental crust is about fifty parts per million but in a good volcanic ore body it may be as much as 3 per cent or 30,000 parts per million!

This process can be seen at work in the Andes. Here, as was mentioned earlier, the active volcanic belt is paralleled about a hundred kilometres to the west by an older chain of 'porphyry copper' ore bodies. The most famous of these is the site of the Chuquicamata copper mine, where copper ores averaging over 2 per cent copper are extracted from an open pit, for a long time the world's biggest hole in the ground. Now the volcanoes which might once have sat on top of these intrusions are long since gone, but the present volcanic chain is almost certainly underlain by similar intrusions. The youngest volcanoes are perfectly fresh – a few are still active – but the older ones are deeply dissected by erosion, and their heavily-altered cores are exposed, some of them gaily-coloured with yellow fumarolic sulphur deposits and reddish ochres of various iron oxides. In other, still older, volcanoes, the core has been thoroughly permeated by copper-rich hydrothermal solutions, giving the rocks a pastel-green colour. A few copper mines have been opened in these old volcanoes, but they are small compared to the open-pit mines in the intrusive rocks. So although the present volcanic belt in the Andes is not important today as a source of copper it is at least useful in these days of concern about the alarming rate of consumption of the Earth's resources to know that in the Andes copper ores are being formed at the present day, and that in the fullness of time, workable ores will be available to our distant descendants, should we have any.

Let's turn now from generalities to specific cases. In the next few pages significant examples of gold, silver, copper, iron, and sulphur ore bodies will be described. Instead of selecting examples at random from all over the world, only mines located on the American part of the circum-Pacific volcanic belt have been chosen.

## Gold

Volumes have been written on the geology of gold deposits; not surprisingly in view of the importance that gold has had in shaping the history of civilized man, and the immense efforts that so

many individuals have made to acquire it. Much the most difficult way of getting large amounts of gold is to try and mine it
directly from the ground; far more people have become rich
through trafficking in gold than through mining it. Despite its
apparent scarcity, gold does occur in small quantities all over the
world, in all kinds of unlikely places – even sea water contains
over five cents' worth of gold per million cubic metres. The average content of gold in the continental crust, however, is only about
0·004 parts per million, so profound concentration processes have
to operate to produce an economically workable gold ore. Volcanic activity is one of the ways in which this concentration takes
place.

A fine example of a gold deposit in the roots of an old volcano
is at Cripple Creek in Colorado, U.S.A. This was once a booming
mining camp which reached its peak in about 1900, ten years after
gold was first found there and over fifty years after the sensational
discovery of gold in California in 1848, which triggered off the
great gold rush of '49. No less than sixty-four individual mines
were opened at Cripple Creek, many of them with stirring names
such as the 'Vindicator', 'Golden Cycle' and 'Stratton Independ-
ence'. All were excavated in a complex mass of basaltic breccia
about four kilometres across in which nine separate volcanic necks
can be identified, tapering downwards in carrot-shaped pipes,
once forming the feeders to an ancient volcano. The present surface level of the mining area varies between 2,700 and 3,000 metres
above sea level, but studies of the pyroclastic rocks which flanked
the old volcano suggest that the top of the original cone was at

*Fig. 68 Sketch section across the Cripple Creek gold mining area, showing the many separate volcanic vents which once fed a volcano on the same site.*

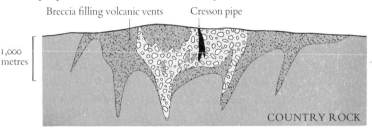

Breccia filling volcanic vents     Cresson pipe

1,000
metres

COUNTRY ROCK

about 3,600 metres. About 600 metres of the old volcanic pile have therefore been eroded away to reveal its mineralized core. Since the necks taper off downwards, the amount and quality of useful ore also decrease downwards, so none of the mine workings extends much below 1,000 metres below ground level, quite shallow compared with some of the great South African gold mines which are three times as deep.

The ore itself occurs in irregular sheets and veins cutting across the basaltic breccia, with the individual veins ranging in size from hair-line cracks to complex zones twelve metres or more across. Much of the romance and excitement in mining comes from the wholly unpredictable vagaries of the ore body. A poor vein which hardly seems worth excavating, may at the next blasting, open up into a rich 'ore shoot', with a heavy concentration of ore, while on the other hand a productive vein which has been followed for hundreds of metres may suddenly come to an end, being cut off abruptly by a fault. At Cripple Creek a late explosive eruption in the central part of the complex produced the Cresson breccia pipe, about 200 metres in diameter, and 640 metres deep. This pipe was discovered in 1915, and the discovery caused a second boom in the mining camp, since it turned out to be what miners of the old West liked to call a 'bonanza', a mass of exceptionally rich, easily-won ore. The Cresson bonanza, apart from setting off a good many wild drinking sprees in the mining camp, yielded over 1,800,000 tons of ore worth thirty-two million dollars; one small cavity or 'vug' within the pipe alone producing 1,200,000 dollars' worth. In some of the legendary bonanzas of mining history, the fortunate miners are supposed to have been able to hack away bits and pieces of gold from the working face of the mine with tin snips and pliers, but not so in Cripple Creek. Here the ore was not metallic or 'native' gold, but mainly a rather complex, pale yellow mineral called *calaverite*, a gold-silver-telluride (Au Ag Te$_2$), somewhat less appealing than gold itself, but very nearly as valuable. Several other telluride minerals also occur, and the occurrence of gold as a telluride is characteristic of many volcanic associations. As if to emphasize this fact, the early miners named one of the mining camps in Nevada 'Telluride'. It's now a flourishing town.

## Silver

The Comstock Lode in Nevada was the scene of one of the biggest mining booms in the history of the opening up of the American West. It was discovered in 1859, but productivity did not reach its peak until the 1870s when many bonanzas were discovered. A large number of mines are scattered along the five-kilometre length of the lode, which is basically a mineralized fault zone, separating geologically young andesite and dacite lavas from older rocks. The lode forms a flattish sheet, inclined at about 40° to the horizontal, and reaches a maximum thickness of 120 metres and a depth of 1,000 metres, although most of the richest ore was found well above this level.

As in so many of the world's mines, the mining operations on the Comstock Lode have been severely hampered by water flooding into the workings. At Comstock, though, the problems are particularly acute, since the water is extremely hot, reaching 64°C in some places. For a long while this near-scalding water made it impossible to mine much below the 1,000-metre level and many miners were killed by it, either directly by falling into the water, or indirectly through the effects of over-exertion in the very high temperatures of the mine galleries – no less than fifty-three died in one period of twenty-two months up to May 1877. To combat this it was decided to dig a six-kilometre-long tunnel to drain and ventilate the upper parts of the mine workings. This tunnel, which became known as the Sutro tunnel, took many years of desperately hard work to complete, and the succession of physical obstacles and financial crises that were successfully overcome in its construction have become legendary, comparable in some ways with the heroic engineering in the laying of the first trans-continental railway across America.

Geologically, the presence of such large volumes of hot water is immensely significant, since it implies that beneath the Comstock Lode there is still a large mass of hot igneous rock, which may be producing mineralization at greater levels. The ore in the Comstock Lode consists mainly of simple silver minerals such as argentite (silver sulphide, $AG_2S$) together with more complex ones such as polybasite ($Ag_{16}Sb_2S_{11}$). Gold also occurs with the silver in about a 1:40 ratio and helps to make the mining even more profitable.

Rich though it was, the Comstock Lode could not hold a candle to the Cerro Rico, the 'Hill of Silver' at Potosi in Bolivia, which was discovered in 1544, almost immediately after the Spanish conquest of Peru. The Cerro Rico is in fact quite high, reaching over 4,800 metres, but it rises only about 1,000 metres above its surroundings. Like Cripple Creek, it is the eroded stump of an old volcano, but its geology is much less well-known. The central feature of the hill seems to be a plug or neck of 'rhyolite porphyry', a fine-grained acid lava containing phenocrysts of feldspar, and this is surrounded by outward-dipping sediments and pyroclastics which are reported to be about ten to fifteen million years old. More or less the whole mountain is mineralized by hundreds of closely-spaced veins reaching up to four metres in thickness, which contain a variety of silver minerals including native silver, argentite, and cerargyrite (silver chloride, $AgCl$). These minerals are all characteristic of the upper parts of ore bodies where the ore has been enriched by surface 'oxidation', and the ores from the upper levels of the Cerro Rico in its heyday averaged about 0·3 per cent silver. This rich ore was exhausted long ago, but mining is still going on at the present day, 400 years after the mine was first discovered. The modern workings are at very deep levels in unoxidized ore which contains only about 0·03 per cent silver, but up to about 4 per cent of tin, and it is now only the tin which makes mining economically viable.

During the seventeenth century Potosi enjoyed a period of enormous prosperity, and thanks to the riches coming from the silver mines it became known as the 'Imperial City' of the Spanish New World, and was for a long time the biggest city in the Americas, with a population of over 150,000. The value of the

51. *The Cerro Rico, rising above the rooftops of Potosi, Bolivia. The conical hill once formed part of a volcano, and has subsequently been honeycombed with silver mines. The tip heaps all over the hill testify to the intense mining activity that has continued through the centuries.*

silver exported from Potosi is difficult to assess in present-day terms. Suffice it to say that it gave rise to a common Spanish expression 'worth a Potosi', and that the colossal volumes of cheap silver flooding into seventeenth-century Spain undermined its economy and society and helped to cause its collapse as a major colonial power. All of the silver that reached Spain, of course, had to be transported from Potosi, deep in the heart of South America. Most of it went by mule or llama train via La Paz to Arica on the coast of Chile, and thence by ship to Panama where it had to be offloaded, carried by mule again across the Isthmus of Panama, and reshipped from Portobello to Spain. Much of it was lost on the high seas to marauding pirates and the weather; but nevertheless a large proportion of it reached its destination. An English friar, Thomas Gage, gave a good impression of the immense quantities involved when he described the scene at Portobello in 1647 just before a convoy of treasure ships set sail for Spain:

... what I most wondered at was to see the *raquas* (droves) of mules which came thither from Panama, laden with wedges of silver; in one day I told (counted) 200 mules loaded with nothing else, which were unloaded in the market place so that there were heaps of silver wedges like heaps of stones in the street.★

## Copper

80 per cent of the world's copper comes from only four major producing areas: the south-western U.S.A., the Andean cordillera, the Canadian Shield, and Central Africa. The two examples described here are both of volcanic origin, but could scarcely be more dissimilar.

2,700 metres up in a deep narrow valley in the Chilean Andes, eighty kilometres south-east of the capital Santiago, is one of the largest underground mines in the world, El Teniente. Working conditions in the mine are difficult – up to twelve metres of snow falls in the Andes in winter – and most of the surface plant is located down the valley in more agreeable conditions. Such a large mine in such an unpromising area clearly requires a very rich ore to make it economical, and the El Teniente mine should eventually be extracting up to 63,000 tons of ore per day containing over 2 per cent of copper. This may not sound a great deal, but in many areas, copper is profitably mined at as little as 0·4 per cent. The mine itself is developed around an explosion breccia which occupies a diatreme-like structure which was probably once linked with a volcanic crater at the surface. The breccia itself is not mineralized, but it cuts through a thick sequence of old andesite lavas and a small four-million-year-old dacite intrusion. These are mineralized throughout with a wide range of copper minerals and constitute the ore. It's thought that the mineralization was linked with the production of the breccia pipe. Reserves have been estimated at over 250 million tons of high-grade ore, so the mine will be supplying copper for many decades to come.

★ George Pendle, *A History of Latin America*, Peter Smith, 1963; Penguin Books, latest edition 1973.

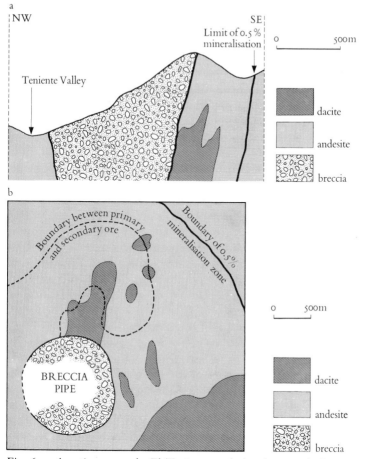

*Fig. 69a A section across the El Teniente ore body, showing the breccia pipe cutting the older lavas and dacite intrusion.*

*Fig. 69b Sketch plan of the El Teniente mine at the 800-metre level.*

The second copper deposit occurs on the Keewenaw peninsula, a long arm of land jutting out into Lake Superior in Canada. The peninsula contains a belt of very old basalt lavas about five kilometres wide and about 160 kilometres long, the upper parts of which contain on average about 1·25 per cent of native copper,

better-known as metallic copper! The copper was first worked by
the indigenous Indians of Canada until it was 'discovered' by the
Jesuits in the seventeenth century, and mining on a big scale
started in 1845. Over a hundred mining companies were active in
the area which was the biggest copper mining region in North
America until 1887, when it was surpassed by one of the
'porphyry' coppers. During its active life profits totalling some
315 million dollars were made, but the field is now worked out.

It is estimated that on the Keewenaw peninsula there were
originally about 400 individual basalt lavas forming a pile about
6,000 metres thick, and that the flows are not less than 2,000 million years old! (Remember that almost all modern volcanoes have
been built in the last ten million years or so.) The volcanic setting
which gave rise to these flows, then, is much older than anything
discussed so far, and it is difficult to speculate on what relation it
may have had to the Plate Tectonics of 2,000 million years ago.
Native copper, however, is not exceptional in lavas; there are
several localities around the world where it is found in small
amounts in much younger flows . . . In these cases, as at Keewenaw, the copper is concentrated in the vesicular, scoriaceous
tops of the lava flows, where it often fills in the open spaces completely. Most of the individual bits of copper metal are quite small,
but some larger lumps have been found – the biggest of them a
230-kilogram mass. The tops of the Keewenaw lavas are all red-
dened and oxidized, a fairly common condition for basalts, and
it has been suggested that oxygen derived from iron oxides in the
basalt combined with the sulphur from earlier copper sulphide
minerals, effectively 'reducing' them to native copper. The copper sulphides themselves are supposed to have come up in hydrothermal solutions from intrusive rocks underlying the lavas. Like
most hypotheses on the origin of ores, though, this suggestion
owes more to speculation than observation, and many mining
geologists have argued strongly against it.

## Iron

There are scarcely any large iron mines developed in volcanic rocks, but mention of the oxidized zone at the top of the Keewenaw flows provides a splendid opportunity to take into consideration a rather small and obscure iron ore deposit, but one which is exceptionally interesting and, so far as is known, unique. It's quite common for extensive oxidation of basaltic lavas to occur, when steam or other gases blast up through them, producing concentrations of iron minerals such as haematite ($Fe_2O_3$) and magnetite ($Fe_3O_4$). Now iron is such a common element that its ores have to be extremely rich before they are economically workable (most are well over 30 per cent iron), which is why oxidized lavas are not usually worked for iron. El Laco, on the borders between Chile and Argentina, however, is the exception. Here there is a large lava which consists almost entirely of the minerals magnetite and haematite! This peculiar mass of high grade iron ore (magnetite is 70 per cent iron) was certainly once a moving lava flow – it has all the typical features of a lava – but it seems that through some exceptional combination of circumstances, a much larger mass of andesite lava was completely oxidized *while still below ground*, and the iron ore was concentrated somehow into a homogeneous liquid, probably saturated with water vapour, which was erupted at the surface. Although this iron ore lava is unique, it's not such an improbable oddity as it may sound – the average andesite is always about 5 per cent iron oxides, partly as magnetite and haematite, and mainly combined with other elements in silicate minerals. The El Laco flow is currently being developed, and is likely to prove a valuable source of iron for both Chile and Argentina. It's a pity that there aren't a few more flows like it in the world!

## Sulphur

This is how Milton described Hell:

A dungeon horrible, on all sides round,
As one great furnace flamed,
Yet from these flames no light, but rather darkness visible
Served only to discover sights of woe
Regions of sorrow, doleful shades where peace
And rest can never dwell, hope never comes
That comes to all, but torture without end
Still urges, and a fiery deluge, fed
With ever burning sulphur unconsumed.

*Paradise Lost*

Many of the descriptions of Purgatory in literature, like this one, owe at least something to contemporary accounts of volcanic eruptions, and during the Middle Ages volcanoes were supposed to be gateways to Hell or prisons of the damned. Dark and dismal disasters of all kinds have also traditionally been associated with 'fire and brimstone'. Even a major landslide on the otherwise placid chalk cliffs of Dorset on a dark night in the nineteenth century was reported by one badly-frightened witness to have been accompanied by 'a strong smell of sulphur'. A smell of sulphur, or strictly speaking of sulphur dioxide (tear gas, $SO_2$), is certainly an unmistakable feature of many volcanic eruptions, since the gases emitted from the vent contain a large proportion of it. Usually, the drifting, acrid clouds do no more than make their presence unpleasantly felt, leaving the unfortunate sufferer with nothing worse than smarting eyes and a dry, coated mouth. However, if the gas is able to accumulate by rolling into a hollow, for example, it can become intolerable and deaths have occurred in some cases through asphyxiation. Interestingly enough, after the main part of the eruption is over, the gases that continue to be emitted tend to change in composition, and the much smellier (and more poisonous) gas hydrogen sulphide ($H_2S$) often predominates over sulphur dioxide.

Whether or not it feeds the dismal fires of the Infernal Regions, sulphur plays a conspicuous part in volcanic eruptions, and it becomes even more important in the fumarolic stage of a volcano's life when wholesale alteration of the core of the volcano may cause deposition of huge amounts of it. It is perhaps surprising, then, that volcanoes actually contribute only a fairly small proportion of the world's economic sulphur requirements. Most of it comes from a rather queer source, in sedimentary rocks draped over big, upward-pushing salt domes (large intrusive masses of salt which force themselves up towards the surface) and this sulphur probably has a complex biological origin. The southern United States is the principal source of sulphur of this kind.

There is no shortage of sulphur-rich volcanoes in the world, but unfortunately the low price of sulphur means that most of them are uneconomic as mining propositions. Two of the biggest volcanic sulphur mines in the world are in north Chile, an area where volcanoes with names like 'Azufre' and 'Azufreras' abound (Azufre is Spanish for sulphur), but the two which are actually mined have much less informative Indian names: Aucanquilcha and Ollague. The mine on Aucanquilcha has the distinction of being the highest mine in the world, some of its open pit workings reaching up to 6,000 metres. The mine is situated in the core of a complex andesite volcano, which still has a faintly active fumarole on it, wafting out warm, damp, sulphurous fumes, and the whole central part of the volcano is yellow with sulphur. The fumaroles are also depositing small traces of bornite, a copper sulphide mineral. At the beginning of the century the mine was worked by a small number of men and trains of llamas toiling up and down the volcano; now there is a road right to the top and immensely powerful diesel lorries regularly grind their way up to the workings at the top, take on a load of ore, and grind equally slowly back down again, making about five round trips a day. The ore, which contains about 30 per cent sulphur, is crushed and processed at a plant much lower down on the slopes of the volcanoes at about 3,500 metres and is then shipped off by rail to the Chuquicamata copper mine, about 100 kilometres away. There it is converted into sulphuric acid for use in the mine's huge electrolytic refinery. Apart from being the highest mine in the world, Aucanquilcha also boasts the world's highest permanent human habitation at over 5,300 metres and the highest football pitch. This distinction is not much of a consolation for the miners who work on the mountain. Almost all of them are barrel-chested

Indians from the Bolivian *altiplano* or high plateau, the only people who can tolerate the constant ordeal of living and working at a high altitude under desperate conditions. It may sound like fun to drive to the top of a mountain in the morning to start work, but after a few hours in the thin, bitter cold air, with sulphur dust billowing around in the wind and stinging the eyes, the attraction fades. Respiratory diseases are common amongst the miners and their life expectancy is very short.

Two separate mining companies are extracting sulphur from Ollague volcano, only a few kilometres from Aucanquilcha, and they have some tricky problems to deal with. The frontier between Chile and Bolivia runs exactly through the summit of the volcano, and although there is a good deal of ore on the Bolivian side, the only two roads up to it are in Chile. Apart from this political puzzle, the miners also have to contend with a vigorously active fumarole, pluming off a column of steam hundreds of metres into the air. The volcano is much more lively than Aucanquilcha, and the temperature in some of the excavations is unpleasantly high. The miners are scared stiff that their workings

52. *A working sulphur mine on the Aucanquilcha volcano in northern Chile. To get at the sulphur, lorries like the one unloading in the foreground have to negotiate the perilous zig-zag road to the top of the volcano at nearly 6,000 metres.*

will break through into a sensitive spot in the volcano's anatomy, blowing them sky high: at 5,500 metres they're half-way there already.

## Geysers and geothermal power

'Iceland' really is an inappropriate name for that country. Sitting astride the Mid-Atlantic Ridge, it is an area of highly-active volcanism, which means that while Londoners are shivering their way through damp, chilly English winters, worrying about whether to install central heating or spend the money on a decent holiday instead, the people of Reykjavik are sitting snug and warm in houses heated with cheap natural steam, and worrying about which variety of tomato to plant in their steam-heated greenhouses. Iceland is fortunate in having abundant supplies of naturally-heated water and steam, but is probably most famous for its geysers. The 'Great Geyser', active in the 1770s, was the grandfather of them all. Proper geysers are uncommon because the conditions that produce them are rather special. Probably the best-known geyser outside Iceland is 'Old Faithful' in the Yellowstone National Park, which is as thoroughly American as party political conventions – predictable, spectacular and a lot of gush. Less well-publicized geysers also occur in New Zealand, Chile, Japan, Indonesia, Kamchatka, and the Aleutian Islands.

A true geyser spouts a jet of boiling water at intervals high into the air – the record is 500 metres for a now extinct geyser in New Zealand – but these intermittent fountains are almost always associated with many less spectacular sources of boiling water, which bubble, hiss and splutter continuously, like small indignant steam engines. Geyser water, like that of the hot springs with which they are related, usually contains a lot of dissolved minerals, and these tend to be precipitated around the mouth of the geyser as *siliceous sinter*, sometimes forming wide, flat terraces, and sometimes building up round the mouth to form a sort of chimney, rather like a stalagmite with a hole in the middle.

53. *A beehive-shaped mound of siliceous sinter built up by a small geyser at El Tatio, Chile. In the background is a small white plume of steam. This unimpressive steam source is capable of supporting a fifteen megawatt power station.*

One of the most attractive aspects of these deposits round geysers is that they are often brightly coloured, both by minerals and by strains of algae that flourish in the somewhat peculiar conditions of the hot, mineral-rich water. One of the most widely-known features of nineteenth-century New Zealand was a set of magnificent pink and white terraces near Lake Rotomahana, produced by the deposition of siliceous sinter by hot water. These were unfortunately destroyed by the eruption of the volcano Tarawera in 1886, but there are many other smaller examples in the world which give some idea of how splendid these coloured terraces were.

There's been a good deal of debate about what makes predictable geysers like Old Faithful work. One of the most widely-accepted ideas is that first put forward by the German chemist Bunsen (of burner notoriety) after visiting Iceland in the 1880s. He suggested that beneath the mouth of the geyser is an irregularly-shaped column of hot water, which is heated from below by conduction of heat directly from hot volcanic rocks, or else indirectly by rising hot water, heated by contact with hot rocks deeper down. Eventually, the water at the base of the column reaches boiling point, although the water at the top is still well below it. Small bubbles of steam form, and these float upwards, expanding as they go, and the expansion of the bubbles pushes some of the water out of the top of the column. This in turn has the effect of reducing the pressure in the water below, and triggers off a violently-accelerating chain reaction, since as the pressure of the water at the base of the column decreases, its boiling point also decreases, so it boils faster, producing more steam, which expands faster and blows the whole mass of steam and water in the column clean out of it in a single powerful but short-lived jet. The interval between one gush and the next, which is about an hour for Old Faithful, is governed only by the time it takes for fresh water to seep back into the geyser and for it to be heated up again. A lot of the water is undoubtedly recycled many times over.

Most geysers are fairly short-lived, in geological terms, and the period between their eruptions usually gets longer as they age. Often, they become so lethargic that they disappoint the eager spectators who come to watch them. To counteract this distressing tendency, the Icelandic geysers are often 'tickled' into activity by pouring a bucket of soapflakes down the throat of the recalcitrant individual. It's not known quite how this works, but it certainly does. Probably the soap reduces the surface tension of the water in the column, making it froth, which reduces the pressure in the column and thus propagates the chain reaction, but with a sensitive geyser, the same effect can sometimes be obtained by stirring it up with a stick. The practice of soaping and tickling geysers, however, is frowned upon by the warders of the geysers in the

Yellowstone National Park, probably because a good deal of rubbish has been thrown into them by many thousands of tourists anxious to get their money's worth out of their visit.

Geysers, in fact, are only economically significant in so far as they provide an attraction to tourists, so it may be asked why they have been included in a chapter on volcanic economics. The reason is that most geyser fields could be worked into geothermal power supply systems, but then their value to the tourist trade vanishes. Who wants to look at a few well-lagged pipes coming up out of the ground and disappearing into a power station? So when plans are put forward for developing a geyser field into a geothermal resource, the planners have to decide whether the benefits of cheap power are not outweighed by the quantifiable loss of tourist revenue, and the unquantifiable loss of a rare natural phenomenon. This problem has already arisen in New Zealand, where it has been found that tapping reservoirs of underground steam adversely affects the surface displays.

Not all natural steam sources are linked to surface geysers, but even if they aren't there is only a small chance that they will be suitable for geothermal development. Innumerable volcanic areas produce a great deal of steam, but it's only in a few that conditions are sufficiently favourable for it to be used – the steam must be hot, dry and at a high pressure. (The steam that comes out of a boiling kettle is just the reverse; it's cold, only just at boiling point, at low pressure, and wet, since it's condensing all the time. The visible 'steam' coming out of the spout of the kettle is in fact a mist of liquid water particles.) On top of all this, the steam ideally should also be fairly pure, and free from corrosive acids which might eat through any plumbing set up to carry it. (Remember what happened to the pots and pans of the Griggs expedition to the Valley of Ten Thousand Smokes!) Modern technology has fortunately made great strides in coping with this problem.

The best-known and longest-established geothermal power station is at Lardarello in Italy. Here, natural steam vents occur at the surface over an area of about 200 square kilometres, but there is no *direct* link with any volcanic rocks. It is thought that the whole area is underlain by a large mass of hot granitic intrusive rocks, which may be related to volcanic rocks elsewhere. The many steam sources here have been known for centuries, but it wasn't until the seventeenth century that anyone thought of a use for them. Initially, the steam was only used as a source of borax, which is present in small quantities as boric acid in the water condensed from the steam and was obtained by evaporating the boric acid to dryness. In 1827 Count Francesco Lardarel had the bright idea of using the natural steam to provide the heat for the evaporation process and started off a successful chemical industry. As the science of chemistry progressed during the nineteenth century, and analytical techniques improved, more and more elements were found to be present in the Lardarello steam and a great discovery was made in 1895, when a chemist called Nasini detected the rare gas helium in it. This element had been known since 1868 from analyses of the sun's spectrum; but this was one of the first occasions when it was identified on Earth.

It was not until 1904 that an engineer named Ginori Conti first devised a way of using the steam to generate electricity, and even then it was only used to provide electric light for the chemical plant – at that time, of course, there were few consumers who could make use of electricity, however cheap. A bigger turbine was installed in 1913, driven directly by steam from the ground, but corrosion by the acids in the steam proved such a problem that this approach was abandoned, and the natural steam was used only to heat pure water for the turbine, entailing the waste of a considerable amount of heat. In 1923, methods were devised of purifying the steam, and with the increasing availability of corrosion-resistant materials, it became possible to generate cheap electricity on a large scale and the installations at Lardarello went on from strength to strength, apart from a set-back during the Second World War when the retreating German armies wrecked them.

At the present day, Lardarello supplies about one thirtieth of Italy's total electricity requirements, from about a hundred bore holes supplying steam at 230°C and 25 atmospheres pressure, at a cost reported to be about one fifth of that of a hydro-electric generating station. 200 years after its inception the chemical industry at Lardarello is still going strong, and it produces annually thousands of tons of boric acid and borax, as well as other odd-ments such as ammonia, ammonium carbonate, aluminium chloride, manganese borate and sodium perborate.

Geothermal power from the volcanic province of North Island, New Zealand, provides about 11 per cent of that country's power needs, and there is no doubt that it could provide more. New Zealand, though, is fortunate in having abundant supplies of rela-tively cheap hydro-electric power and has recently discovered supplies of natural gas, so there is less pressure on the geothermal supplies and hopefully the geyser fields will survive to spout for many years to come.

The only other major geothermal station in the world is at The Geysers in California, U.S.A., where electricity is generated at a cost about 20 per cent less than near-by conventional sources. This field is being expanded steadily, because although developing a natural steam resource is a chancy and expensive business – a bit like drilling for oil – money can be saved in the long term, and, of course, the electricity is completely 'clean', no fossil fuels are burned, and no pollutants are ejected into the atmosphere. By 1978, it is estimated that the electrical output of The Geysers should be about 450 megawatts, nearly enough to supply a city as large as San Francisco. Many of the developing countries, such as Guatemala and Indonesia, are trying to develop their own reserves of natural steam. In Chile a small natural geyser field at El Tatio, 4,200 metres up in the Andes, is being developed as a fifteen-megawatt geothermal power station, but unfortunately it is rather remote from the nearest potential consumer (the Chuquicamata copper mine) and thus the development costs are likely to be great. It should also be possible, however, to use the geothermal energy to power water desalination plants to provide fresh water for vil-lages in the Atacama desert. One of the unfortunate consequences of the El Tatio development is that the performance of the geysers has been sadly diminished already, and a splendid natural swim-ming pool of hot water that weary travellers used to freshen up in is now a sad, muddy puddle.

Natural sources of steam, then, are a valuable means of generating cheap electricity. The energy involved in these sources is however only a tiny fraction of that locked up in volcanoes as a whole. The single eruption of Kilauea in 1952 is reckoned to have dissipated heat energy equivalent to $1 \cdot 8 \times 10^{24}$ ergs, or, in plain English, enough energy to supply two fifths of the power requirements for the whole of the U.S.A. during the period of the eruption. One eminent British geologist has pointed out that volcanic heat, *if* it could be tapped, could supply all the world's power needs for the foreseeable future. This is undoubtedly true, but it's a big 'if'. The American vulcanologist Gordon Macdonald has suggested how it might be done. He proposes that nuclear explosions should be used to shatter large masses of hot volcanic rocks, forming spherical or chimney-shaped shatter zones, and that water should then be pumped into these zones to be turned into steam, which would be tapped at the surface and used in the usual way. He even goes so far as to suggest that heat exchangers could be introduced directly into large volumes of molten magma, the ultimate source of volcanic heat.

As the world gets more overcrowded and polluted, and fossil fuels run out, there will be an increasingly urgent need for 'clean' sources of energy. Nuclear power at its best is rather an inadequate solution, since it generates large volumes of radioactive waste, which is extraordinarily difficult to dispose of, and also causes 'thermal' pollution, since it liberates stored energy into the environment. The only 'clean' sources of energy which can't upset the world's heat balance are geothermal, solar, wind, wave and tidal sources. The last three are rather unimportant, and it is likely to be a long time before solar energy can be used on anything other than a trivial scale, so it looks as though geothermal energy will be our main hope for the future.

While this book was being written, the whole world energy situation deteriorated, almost overnight, as a result of the Arab–Israeli war, and politicians all over the world suddenly woke up to the realization that the 'energy crisis' was not something to be tackled within the next century, but within the next decade. In every developed country in the world, means of economizing on energy were rapidly devised, and sources for the future urgently

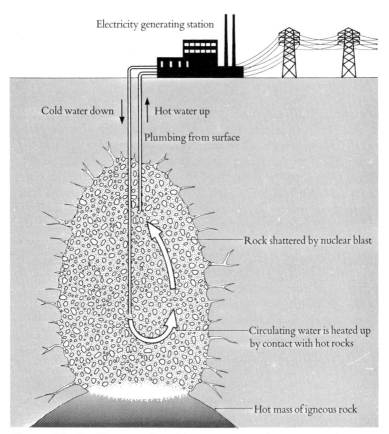

Electricity generating station

Cold water down    Hot water up

Plumbing from surface

Rock shattered by nuclear blast

Circulating water is heated up
by contact with hot rocks

Hot mass of igneous rock

*Fig. 70  Macdonald's suggestion of how to generate electricity on a large
scale from geothermal sources.*

looked for. Geothermal energy is bound to become much more
important to the world than it is now. It is likely that future geothermal source areas will not be obviously related to volcanic
rocks, and will certainly not be located beneath obvious surface
displays of steam. They will probably be located at great depths,
and will require highly-sophisticated techniques both to locate
them, and to extract useful amounts of heat from them. One can

only hope that energy from such sources will be available before the world has got itself into a worse mess than it is in at present.

# Chapter 10  Predicting volcanic eruptions, and what to do once they've started

## The problem

Some fifty-six kilometres south of the city of Manila in the Philippines is a lake, about twenty-five kilometres across at its widest, with a small island near its centre. This island is one of the world's most dangerous volcanoes, called Taal. It has a long history of eruptions going back to 1572, shortly after the first Spanish colonists arrived in the Philippines. Because the population was sparse in those days, with few people living on Taal itself, there were not many casualties in the earliest recorded eruptions – a big one in 1754 killed only twelve people. As time passed, however, more and more peasants settled on Taal and around the shores of the lake, forgetting or ignoring the fact that the land they were occupying had frequently been devastated in the past. For a long while, there were no serious eruptions. But in 1911, a major eruption of Taal took place, generating an ash-cloud visible over 400 kilometres away. Of the 500 or so people then living on the island only about fifteen survived; a further 800 living around the shores of the lake also died. Those who escaped had appalling tales to tell of the chaos and terror that the eruption brought, and one might have thought that they would have been discouraged from ever living near the volcano again. Not a bit of it. Taal remained quiet; the survivors had nowhere else to go; the pressure of population meant that they had little choice but to drift back into the devastated area around the shores of the lake, and hope for the best. Even Taal itself, the centre of the eruption, was re-populated.

In 1965, after fifty-four years of inactivity, when memories of

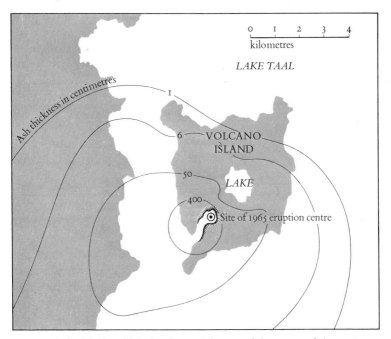

*Fig. 71 Lake Taal and Taal volcano. The site of the centre of the 1965 eruption and the thickness of the ash deposits laid down are shown. The amount of ash in fact is relatively small, and quite unrelated to the violence of the eruption.* (After J. G. Moore)

the 1911 tragedy were fading, Taal erupted again. The whole affair lasted only for about forty-eight hours, but it was extremely violent. Powerful horizontal blasts swept out sideways from the vent in base surges (see chapter three) from the vertical column of ash and steam, whipping across the lake and on to the shore. Near the vent, trees were uprooted or broken off; further away they were stripped bare and the sides facing the volcano deeply scoured, with up to ten centimetres of wood eroded by the hurricane-force ash-laden blasts, while on the side facing away from the vent the bark was unaffected. The effects of these base-surge blasts extended up to about six kilometres from the vent, and ash carried by them accumulated to a thickness of over a metre round the shores of the lake. Although in some respects similar to *nuées ardentes*, these lateral base surges were comparatively cool; none of the trees in the affected area showed signs of burning or charring.

Fortunately, there was a small observatory on Taal which gave warning of danger when the temperature of the lake water rose to an abnormally high level. This warning led to a partial evacuation of the area round the volcano, and when it came the eruption killed only 190 people. Clearly, this represented an improvement over the 1911 situation, but none the less those 190 people died needlessly. After this second demonstration of the unwiseness of living near a volcano like Taal, one might have thought that there was more reason than ever for keeping clear of it. But only a few days after the eruption had finished, families were moving back to reclaim their land and start afresh, no doubt hoping that the next eruption would not come in their lifetimes. Unfortunately though, there is every possibility that Taal *will* erupt again within the lifetime of some of them, and that there will be more deaths, unless clear warning of the eruption is given and the areas at risk *completely* evacuated.

Taal is not unique in this respect by any means. All round our over-crowded world there are potentially dangerous volcanoes with tens of thousands of people living on their flanks. In many of these cases, the danger to life is not great. On Etna, for example, real-estate developers are building houses on lava flows only seventy years old to accommodate the needs of the spreading city of Catania. It's inevitable that some of these houses will be demolished by lavas within the next hundred years or so, but it will be easy enough for the unfortunate house owners to evacuate before the lavas arrive.

It's only rarely, in fact, that lavas cause anything other than damage to property, and those few people that get killed by them are usually foolhardy spectators who are lured by their own ignorance and curiosity into unhealthy situations. Perhaps the worst case of this kind was in 1872 when a party of twenty-two young Italians went up to watch the spectacle of flowing lava in the Valle dell'Inferno on Vesuvius. Unthinkingly, they allowed themselves to be trapped between two tongues of advancing lava and the precipitous cliffs of the Monte Somma caldera, a combination of circumstances that would be well worthy of a modern James Bond film, but which in real life led to twenty-two peculiarly unpleasant deaths.

Ash-falls are a different matter; they are not so easy to avoid, so the dangers are much greater. Even so, intelligent analysis of the situation and appropriate action can save lives and property. Naturally, in the pitch-darkness of a heavy ash-fall, it is easy to succumb to panic, but panic doesn't save lives. Nor, apparently, does prayer. During the 1906 eruption of Vesuvius, the terrified villagers of San Giuseppe assembled in their village church and stayed there during the worst part of the eruption, thinking that they would be safe; many of them were killed when the roof of the church collapsed under the weight of the ash piling up on it. Had the villagers all stayed at home, instead of crowding into the church, they could have saved both their lives and their homes by shovelling the ash off their own roofs. Fortunately, there has not been an eruption of Vesuvius in modern times to compare in magnitude with that of A.D. 79, but there is no reason to suppose that such an eruption could not occur again in the future, and since the density of population in the area is now many times greater than it was in Roman times, the potential loss of life and property is also many times greater.

There are some even more unpleasant possibilities. Some thickly-populated areas of Italy are underlain by ignimbrite sheets, a number of them geologically very young. Ignimbrites travel swiftly and spread widely; the mortality that would result from a sudden unexpected ignimbrite eruption in these areas at the present day would be comparable with that of a nuclear attack. It is not only Italy that is at risk; it merely happens to provide useful European examples. Similar hazards exist all over the world – Japan is another country which is particularly vulnerable, because of its high population density. This may all sound rather alarmist. It's not intended to be, but it is inescapable that volcanic eruptions are *bound* to take place in the future, and as population pressure around the world increases, more and more people are *bound* to be affected by them. So it is becoming increasingly important that we should be able both to predict when eruptions will take place, and to devise ways of minimizing the damage done by them.

## Methods of prediction

Great strides have been made in methods of monitoring volcanoes during this century, but even so, the number of volcanoes which are kept under detailed observation is distressingly small. Of course, even with a fully-instrumented volcano, the job of making predictions is not easy. To be worthwhile, a prediction must above all be *reliable*; that is, if an eruption is predicted for a given volcano on a given date, one must be fairly certain that it *will* actually happen. If it doesn't, a situation will arise comparable with that at Hawaii in 1960 when the Chilean *tsunami* was predicted, and the people failed to respond, since they had been misled too often in the past. It's the old, old problem of not crying 'wolf' too often if you want people to believe you.

Basically, there are four ways of predicting eruptions: studying the eruptive pattern of the volcano, making geophysical observations of its magnetic and thermal properties, keeping a careful survey of its topography, and monitoring the seismic activity associated with it. Some examples of volcanic phenomena that have more or less predictable rhythms have already been mentioned; they range from the crude twenty-five to thirty-year cycle for Vesuvius to the roughly hourly gushes from the Old Faithful geyser. It's unfortunate as far as volcanoes are concerned that these cycles are so hopelessly unreliable – Vesuvius is at the time of writing many years behind its widely-quoted schedule. However, any cycle, however crude, is valuable in that as time passes, the probability of an eruption taking place increases, so that volcano watchers will become more and more alert in looking for significant changes and warning signs in the state of the volcano.

Geophysical methods of diagnosing what's going on inside a volcano are still in their infancy. They depend on the fact that before an eruption starts, a large volume of hot magma is introduced deep below the volcano. This hot magma makes its presence felt, or rather detectable, by heating up the rocks round it. This heating up may cause a rise in temperature of the rocks at the surface, and if it does, the area of hot rocks will show up clearly on infra-red photographs. So by flying regular infra-red aerial photographic missions over the volcano, it may be possible to predict the sites of new activity precisely. The method has yet to be fully tried and tested, though, and, although it looks promising, it may not be particularly useful because the surface temperature changes may not be detectable sufficiently long before the eruption starts for much to be done about it.

A second effect of the heating up of the rocks in a volcano is that their magnetic properties are changed. It was mentioned in chapter one that the basaltic rocks of the oceanic crust have a magnetic fabric printed into them when they are formed at the mid-oceanic ridges, and that this magnetic fabric provides a permanent record of the Earth's magnetic field at the time when they cooled down. Now the rocks of an ordinary terrestrial volcano have a similar magnetic fabric, but if they are heated up by the arrival of new magma, the fabric is disturbed and the changes are detectable either by measurements on the ground or in the air. The eruption of O-Shima volcano in Japan in 1950 was preceded by considerable changes in the magnetic fabric of its rocks, and this gave rise to the hope that such changes would be useful indicators of forthcoming eruptions. Unfortunately, though, it looks as though the method will only work when the mass of new magma comes up to a shallow level, perhaps only a couple of kilometres below surface. Where the magma remains deep down, as it usually does in Hawaii, for example, no changes are detectable at the surface. Work is still going on in this field, though, and there is hope something more may come out of it yet.

The topographical changes that take place in some volcanoes are much more reliable indicators of forthcoming eruptions. The most detailed studies of these have been made in Hawaii, where it has been known for a long time that eruptions of the major basaltic shield volcanoes are preceded by a general swelling up or *tumescence* of the whole thing, followed by a general deflation as the eruption proceeds. It's a bit reminiscent of the frozen chicken pie of chapter six: as the pie cooks, the crust tends to lift and swell; if gravy erupts at the surface, it subsides. The tumescence of the Hawaiian volcanoes, however, is slight, only one metre or so at the summit, and since the volcanoes are over 3,000 metres high this represents an extremely small proportionate swelling. Accurate surveys are needed to detect changes as small as these, but it can be done with normal theodolites and the like. (A similar effect was in fact first observed as long ago as 1914 by a Japanese geophysicist who observed that the ordinary bench-marks round the Sakurajima volcano were displaced by as much as one metre by a large eruption in which about two cubic kilometres of lava were released.)

There are easier ways than conventional surveying, though. One of the simplest is to use a *tiltmeter*. This consists of two separate liquid reservoirs, widely spaced, and connected by a tube. The levels of liquid in each reservoir are carefully measured and recorded, so that if subsequently one reservoir is raised relative to the other, as a result of the swelling of the volcano, liquid will run downhill from the higher into the lower reservoir, and the differences in levels will be immediately obvious. The method sounds a little crude, but it is actually remarkably sensitive and a modern tiltmeter can detect a tilt of as little as one millimetre per kilometre. So with a number of tiltmeter stations spaced out round a volcano, it is possible to keep a very close watch indeed on what is happening.

An example of the sensitivity and usefulness of tiltmeters is the 1959 to 1960 eruption of Kilauea, a volcano whose eruptions are usually preceded by a swelling of the summit, and outward tilting of the ground round the summit crater. For not less than *two years* before the 1959 to 1960 eruption, gradual swelling had been recorded on tiltmeters, and the rapid acceleration of the swelling rate in November 1959 demonstrated clearly that something was about to happen; it did, on the fourteenth of the month. As the first lavas poured out on to the surface, the tiltmeters showed a sudden deflation, but then the eruption ceased temporarily, and

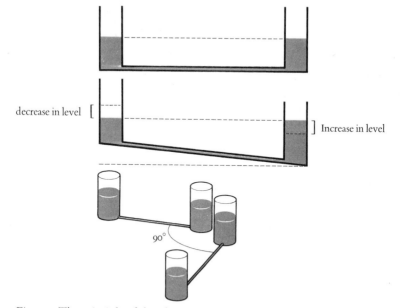

decrease in level [                                                                    ] Increase in level

*Fig. 72 The principle of the tiltmeter. When one reservoir is raised relative to the other by swelling of the volcano, the liquid level in both reservoirs changes (upper diagram). Usually, two instruments at right angles are used (lower diagram), so that the direction of the tilting can be established.*

swelling recommenced until a fresh outburst started on 26 November. This went on until well into December, and finished with the volcano still very swollen up, more so than at any previous time. It was plain that there was more to come in the eruption, and on 13 January 1960 a major fissure opened on the flanks of the volcano, releasing in the following five weeks 120 million cubic metres of lava. After this the summit area subsided rapidly, and remained deflated until the next eruption was on its way.

Laser beams are now being used in some cases to supplement tiltmeters. These sound at first much more sophisticated, but in fact they are only a different tool to do a different job, and are no less and no more useful as scientific instruments. Basically, all that needs to be done is to establish survey stations at well-defined points all round the volcano, and then measure the distance between them precisely, to within a few millimetres. An expensive piece of electronic gadgetry, incorporating a laser, is used for this, but its workings need not concern us. Any changes which have taken place in the volcano will be detected when the same measurements are repeated, after a given period of, say three months. Like the tiltmeter, though, this method relies for its usefulness on having a previous, detailed knowledge of the volcano and what is likely to happen to it before an eruption. Sadly, there are few volcanoes outside Hawaii which have yet been studied in this degree of detail, and it's possible that other volcanoes, with different styles of eruption, will not show the same kind of behaviour.

Probably the most obvious and widely useful method of prediction is the detection of seismic activity associated with an oncoming eruption. Earthquakes or tremors usually precede major eruptions, though they are not often severe, and if correctly interpreted they can save a lot of lives rather than taking them. Quite often, no special sensing apparatus is needed – the shaking is strong enough to be felt by anyone living in the area. The great eruption of A.D. 79, for example, is supposed to have been preceded by increasing seismic activity during the previous *sixteen years* – and there was no one around with a seismometer in those days! Nor does one need sophisticated apparatus to amplify seismic vibrations perceptibly. During the 1906 eruption of Vesuvius, Frank Perret, the character we met in dealing with *nuées ardentes*, detected the first signs of a major new development by biting on his iron bedstead! However, although some seismic effects may be detectable in this way, since the bed-frame amplifies small vibrations and transmits them through the teeth to the bones of the head, no one is going to pay teams of vulcanologists to lie around all day with their teeth sunk into their bedsteads, and it is clearly desirable to pick up the earliest, faintest signs, rather than wait until things have built up to a climax before taking action – in most cases, the shocks perceptible to humans precede an eruption only by hours or days. The apparatus used is basically simple – even Perret did actually employ an earth contact microphone most of the time – but few volcanoes have even the simplest kinds of seismometer to monitor their state of health. Hawaii is again by far the best-equipped area in this respect, so a single eruption of Kilauea again provides a good case study.

In January of the year 1955 the number of seismic tremors recorded at the Pahoa seismometer station on the volcano averaged six per day. Between 1 and 23 February the average had risen to fifteen per day. On 24 February about a hundred were recorded, on 25 February, 300. Many of these shocks were perceptible to the people living in the area. To quote Gordon MacDonald, who was there at the time:

Harold Warner ... informed us that Mrs Warner was feeling 'quakes every few minutes', that many of them were accompanied by rumbling and booming noises, resembling blasting, and that the ranch dogs were behaving peculiarly, digging in the ground and snuffling excitedly in the diggings as though they were pursuing some burrowing animal . . . Were the dogs able to smell volcanic gases that were leaking through the rocks to the surface? We also sniffed the holes but could smell nothing . . .*

On 26 February no less than 600 tremors were recorded, and the seismometers themselves were beginning to suffer from the tilting they were experiencing as the volcano tumesced. It was clear that an eruption was approaching, but with true scientific caution, MacDonald hesitated about issuing a public warning, as there had been a similar series of tremors previously which had led to nothing. He decided to delay his announcement until a routine press bulletin at the end of February. Ironically, the eruption just beat him to it, and broke out on the morning of the twenty-eighth! The first phase of the eruption lasted only a short time, and when it died away, it was widely thought that the whole thing was all over. The seismometers, however, continued to be busy, and it was clear that the eruption had not finished. The second phase commenced on 1 March, close to the spot predicted

* G. A. Macdonald, *Volcanoes.*

by geophysicists, near the village of Kapoho, which fortunately had been evacuated in good time.

So seismic evidence can be very useful. The trouble is, though, that whereas many eruptions are accompanied by seismic activity, the reverse is not always true; not every episode of seismic tremors in a volcanic area necessarily leads to an eruption. And, of course, even if an eruption *does* take place, it may prove to be a damp squib. In 1971, a new basaltic andesite lava dome began to grow slowly and quietly in the crater lake of La Soufrière, the Caribbean volcano which erupted vigorously in 1902. The local authorities, naturally, were afraid that a major explosive eruption might develop, leading to a large-scale disaster comparable with that in 1902 when 1,350 people were killed by mudflows and *nuées ardentes*, so they took appropriate precautions, even preparing for the evacuation of the inhabitants of the areas at risk. The dome went on growing, although there was remarkably little seismic activity. Further seismometers and scientists were rushed to the spot from Britain and America. A Royal Navy frigate stood by, complete with helicopter. The atmosphere was taut with suspense and anticipation. Absolutely nothing happened. The dome went on growing quietly for a while, and then stopped and cooled down. Everyone went back to their respective homes, and normal life resumed. Now although this was something of an anti-climax, the non-disaster was significant, because it was one of the few occasions that large-scale coordinated action has been taken to monitor the progress of an eruption of a little-known but potentially highly-dangerous volcano, and to avoid the *possibility* of a disaster. Too often in the past, the authorities have delayed taking action until there was visible evidence of something unpleasant happening, by which time, of course, it was often too late. Let's hope that in future they will be more inclined to err on the safe side.

Developments in space science and telecommunications technology over the last decade have made a global volcano monitoring system feasible. An American proposal, which has been seriously evaluated, suggested that an instrument module should be placed on each of the world's most dangerous volcanoes, perhaps a few hundred in all. Each module would contain a seismometer and an electronics package capable of transmitting the seismic data to an orbiting earth satellite. The satellite would store up the data until it could re-transmit it back down to a control centre on Earth. This control centre would have computer records of the seismic activity of all the volcanoes in the network, and would be able to detect immediately any anomalous seismic data coming in from a volcano. Should the data indicate the possibility of an eruption in the offing, a team could be flown immediately to the volcano to make more detailed observations, and if necessary organize an evacuation.

The instrumentation for this global system of monitoring is already available – it was developed by the American space scientists for the Apollo programme. Three factors have prevented its being implemented. First, of course, the cost would be considerable, and no one has yet been prepared to put up the money. Second, there is a high chance that the monitoring equipment would be destroyed. Not by volcanic activity but by human interference. In developed countries this might take the form of deliberate vandalism; in remote areas it might be the result of the curiosity of an inquisitive tribesman. Third, and most important, it might not prevent a major disaster. Two of the biggest eruptions of this century, those of Mt Lamington in 1951 and Bezymianny in 1956, took place on volcanoes which would almost certainly *not* be regarded as dangerous – Mt Lamington was not even known to *be* a volcano! Hence it would be impossible to make a realistic selection of the volcanoes to be monitored, and it would certainly be impossible to monitor all those that just *might* erupt.

## Minimizing the effects of eruptions

Once a volcano has made up its mind that it's going to erupt, there is precious little that can be done to stop it. Apart from making sure that the people living round the volcano have been given plenty of warning of the eruption, so that they can get well away, there's not much that can be done to minimize the effects. There is absolutely no way to stop a major explosive eruption from carpeting thousands of square kilometres of countryside with ash and causing extensive damage to property, nor is there any way of preventing lavas from being erupted and flowing down the flanks of the volcano, over-running valuable agricultural land and destroying roads, bridges and houses.

In general, lava flows follow natural guidelines down the slopes of a volcano. If there is a gully or valley, then they will follow that until it opens out, or until they fill it completely and over-flow from it. Sometimes, though, it is possible to influence the course that lava takes, so that while damage cannot be avoided, it can be kept to a minimum. So far as we know, this was first at-tempted by one Diego de Pappalardo during the 1669 eruption of Etna. A large flow from the volcano was threatening the city of Catania, so Diego and some stalwart companions decided that they ought to do something about it. They took advantage of the fact that *aa* lavas tend to flow in channels of their own making, with high banks or *levées* built up of solidified lava chunks chan-nelling the flow. Armed with long iron bars and protecting themselves from the fierce radiant heat of the lava with damp cow-hides, Diego and his men attempted to break down one of the *levées* at a point high up on the mountain, and thus divert the flow from its established course. Their thinking was sound and they were partially successful in that they made a breach in the *levée*, and some lava was diverted off through it. Unfortunately, though, the new stream headed off in the direction of the town of Paterno. The indignant citizens of Paterno soon told Diego and his men where to get off, and prevented them from keeping their breach in the *levée* of the main flow open. As a result, it continued on towards Catania, and ultimately broke through the city wall and caused a great deal of damage.

The same problem exists to this day in Sicily. It would have been possible for the authorities to have diverted some of the many lavas that have been erupted over the last few hundred years, but the flanks of Etna are so thickly-populated that a flow diverted from one area would be bound to do damage in another. The authorities, in fact, dare not interfere with lava flows in any circumstances, because if they did, and if the diverted lava subsequently caused damage, they might be held responsible, and liable for the consequences.

In less densely-populated areas, where there might be a choice between a built-up area and open fields or waste ground, diverting lava flows is more acceptable. This situation exists in Hawaii, where lavas are often initiated in the high, barren parts of the island, and then flow down towards more fertile, productive areas. In 1935 for example, lavas were erupted from the northeast flank of Mauna Loa volcano at an altitude of about 2,700 metres, and began flowing down towards the coast, threatening the port of Hilo, some forty kilometres from the vent. Hilo lies in a slight depression, which tends to channel lavas towards the city, so the situation was critical.

The director of the Hawaiian Volcano Observatory at the time was Dr Thomas A. Jaggar, and he came up with the splendid idea of diverting the flows by dropping bombs on them. He called in the U.S. Army Air Corps to provide the necessary hardware, and after a preliminary reconnaissance flight decided that the best hope lay in attacking the lavas in two places, one high up on the volcano near the vent, and the other about a kilometre or so further along the flow. By this time, the flows were only about twenty-five kilometres from Hilo, and a lot of people were getting worried. The bombers went in the day after Jaggar's reconnaissance. There were ten of them, each carrying two 600-pound bombs, and they made two sorties. In the first, they plastered the upper target at about 2,600 metres, disrupting the uppermost channels of the flow, and in the second, they struck the lower target, producing a further breach. They were completely successful. Where the lava had been breached, new flows poured out and spread out on the barren upper parts of the mountain, thus slowing the advance of the main flow front. The 'attack' in fact turned out to be more successful than even Jaggar had hoped, because two days after it, the main flow front stopped moving altogether. Although it's not been proved for certain, it's possible that the lava was so shaken up by the attack that its chemical equilibrium was upset and its viscosity consequently increased

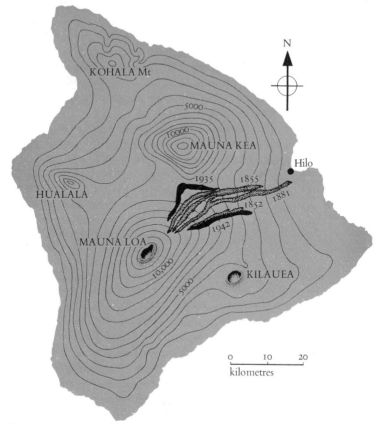

*Fig. 73 Some of the lavas which have been erupted from Mauna Loa during the past hundred years. There is a natural tendency for them to be channelled towards Hilo; the flow of 1881 almost reached it. (After G. A. Macdonald and A. T. Abbott)*

rapidly, so that the whole lava 'froze' solid. It's also possible that the flows might not have reached Hilo even if they had been left to themselves. But the damage that would have been done if they had would have been counted in millions of dollars. The bombing raid cost about 25,000 dollars, a relatively cheap form of insurance.

In 1942, another eruption took place, this time at a height of about 2,800 metres, and large volumes of lava were again spewed out, and looked ominously as though they were going to head down into Hilo. Apart from the danger to the city itself, the flows also seemed likely to disrupt the water supplies, sever the main road round the island, and even damage the harbour installations. Since it was war-time, there was even more incentive than normal to do something to stop the flows, so another bombing mission was mounted. Although the flows were breached, and a minor diversion caused, the bombing turned out to have been unnecessary, since the flows ceased moving shortly afterwards, this time through natural causes.

There are other, simpler ways of tackling lava flows, mostly involving the erection of dams and walls in front of them. These rely for their effectiveness on the fact that basaltic lavas don't behave like bulldozers, pushing everything clear of their path. Viscous acid lavas do behave in this way, and are easily capable of pushing over any obstacles in front of them, such as walls or buildings, but less viscous flows behave in a more liquid fashion and try to flow *round* obstacles. There are many accounts of lavas flooding into buildings without actually destroying them. One of the most graphic cases was the church of San Juan Paricutenango in Mexico. This was completely filled with lava from the eruption of Paricutin so that the main part of the church simply disappeared, but the bell tower survived unscathed, and remained poking up above the surface of the flow when the eruption ceased. More recently, during the 1971 eruption of Etna, the Vulcanological Observatory was, ironically, over-run by lava, and observers were able to enjoy the spectacle of glowing basalt pouring in at the back door and out through the front! Subsequently, however, the building collapsed and was overwhelmed by lava. The significance of this is that since basaltic lavas *don't* bulldoze through walls, they can be dammed, and if a stout dam is built across a valley which is known to be a potential lava channel, then any lava from a subsequent eruption will tend to be ponded up behind the wall. This has two advantages. First, if the flow is a small one, it may prevent *any* lava from getting down to the lower parts of the volcano at all. Second, if it's a big flow, it will ultimately spill over the dam, but at least it will have been held up for some time, providing a breathing space for the people living in threatened areas below, and giving them a chance to move out belongings from their houses or take further preventive steps. Of course, the sort of dam that would be required to hold back completely a really large flow would be impossibly expensive to build, given that there is no certainty that it would ever be needed. So it's only small rapidly-constructed affairs that are really feasible – structures that can be scraped together with earth-moving machinery in a few hours or days if a flow is known to be on its way.

Walls or barriers to *divert* flows from critical areas, rather than dam them are another possibility. These have been tried in Hawaii – about the only area in the world to take its volcanoes seriously. Hastily-erected barriers proved useful in both the 1955 and 1960 eruptions of Kilauea. Although they weren't wholly successful and were eventually overwhelmed by the lava, they did reduce the amount of damage done considerably. Both Jaggar and MacDonald have suggested building substantial permanent barriers around the city of Hilo and its harbour as a precaution against future flows. The kind of barrier they propose would be constructed by bulldozers piling up heavy rock materials into thick walls about ten metres high, and would be intended not to stop the flows, but merely to divert them into other areas where they would do less damage. Although fairly simple, these barriers would be expensive to build, and so far no one has put up the money.

During the 1973 eruption on the island of Heimaey off the coast of Iceland, hastily bulldozed barriers were also used to try and protect the island's main town (Iceland's biggest fishing port) from the lavas erupted from a vent which opened up only a matter of a kilometre or so from the centre of the town. The situation was so critical that fire hoses were also used to flood the advancing lobes of the lava with water, in the hope that this would chill the lava, causing it to solidify rapidly, and in effect build a barrier against itself. High-capacity pumps were flown in from areas as far away as the United States, and a substantial measure of success was achieved.

*Nuées ardentes* and mudflows, which are both much more deadly than lavas, are also much more difficult to deal with. On Kelut volcano, notorious for its mudflows (p. 184), a three-metre-high retaining wall was built in 1905 across the junction between two

54. *An aerial view of basaltic lavas advancing on the town of Heimaey, Iceland. Although extensive damage was done to the town, the lavas did not advance much further than their position here, and, by great good luck, they actually improved the shape of the harbour, making it more sheltered and secure than before.* (Photo courtesy of S. Thorarinsson)

ravines, which had frequently been swept by mudflows. During the next eruption, in 1919, a mudflow ripped down from the crater lake, rushed over the flimsy obstacle as easily as if it had never existed, killed 5,500 people and laid waste a large area of the surrounding countryside.

Because mudflows and *nuées ardentes* travel so much faster than lava flows, and are so much less dense, they may over-run all but the highest and most substantial obstacles, as the Kelut mudflow demonstrated. Probably, a barrier would have to be at least thirty metres high and of massive thickness before it did much good, and it's not likely that many countries would lay out the funds for a structure of that size. Although it's not yet been tried, it may be possible to divert *nuées* and mudflows *at source*. Almost all of the *nuées* from the 1902 eruption of Mt Pelée swept down the same ravine from the growing dome in the crater at the top of the mountain. Concerted bombing on the opposite side might have persuaded the volcano to expend its energies in a safer direction. The same might apply to mudflows originating from crater lakes; judicious bombing of the crater wall could create a breach on the side facing *away* from settled areas, so that mudflows would tend to be diverted in this direction, and most of the devastation would be confined to the predetermined area. Unfortunately, however, quite large-scale bombing would be required in most cases to bring about the necessary changes, and, if the volcano were actually in eruption, there would be a risk of triggering off a major outburst more dangerous than the original situation. Ideally the re-shaping of the volcano should be carried out when it is dormant, to avoid this possibility. The landscape sculpture involved would be easily within the capability of nuclear explosives, but it's most unlikely that the end would justify such drastic means.

# *Chapter 11* Extra-terrestrial volcanoes

One of the concepts implicit in the Plate Tectonic theory is that volcanism is a normal process in the life of our dynamic, evolving planet, and it is known that volcanic activity has been taking place on Earth throughout most of geological history, a period of 4,600 million years. But is this true also of the other planets? Are they evolving in the same way, or are they merely cold, lifeless lumps of rock? Do they have the same structure of core, mantle and crust? Before attempting to answer these questions, it is worthwhile reviewing briefly what is known about the planets, starting with Mercury, the planet nearest the sun.

*Mercury* is a small planet, with a diameter of only 4,980 kilometres, and is only fifty-six million kilometres from the sun. Little is yet known about its internal structure, but in 1974 the Mariner 10 space probe obtained a magnificent series of photographs of the planet's surface, which showed that it looks remarkably like our own Moon, and therefore, by analogy, may have a similar structure. There are a few surface features which may be of volcanic origin.

*Venus*, our nearest planetary neighbour, is nearly the same size as the Earth, with a diameter of 12,200 kilometres, and is about 108 million kilometres from the sun. The surface is masked by a thick, permanent layer of cloud, but Russian and American spacecraft have sent back details of surface conditions. The atmosphere is composed largely of carbon dioxide, and the surface temperature is hundreds of degrees higher than could be tolerated by human life. The density of the planet is similar to that of the

Earth, so it may have a similar structure. Most interesting of all, an American radar survey, capable of mapping the surface despite the blanket of cloud, showed that a number of huge circular structures exist, comparable with those on the Moon. Like Mercury, Venus has no satellites.

*Earth* has a diameter of 12,700 kilometres, and is about 149 million kilometres from the sun. A substantial amount has been learned about the Earth over the last couple of hundred years, but much still remains to be discovered about the early evolution of the Earth, and the extent to which the chance combinations of conditions that make intelligent life possible are typical of other planetary systems in the Universe. Within the solar system, the Earth is rather unusual in that it has a single satellite (the Moon) with a diameter of 3,300 kilometres, over a quarter of that of the Earth itself. (Most of the satellites in the solar system are much smaller than their parent planets.)

*Mars*, the Red Planet, has a diameter of 6,800 kilometres, just over half that of the Earth, but its density is much lower, suggesting that it may not have a metallic core. It is about 228 million kilometres from the sun. The white polar ice caps and some vague surface features can be observed with quite modest telescopes, but there was a good deal of rather wild speculation about the surface details until the Mariner 9 space probe transmitted back to Earth the first close-up pictures of the planet. One of the most exciting features revealed by these pictures was a series of huge volcanoes, one of them the biggest in the solar system. Mars has two satellites, both tiny.

*Jupiter* is different in almost every respect. It is a long way from the sun, about 780 million kilometres, and it is also extremely large, bigger in both mass and volume than all the rest of the planets put together – its diameter is about 142,000 kilometres. Despite its immense size, Jupiter has a remarkably low density, only about 1·33, and it therefore clearly must have a different structure from the Earth. It may have a small dense core, overlain by a 'mantle' of metallic hydrogen, and an immensely thick, dense atmosphere comprised of hydrogen, ammonia and methane.

A Pioneer spacecraft has provided excellent pictures of the structure of the atmosphere, but what lies beneath the clouds is still uncertain. Jupiter has no less than thirteen satellites, the largest of them nearly 5,000 kilometres in diameter.

*Saturn.* Twice as far from the sun as Jupiter, at 1,400 million kilometres, Saturn is also a 'giant' planet, with a diameter of 120,000 kilometres, and apart from its famous ring system is generally similar in make-up. Its density is remarkably low – only 0·71. It has nine satellites; one of them, Titan, is the biggest in the solar system, with a diameter just over 5,000 kilometres, and it is believed to have its own atmosphere.

*Uranus.* Mercury, Venus, Mars, Jupiter and Saturn were all known in the earliest days of civilization. Uranus is so far from the sun (2,800 million kilometres) that it is only just visible to the naked eye, if you know where to look, and it was not discovered until 1781. Its diameter is about 50,000 kilometres, it has four satellites and is probably similar in structure to the two 'giant' planets. Since it is so distant, though, it is difficult to detect much in the way of surface features even with the most powerful telescopes.

*Neptune* is much the same size as Uranus, so it's still in the 'giant' category, but it's so distant (4,400 million kilometres) that its existence was not detected until 1846, when two mathematicians, Adams and Leverrier, independently predicted its existence and also the details of its size and orbit, basing their calculations on irregularities in Uranus's orbit. It has two satellites, one of them discovered as recently as 1950, and a density of only 1·65.

*Pluto.* Aptly named after the Roman god of the underworld, Pluto lies on the extreme fringes of the solar system, and must be a bitterly cold and desolate world, not less than 5,900 million kilometres from the sun. It is a small planet, with a diameter of only 5,800 kilometres and was not discovered until 1930, when it was detected as a tiny speck of light with one of the world's most powerful telescopes after its existence had been predicted by calculations based on observed irregularities in Neptune's orbit.

It's clear even from this brief review that our knowledge of the other planets is still slim. Of the nine planets, only the four nearest the sun, Mercury, Venus, Earth and Mars are possible candidates as sites for volcanic activity. The low-density, 'giant' planets, Jupiter, Saturn, Uranus and Neptune are non-starters, since their internal structures are unlikely to be capable of sustaining the same kind of internal processes that give rise to volcanic activity on Earth.

We need not confine ourselves to the planets in our search for extra-terrestrial volcanoes, however. *Any* body large enough to have a regular internal structure with a hot mantle and a solid crust is a potential candidate for volcanic activity, and, as we have seen, the largest planetary satellite (Titan) is *bigger* than the smallest planet (Mercury). Jupiter has no less than three satellites greater than 3,000 kilometres in diameter, and our own Moon is a pretty hefty object, so these ought also to be taken into account.

In these space-age days, almost everyone knows that the surface of the Moon is covered with a variety of features, such as oceans, seas, craters and the remains of astronauts' picnics, and that at least some of these may be related to volcanic processes. It is possible that similar features are present on the larger satellites of Jupiter and Saturn, but, although a few faint markings are visible through powerful telescopes, nothing more will be known about them until close-up pictures from space probes are available. Since the surface of Venus is obscured by clouds, we shall have to be content with only the Moon, Mars and Mercury.

## The Moon

Although it is only about half a million kilometres away, our knowledge of the Moon remained almost rudimentary until the 1960s, despite the fact that large astronomical telescopes had existed for many years beforehand. This situation arose as a result of the law of diminishing returns; there comes a time when even with a major telescope there is nothing *new* to be seen, and, once the Moon had been photographed in detail under every possible combination of viewing conditions and instrumental techniques, the limit was reached to the amount of worth-while new data that could be obtained from *any* Earth-bound telescope, and astronomers turned their attention to more rewarding problems of distant stars and galaxies. Over the last decade this situation has been reversed, but, before discussing the recent discoveries, we ought to examine what was known about lunar volcanic activity prior to the Space Age.

First, and most important, there was no means of knowing what the structure of the Moon was, so scientists could only speculate on whether or not it had a mobile mantle, capable of sustaining surface volcanic activity. From the earliest times it has been known that the Moon's surface is made up of grey 'seas' such as the Mare Tranquillitatis, and paler-coloured mountainous areas, and it was imaginative speculation about the nature of the 'seas' that led people to identify all manner of strange things on the Moon.

Soon after the invention of the telescope, astronomers found that the 'seas' were smooth, flat plains, with relatively few craters, while the highland areas were much more rugged, and far more heavily-cratered. No one interpreted the seas and highlands in terms of 'oceanic' and 'continental' crust (for one thing, Plate Tectonics hadn't been heard of in pre-Apollo days), but from an early stage there was a school of thought which held that the dark-grey seas or *maria* were plains produced by flood basalts and that they were younger than the surrounding areas. This view was supported by the observation that many of the larger craters have smooth, flat, dark floors and look as though they have been flooded by *mare*-type lavas. Even more convincing, there are many cases where the ghostly rims of old craters can be traced, poking up above the smooth surface of the *maria*, suggesting strongly that they had been partially submerged by the floods of lava forming the *maria*.

One of the chief difficulties facing astronomers who favoured the interpretation of the lunar seas as immense basalt lava plains was that they are quite unlike anything on Earth. Not only are many of them far larger than even the biggest terrestrial basalt plateaux, such as the Deccan of India; but many of them also quite clearly occupy huge circular structures, impossible to interpret in terrestrial volcanic terms. The same problem applied to interpreting the lunar craters – there is nothing on Earth to compare with, say, the magnificent crater Tycho. Natural terrestrial craters can only be formed by volcanic action or meteorite impacts, and this conditioned the minds of astronomers, who tried to interpret the lunar craters in the same terms, and tended to overlook the possibility that processes *might* have operated on the Moon which have never operated on Earth, and of which we would therefore have no direct knowledge. In the pre-Apollo days there were two clearly-defined schools of thought, one arguing that the lunar craters were primarily the result of meteorite impacts, the other that they were volcanic; no one gave any thought to the possibility that they might be both at the same time! This is not to say there were no completely original, even eccentric, ideas on the subject. One British suggestion was that the Moon was originally covered completely with real seas, and that the circular craters were nothing more than the remains of immense coral atolls. Another even more original suggestion was that of an Austrian, Herr Weissberger, who maintained that the craters were not really surface features at all, but merely storms and cyclones in a dense lunar atmosphere!

The fact that the Moon has no atmosphere supported those who favoured a meteorite origin for the craters. Without an atmosphere, they argued, there is nothing to protect the Moon from the steady meteorite bombardment that we *know* the Earth suffers, and therefore there *must* be on the Moon a huge number of meteorite-impact craters. The volcanic school accepted this argument in principle, but pointed out that in many cases the distribution of craters was not consistent with a random meteorite bombardment. The most widely-quoted example was the Hyginus rille, where numbers of small craters, not otherwise distinguishable from other lunar craters, are found plainly aligned along a linear valley, some 180 kilometres long by five kilometres wide and 400 metres deep. How else, the argument went, could such aligned craters be produced except by volcanic activity?

Many other rilles were also known, and a number of these were conspicuously straight and were formed by the subsidence of a long, thin strip of the Moon's surface between parallel fault-bounded sides. This, with the aligned craters, suggested an immediate analogy with the rift valley volcanism known on Earth.

The drawback, though, was that nowhere on the Moon is there a single example of the simple kind of volcano that occurs on Earth. Astronomers spent much time searching for examples, but few of them appear to have stopped to think about whether a volcano erupting under the influence of a gravitational force only one sixth that of the Earth's, and in a vacuum, would necessarily produce a structure like that of Fujiyama or Vesuvius. It seems

55. *A Lunar Orbiter photograph of the Hyginus rille. The rille is conspicuously linear, but is clearly cratered along much of its length.*

obvious now that the mere fact that there is no air on the Moon means that there cannot be any air-fall pyroclastic deposits, and therefore the distribution of volcanic products is *bound* to be different from that of an Earthly volcano.

## The exploration of the Moon

Our knowledge of the Moon was therefore pretty shaky up until the 1960s. The situation changed abruptly when President J. F. Kennedy made his historic declaration to Congress on 25 May 1961: 'I believe that this nation should commit itself to achieving the goal, before this decade is out, of landing a man on the Moon and returning him safely to the Earth. No single space project in this period will be more impressive to mankind . . . and none will be so difficult or expensive to carry out.' This declaration set in motion the most sophisticated and challenging programme of research and experiment that the world has ever seen (or is likely to see again for a long while), which reached its culmination in the Apollo 11 mission. In the ten years before Apollo 11, though, much more was learned about the surface of the Moon than in the three hundred years since the invention of the telescope, as the result of a comprehensive series of unmanned, preparatory missions.

The first major step forward came with the series of *Ranger* probes, the last of which transmitted back detailed T.V. pictures of the Moon's surface before crashing into it. The *Surveyor* and *Lunar Orbiter* programmes followed. The Surveyor spacecraft were designed to soft-land on the surface, and they transmitted back to Earth photographs of the surface, and preliminary data on the composition of the surface materials. The Lunar Orbiter missions provided high-resolution photographs of outstanding quality, which enabled detailed maps of the surface to be made, which were used in the selection of the Apollo landing sites. The Russian lunar programme helped, too, on a more modest scale, and achieved a major success in obtaining the first pictures of the far side of the Moon. Thus the geography of the Moon was known in minute detail before the Apollo missions, and the manned landings have added little to this. Their vital contribution was to supply geophysical data, so that the structure of the Moon could be determined, and to return rock samples so that the geology could be worked out. (To digress slightly, 'geology' is rather an inappropriate word, since it means literally 'the study of the Earth'. 'Selenology' might be more correct.)

## The structure of the Moon

Determination of the internal structure of the Moon was one of the prime objectives of the Apollo programme, since it is of fundamental importance in interpreting the evolution of the Moon. For our purposes, knowledge of the structure is essential in assessing the extent to which volcanic activity was involved in the long evolutionary process.

Seismic stations were set up on the Moon during Apollo missions 12, 14, 15 and 16 as part of a set of geophysical experiments known by the typically N.A.S.A. acronym 'Alsep' (Apollo Lunar Surface Experiment Package). The completed lunar seismic network spans the near face of the Moon in a roughly equilateral triangle with 1,100-kilometre spacing between stations. 'Moon quakes' have been detected by the seismometers at various rates between 700 and 3,000 a year; they are all small by terrestrial standards, ranking at only 1·3 or less on the Richter scale. Meteorite impacts are rather infrequent – only about 100 a year – but produce the strongest signals observed.

Apart from the natural seismic signals from moonquakes and meteorite impacts, the Apollo scientists were anxious to obtain data from some particularly strong shocks, since these would be capable of yielding the most data about the deep structure. One way of doing this would have been to let off small nuclear devices at the landing sites (after the astronauts had left!), but this idea was not pursued, probably because of its unpleasant ethical associations. Instead, it was decided simply to arrange for the discarded Saturn IV-B rocket stages of the spacecraft to crash onto the

Moon. This scheme succeeded splendidly, and the seismic vibrations set up by the impacts of the rockets were detectable at all of the widely-scattered instruments.

The seismic data has shown that the Moon does have a structure somewhat similar to that of the Earth, with 'crust', 'mantle', and 'core', but there are major differences. The outermost few hundred metres is the *regolith*, a layer of shattered, rubbly material produced by millions of years of meteorite impacts. Below this surface layer are solid rocks which extend down to a depth of sixty kilometres, where there is a major boundary, which has been interpreted as the boundary between the lunar crust and mantle. In terrestrial terms, this would be the Mohorovicic discontinuity, but on Earth this boundary is often as little as ten kilometres below the surface.

At a depth of about 1,000 kilometres there is another boundary between the mantle and 'core', which appears to have a radius of about 700 kilometres. Little is known to date about the nature of the core, except that it is probably hot and plastic, but is probably *not* metallic in composition, as the Earth's is.

Almost all the moonquakes detected have extremely deep foci very near the mantle–core boundary. This is very different from the Earth, where the vast majority of earthquakes take place at depths of less than 500 kilometres. The moonquake centres also appear to be unrelated to any surface structures, and are extremely weak – a moonquake that took place on Earth would very likely go undetected.

The feeble seismic activity and the thick, rigid lunar mantle combine to show that internal processes as we know them on Earth are not possible on the Moon, since there can be no convection in the lunar mantle, and therefore that there can be no lunar Plate Tectonics. This in turn indicates that volcanic activity cannot be an important process on the Moon *at the present day*. This comes as no surprise – if volcanic eruptions took place frequently on the Moon, they would be easily visible through Earth-based telescopes. There is, however, plenty of evidence that volcanism played an important part in the past history of the Moon, and many of the youngest visible surface features are of volcanic origin.

## The lunar rocks

Perhaps the most exciting discovery to emerge from the studies of the rocks brought back to Earth by the Apollo astronauts is that all of them, from every part of the Moon visited, are extremely old, ranging from two to four thousand million years. This is a lot older than most (but not all) of the rocks on Earth. The basaltic rocks making up the oceanic crust, for example, are for the most part less than 100 million years old. Therefore, while it is still correct to say that many of the youngest visible features on the Moon's surface are volcanic, the volcanic activity took place aeons before any of the present day terrestrial volcanoes were formed, and the Moon has in effect been 'dead' throughout most of the known period of the geological history of the Earth.

Turning to the rocks themselves, the very first samples to be returned to Earth included specimens of volcanic rocks. The Apollo 11 astronauts collected a few kilograms of material from their landing site in the Sea of Tranquillity. These specimens, worth hundreds of times their weight in gold, were distributed to specialist laboratories all round the world, and subjected to the most rigorous programme of analysis and investigation that any rocks have ever undergone. The results of all these studies revealed that many of the specimens were nothing more unusual than good old basalt, comparable in many ways to ordinary terrestrial basalts, right down to the last phenocryst and vesicle!

When these eagerly-awaited samples were examined in the special Lunar Receiving Laboratory in the United States, the scientists who were privileged to make the first examinations must have experienced something of a let down, for most of the Apollo 11 sample consisted of dirty grey, ashy material, with only a few sizeable chunks. Everything was covered in grey powdery dust, so inherently the whole operation was not much different from raking over a heap of boiler slag. However, the specimens did not come from a slag heap, and when they were examined, it was found that a variety of different types were present, ranging from fine-grained highly vesicular basalts to much coarser-grained, sparsely-vesicular types. The mineralogy of the basalts proved to be similar to Earthly ones, and, just as on Earth, some varieties were found to be particularly rich in olivine, and others in pyroxene.

It would have been sad if there had been *no* differences at all between the lunar and terrestrial rocks, and the detailed laboratory work on the several sets of specimens now brought back have shown some interesting, subtle differences. Some completely new minerals have been discovered in the lunar rocks (one of them has been named *Armalcolite*, after *Arm*strong, *Al*drin and *Col*lins, the Apollo 11 astronauts), and some minerals which are exceedingly rare on Earth have been found to occur commonly in the lunar basalts. In particular, ordinary native iron occurs in some of the basalts, and this indicates that the lavas must have been erupted in oxygen-poor conditions, because otherwise the iron would have been converted to one of its oxides. This is significant, since it helps to refute suggestions that the Moon may once have had an oxygen-rich atmosphere similar to our own.

Chemical analyses also revealed some important differences. The basalts collected at each individual landing site tended to be similar to one another, but there were significant differences between the rocks from different sites. This indicates that the basalts were derived from more than one primary source, rather than from a single common 'pool' of magma as some earlier speculations had suggested. In general the lunar basalts turned out to be much richer in titanium than their terrestrial counterparts, and much poorer in the alkali elements, sodium and potassium. Other differences are shown in the trace element contents of all the lunar rocks. These are not just random variations, however, and they provide vital clues to the mechanism of the Moon's evolution 4,600 million years ago. For example, the Moon rocks are depleted in 'volatile' elements such as sodium and potassium, but enriched in 'refractory' elements such as calcium, aluminium and barium. This provides a pointer to the way that the Moon evolved out of the primordial gaseous nebula around the Sun from which it and all the planets condensed. The Moon must have accreted from material that condensed *prior* to the condensation of significant amounts of iron. The uncondensed material in the nebula, including most of the iron and elements more volatile than iron were swept away, or captured by the much more massive Earth.

Both the Earth and the Moon have large 'oceans', and both are comprised mostly of basaltic material, but it is really rather unfortunate that the term 'ocean' was ever applied to the lunar basalt plains, such as the Oceanus Procellarum, or Ocean of Storms, because it creates a tendency to think that they must be the counterparts of the Earth's oceanic crust. It is worth emphasizing here that sea-floor spreading is not, and appears never to have been, a significant process in the shaping of the lunar seas and oceans. The lunar basalt plains are now generally referred to by their Latin name, *maria* (seas), and this usage may help to avoid confusion.

In some respects one can consider the rocks of the rugged lunar highlands as being the counterparts of the Earth's continental crust, but again the comparison must not be too closely drawn. It had long been thought that the pale-coloured rocks of the highlands would turn out to be older and of different compositions from the lavas filling the circular mare basins. The Apollo results showed that the highland rocks did indeed form a separate, distinct suite. Chemically they are much richer in calcium and aluminimum than the *mare* basalts, and poorer in magnesium, iron and titanium. They consist mostly of plagioclase feldspar minerals. These fascinating rocks are known as *anorthosites*, and interestingly enough the terrestrial equivalent anorthosites are found *only* in the oldest parts of the continental crust. It has even been suggested that in the lunar anorthosites we are looking at the kinds of rocks which may have formed part of the very first solid crust on Earth, and that the early histories of the Earth and Moon were similar, so that about four thousand million years ago the Earth may have looked much like the Moon does today. The Apollo data show that the anorthositic lunar highlands were formed between about four and a half and four thousand million years ago, and that there was then a period during which the Moon experienced an immensely heavy bombardment by massive objects the size of asteroids. This period of intense bombardment has been described as the 'lunar cataclysm' by American scientists, since it was so far-reaching in its effects. In particular, the massive impacts were responsible for the formation of all the circular *mare* basins. The bombardment appears to have ceased about three thousand million years ago and, after this, the basins excavated by the impacts were slowly filled by accumulations of basalt lavas. The youngest lava is just over three thousand million years old.

An event taking place four thousand million years ago is very difficult to conceive, but it was an important milestone in the history of the Moon, for subsequently few major changes took place, apart from the formation of craters by impacts from bodies of a more conventional size. During the same period the Earth evolved drastically, and the rocks we now see on the Earth's surface can tell us little about when or how the continental and oceanic crust came to be differentiated. The work on the lunar rocks, then, has given us a profound insight into the origins of our own planet, and many geologists now believe that it is by studying the Moon and our neighbouring planets that we can best progress in our understanding of the early history of the Earth.

## *New interpretations of lunar surface features*

The superb Lunar Orbiter photographs, the manned Apollo landings, and the rocks returned to Earth have provided a great flood of new information about the Moon, and have thrown fresh light on some of the oldest and most puzzling problems of the Moon; the origins of the great *mare* basins and the thousands of craters. It is now abundantly clear that these are both primarily impact structures, but it is still worth examining what is now known of them, and in particular the part that volcanic activity may have played in modifying the primary structures.

## The role of meteorite impacts

It is abundantly clear that the whole surface of the Moon has been influenced by meteoritic bombardment. The Moon has no atmosphere to speak of, and therefore, unlike the Earth, every speck of cosmic dust that it encounters piles into it at high speed and leaves its mark. Since the Moon's surface is so old, the total number of separate impacts that have occurred is almost infinite, and the surface as a whole has been shaped and moulded by meteorite and micrometeorite impacts. These are the only agents of erosion on the Moon, but, over the course of hundreds of millions of years, they have succeeded in rounding the whole lunar topography into soft, gently-rolling contours.

Although meteorite impacts are important in this secondary role, they have of course also played a primary role in the formation of seas and craters. The irregularly circular shapes of seas such as Mare Crisium (the Sea of Crises) were well-known before the days of Apollo, and the manned landings served to confirm long-held views that the smooth, monotonous expanses of the *mare* were vast lava plains. The Lunar Orbiter photographs even showed up the fronts of individual lava flows on the surface of the Mare Imbrium. These have exactly the sort of lobate flow-fronts that one would expect of a fluid basalt lava spreading out on a flat surface. Prior to Apollo, however, little was known about how the lavas were related to the formation of the circular structures which they fill.

This problem was made particularly acute when the first photographs of the rear side of the Moon (which is always hidden from the Earth) were obtained by the Russian spacecraft Zond III. The photographs showed an enormous circular structure, no less than 700 kilometres in diameter, the central part of which was occupied by dark grey, smooth mare material. This peculiar structure, known as the Orientale Basin, was subsequently photographed in detail by Lunar Orbiter IV, and these photographs showed it to consist of a spectacular series of four circular scarps, arranged con-

56. *A number of individual lava flows can be seen here, snaking across the flat surface of the Mare Imbrium. Although they cover large areas, the flows are relatively thin, and can only be seen under conditions of low-angle illumination. The long shadows cast by the hills at the top indicate that the sun was extremely low when this Apollo photograph was taken.*

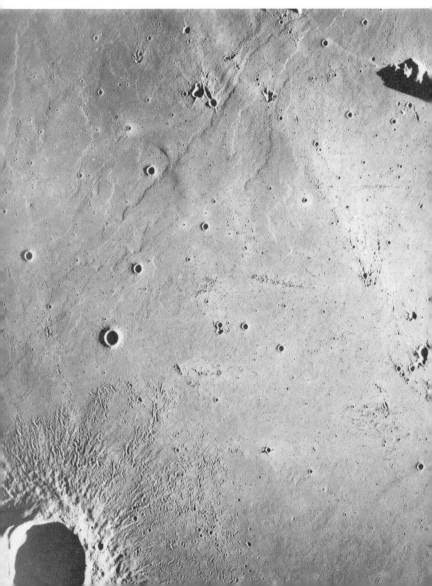

centrically round the central lava plain, itself about 200 kilometres in diameter.

The size and regularity of these concentric structures clearly present problems. It's likely that they are the result of the impact of an asteroid-sized body on the Moon, the actual point of impact being at the centre of the inner mare basin, while the concentric ridges around it were thrown up by the shock waves propagated by the impact. Alternatively, the concentric ridges may represent collapse features, where the Moon's crust, weakened by fracture during the impact event, subsided along concentric rings a short time later, as a result of the extrusion of large volumes of basalt at the surface to form the central lava plain.

The lava itself must have been originated deep down in the Moon, probably in the lunar mantle, and it seems as though the scale of the impact was so great that in effect a hole was blasted through the crust, enabling magma derived from the mantle to well out on the surface. If the eruption of these large volumes of magma was responsible for large-scale subsidence, then the Orientale Basin may have some affinities with the formation of terrestrial calderas, in which subsidence is also believed to play a major part. The Orientale Basin, however, is nearly a hundred times larger than a caldera like that of Mt Katmai, for example.

It's now generally accepted that most of the other major *maria* had similar origins, with a large-scale impact followed by extrusion of lava. A similar combination of impact and volcanic phenomena may have been responsible for the formation of many of the largest craters, especially those that are floored by dark *mare* lavas. There are many thousands of other, smaller craters which are more difficult to interpret. Many of them are certainly straightforward meteorite impact craters, but many display some puzzling features. Often, the walls of the crater are made of a series of concentric terraces, and this has led many observers to suggest that some kind of subsidence has taken place, with the floor of the crater being lowered relative to its surroundings. This, of course, again sounds reminiscent of caldera formation, but even a modest lunar crater is still ten times the size of the Mt Katmai caldera.

57. *The magnificent Orientale Basin on the far side of the Moon. The scale of the structure can best be judged by comparing it with the size of the Moon as a whole, since the edge of the Moon can be seen in the same photograph.*

The superb crater Tycho, eighty kilometres in diameter, provides an excellent example. Tycho is particularly famous for the magnificent 'ray' system radiating out from it, which can be seen with even the most modest pair of binoculars, but it is an extremely impressive object in itself. It consists of a fresh-looking, steep-walled depression with a fine central peak and it is surrounded by a blanket of ejected material which can be divided into three concentric rings: an inner bright one, a middle dark one,

58. *A near vertical view into the crater Tycho. The central peak stands out plainly, casting a long shadow, and the concentric structure of the crater walls is evident.*

and an outer light one. The inner ring has a distinctive hummocky topography and a series of concentric markings, but the middle ring is quite different and is characterized by radial ridges and valleys. Both of these are probably entirely the result of the violent ejection of fragmental material as a consequence of a meteorite impact, but the main floor of the crater is covered with what looks like a series of lava flows, which have been ponded within the crater and now have a cracked and crenulated surface, a little like the solidified surface of a lava lake. These lavas must have flooded into the crater *after* the meteorite impact which actually excavated it, but there is no doubt that the eruption of the lavas was part and parcel of the whole crater-forming episode. On the inner and middle rings of the ejecta blanket there are also irregular wormy-looking features which look suspiciously like viscous lava flows, possibly erupted at the surface at the same time as those actually within the crater itself. It's also possible, though, that they are some kind of pyroclastic flow, or else flows produced by the shock melting of large volumes of rock when the meteorite struck.

The radial pattern of bright streaks or 'rays' centred on Tycho can be traced over a large part of the Moon's surface. Many other craters have similar, but less impressive ray systems. There can be little doubt that these are primarily the results of meteorite impacts, but close-up Lunar Orbiter photos have shown that the rays can be traced back into the thick blanket of debris round the source crater, and, in this region, structures reminiscent of pyroclastic flows are found. Mostly, the patterns of rays are strictly radial, but in a few places they are clearly 'braided', that is, the lines criss-cross one another producing patterns identical to the flow ridges on the surface of hot avalanche and *nuée ardente* deposits. Even more significant, in some places there are sets of low, dune-like ridges running *perpendicular* to the ray direction. The only comparable structures on earth are produced by *base surges*, which were first recognized by observers of nuclear test explosions, who noticed that apart from the familiar upward-directed mushroom cloud, a circular ring-like cloud also rolled away from the base of the main stem of the mushroom, hugging the surface (chapter three). Subsequently, the same kind of ring-shaped cloud was noticed at the base of the eruption column of several volcanoes, such as Taal in the Philippines, and it was found that the base surge was in many ways just like a sort of radial *nuée ardente*: a dense, turbulent cloud of pyroclastic material supported by a large volume of expanding gas which rolled outwards and down the slopes of the volcano. Where these radial *nuées* ran out of steam and began to deposit their loads of ash, the gas blast was still strong enough to mould the ash into low dunes, which were all arranged round the volcanic cone in such a way that their longest axis was parallel to the slope, and therefore perpendicular to the blast. It seems likely that the lunar dunes were formed by the same kind of base surge blast, so although this may not have been primarily a volcanic effect, it is at least comforting to know that a

59. *A number of different examples of the sinuous rilles which are common on the Moon's surface. Many of these appear to originate near well-formed craters and subsequently peter out; others seem not to be related to craters at all.*

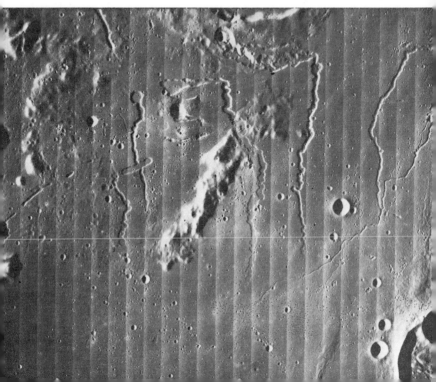

meteorite impact could trigger off a distinctly volcanic phenomenon.

Fascinating though these observations are, it is, unfortunately, impossible to be sure of their correctness, and until geologists have an opportunity to examine a crater like Tycho and the ray system around it in minute detail, the nature of the mechanisms which operated to produce the structures that we now see will remain speculative. There is no doubt, though, that the major lunar craters are primarily impact features, which have been extensively modified by the effects of secondary volcanic activity, triggered off by the impact.

### The origin of the lunar rilles

It was pointed out earlier that rilles had long been considered as being possibly volcanic rift valleys, and the Lunar Orbiter photographs certainly supported the suggestion that the famous Hyginus rille was volcanic. But the Lunar Orbiter photographs raised far more problems than they solved. Not only did they reveal that rilles are more abundant than had been expected, but also that many of them are anything but rift valleys, and are much more like wriggling, meandering river valleys. Early on in the planning of the Apollo programme it was decided to devote one mission to the examination of one of these strange rilles. The one that was selected was the Hadley rille, which is located at the foot of the Appenine mountains, near the Mare Imbrium.

This rille is about 135 kilometres long by one kilometre wide and 370 metres deep, and it was mapped in detail from the Lunar Orbiter photographs. Traces of what looked like rock outcrops in the upper walls of the rille were identified on the photographs, and it was hoped that these would provide a new perspective on lunar geology, because all the earlier missions had found only shattered, out-of-place rocks forming the regolith. The Apollo 15 astronauts found in the walls of the rille and in the near-by Mt Hadley a succession of parallel stratiform layers, and those in the rille turned out to be basalt lava flows of the kind underlying the whole of the Mare Imbrium. The presence of the basalt flows also suggested the

60. *The Mare Imbrium (left), the Hadley rille (centre) and the Appenine Mountains (right). The Apollo 15 landing site is shown by the white arrow. The photograph was taken from the Apollo 15 command module.*

possibility that the rille might have been formed by the collapse of a long lava tunnel. In chapter four, terrestrial lava tunnels were described, and it was pointed out that some of them are very long. Now there are also a good many cases known on Earth where the roof of such a lava tunnel has collapsed, producing a long irregular groove or valley.

Apart from the general similarity in appearance, there are other

*Fig. 74 A sketch map of the area shown in photograph Plate 61. The cross-sections reveal plainly how the rille is elevated above its surroundings.*

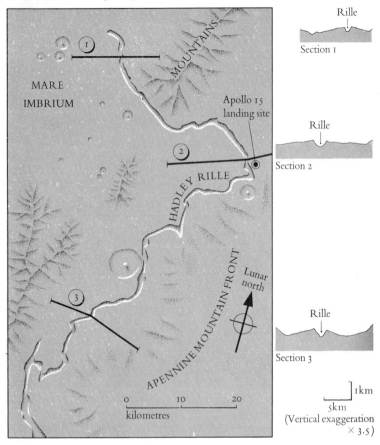

reasons for thinking that the Hadley rille is a collapsed lava tunnel. Experimental work has shown that the lunar basalts are likely to be even more fluid than their terrestrial counterparts, and therefore they are likely to flow farther, and to produce longer lava tunnels. Furthermore, all the sinous rilles are found on the flat mare surface – none occur in the highland areas. Any stream of liquid flowing over a flat surface will meander all over the place, in a random fashion, and this may account for the extraordinarily squiggly outlines of the rilles, Hadley included. The detailed mapping of Hadley showed a rather unexpected feature – the rille itself is elevated above the general level of the mare surface. This is a feature which is characteristic of lava channels everywhere, and lends more support to the lava tunnel idea.

But what could have caused a collapse? One might think that since erosion by wind and water cannot take place on the Moon, there can be no way in which a lava tunnel could be induced to collapse. But the constant rain of meteorites and micrometeorites is more than adequate as an agent of erosion, and what's more, the impact of a *large* meteorite in the vicinity would cause any tunnel to collapse, even if it fell some way away, since it would set up powerful and destructive moonquakes.

Apart from lava channels, a variety of other ideas, some of them rather wild, have been advanced to explain the sinuous rilles. Several have invoked ordinary surface rivers, flowing at a time when the Moon is supposed to have possessed an atmosphere similar to the Earth's. Unfortunately, though, there is no evidence that the Moon ever did have such an atmosphere, let alone rivers on its surface, and anyway the characteristics of the rilles are in detail quite different from river valleys – one of their most remarkable features is their extraordinarily uniform width, some of them not varying by more than a few per cent over hundreds of kilometres. Unless one invokes some kind of lunar 'canal' system, it is therefore extremely difficult to explain the origin of sinuous rilles by any sort of surface flow of water. It has been suggested that even if water is excluded, flow by some other medium must have been responsible, and that *nuées ardentes* may have been involved. These do have a considerable erosive power, and it's possible that a series of *nuées* could excavate a deep channel in the loose surface material of the moon. But even these would be un-likely to produce the long, thin channels typical of rilles, so it looks at the moment as if the most likely origin of sinuous rilles is in the collapse of lava tunnels; but there is a high chance that future students of the Moon will come up with some better ideas.

## Lunar volcanoes

There are *no* immediately recognizable Mt Fuji-like volcanoes on the Moon, nor, in view of the vastly-different environment on the Moon, should one expect to find them. There is no atmosphere on the Moon, and the force of gravity is only one sixth that of the Earth. Thus, if a volcanic eruption comparable to that of Pari-cutin in Mexico were to take place on the Moon, one would *not* find a similar scoria cone as the end result. The absence of atmo-sphere and the lower gravity both combine together to ensure that pyroclastic material ejected from the vent will be thrown higher, and travel farther, than on Earth. The volcanic structure that would result would therefore be much broader and flatter than a terrestrial scoria cone. Some volcanoes of this kind have been tentatively identified on the Moon; they look extremely similar to meteorite impact craters, but are usually surrounded by a dark-coloured halo of pyroclastic material.

Apart from these rather dubious volcanoes, the nearest ana-logues of terrestrial volcanoes on the Moon are extrusive lava domes, somewhat similar to those described in chapter four. These usually occur as low, swelling hills rising up above flat *mare* plains, and it is thought that they result from the extrusion of viscous acid lavas.

## Lunar volcanic eruptions

It is evident from the evidence obtained from the Apollo landings that volcanic activity played a major role in the early history of the Moon, particularly in the filling of the *mare* basins with basalt lavas. It's equally evident that volcanic activity at the present day can only be at an insignificant level. But are there any eruptions at all, or is the Moon completely dead?

There have been a number of reports of short-lived phenomena taking place which *might* have been associated with volcanic eruptions, but most of them have been rather vague accounts of tiny craters changing in shape, or of small areas varying in colour or brightness. Most of these reports are not reliable, since they usually stemmed from a single observer examining fine detail at the extreme limit of resolution of his telescope, probably in less than optimum viewing conditions. So far, the Lunar Orbiter photographs have revealed no signs of changes taking place whatever, so the reports made by ground-based astronomers in the past should be treated with caution. Having said this, though, there are some cases which have been known for a long time, and have acquired a certain respectability through being widely-quoted.

Perhaps the most famous case of all is the 'disappearance' of the crater Linné. This event, if it was an event, took place in about 1850 and it caused a great stir amongst the astronomers of the day, who considered the Moon to be a dead, unchanging world. In 1886, a dedicated, precise observer named Schmidt realized that Linné, a crater that he had himself mapped several times between 1841 and 1843, had disappeared. His announcement of this startling change awoke new interest in the Moon, and a great many observers began systematic work to find similar cases. It is difficult at this remove of time to know what to make of this reported change. Even though the telescopes of the day were much inferior to modern ones, Linné as originally described by Schmidt and other workers was a fairly conspicuous feature about nine kilometres across, and since it was situated in the broad, open expanse of the Mare Serenitatis, it was one that would not be easily confused with others. The present site of Linné is uncertain. The Lunar Orbiter photographs show several separate small craters in the general area where Linné is believed to have been located. Accepting that it did once exist as an entity, two things could have happened to Linné: it could either have been hit by a meteorite, or it may have been destroyed by a volcanic eruption. In either case, however, one would expect to see some kind of *new* structure, as well as modification of the old. None of the present craters which might be related to the original Linné is in any way out of the ordinary.

Somewhat better evidence than this comes from the crater Alphonsus, which has been notorious for reports of transient events taking place in it. (But this may of course be the result of a vicious circle; the more 'events' that are described, the more people look at the crater, and the higher the probability of 'events' being observed.) Fortunately, though, the evidence for Alphonsus is both recent and reliable. On 3 November 1958 a Russian astronomer, Nikolai Kozirev, was observing Alphonsus with a fifty-inch telescope at the Crimea Observatory. Quite suddenly, he noticed that there was a small red cloud near the centre of the crater, and that it was moving slowly. Although the cloud was only visible for half an hour or so, Kozirev was able to take some temperature measurements and discovered that the cloud was hot, possibly 2,000°C or so. About a year later, Kozirev again reported activity in the area, but it was much less obvious. There seems little doubt that it was some kind of volcanic eruption that Kozirev saw and some geologists have suggested that it may have been the emission of a *nuée ardente*.

## A brief lunar recap

Our thinking about the Moon has advanced so much in the last few years that it's probably worth summing up the most important discoveries. First, it's now known that the Moon has a structure broadly similar to that of the Earth, with a core, mantle and crust. Second, the crust is divided into two fundamental types, in some ways akin to that of the Earth: the seas, which are extensive flood basalt plains; and the highlands, which are composed mainly of gabbroic anorthosites. Third, the Moon is not 'dead', in that moonquakes do occur deep within the mantle, although they are very feeble compared with earthquakes, and this suggests that some kind of internal process is continuing. Fourth, all the lunar rocks are extremely old, most of them older than any rocks exposed on Earth. This could mean that when we look at the Moon

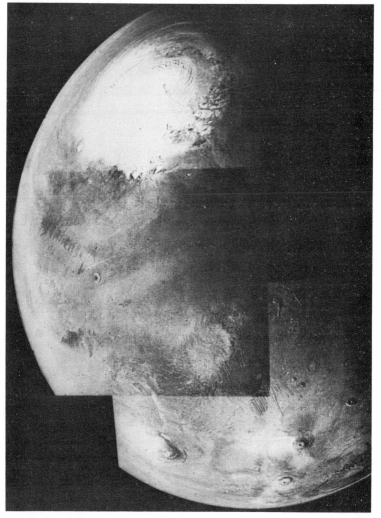

61. *A view from Mariner 9 of the surface of Mars. The northern ice-cap shows up plainly at the top of the picture. The pimply excrescences in the lower part are huge volcanoes, and the white patches indistinctly visible to the left of each volcano are due to clouds formed in the thin Martian atmosphere in the lee of the high volcanoes.*

we are seeing something of what the Earth looked like about 4,000 million years ago. Fifth, the most prominent features of the Moon's surface, the seas and craters, were probably formed as the result of impacts of asteroids and meteorites, which triggered off the eruption of lavas and other volcanic phenomena. Sixth, although there are large volumes of volcanic rocks on the Moon, there are few obvious volcanoes, and volcanic eruptions on the Moon at the present day are extremely infrequent.

## Mars

Mars, the Red Planet, is much the most notorious object in the Solar System, and is always associated with flying saucers, green gremlins and the like. But these are relatively recent additions to the legends about Mars, which has been regarded as a particularly significant and portentous planet since the days of the earliest astrologers who associated its fiery red colour with the god of war. Its surface features first became known in the seventeenth century, when the Dutch astronomer Christian Huygens recorded faint, dusky markings on its red disc in 1659, and shortly afterwards Cassini detected the white polar ice-caps which have played an important part in all the subsequent speculations about the possibilities of there being some form of life on Mars. Subsequently, the polar ice-caps were found to show a considerable variation in size with the passage of the Martian seasons, and the dusky markings on the rest of the planet also appeared to show regular variations in colour and extent. This gave great impetus to the burning question 'Is there life on Mars?' since many observers thought that these variations in the dusky areas were due to the seasonal growth and recession of extensive areas of vegetation, which of course implied that Mars might be a sufficiently congenial planet to support human-like life.

This tantalizing possibility received a considerable extra boost in 1877 when Giovanni Schiaparelli observed for the first time the so-called 'canals' on Mars, features which he saw as faint linear streaks running across the surface of the reddish Martian deserts, and which he tentatively suggested could be artificial waterways constructed by intelligent Martians. His suggestion was seized upon by Percival Lowell, a wealthy American, who built himself a well-equipped observatory in Flagstaff, Arizona and settled down to a study of Mars. He soon developed something of an *idée fixe* about the canals, and was convinced that Mars was inhabited by a race of intelligent and resourceful Martians who were struggling against the progressive dessication of their planet by building an enormously complex series of canals to carry water from the polar ice-caps to the equatorial areas. His imaginative and thought-provoking ideas kept interest in Mars at a high level for decades, and sparked off innumerable science-fiction stories of varying degrees of idiocy about life on the 'dying' planet and the attempts of the Martians to escape from it, and also lent weight to the periodic bouts of tall stories about flying saucers which were used to pad out newspapers on quiet days in the fifties.

The true nature of the 'canals', however, could never be resolved purely by telescopic observation, and most astronomers knew this. Mars is a small planet, only about half the size of the Earth, and it's a long way away, fifty-six million kilometres at its nearest. To make matters worse, it has an atmosphere in which large dust storms periodically blow up, obscuring parts of the surface. So our knowledge of Mars remained largely static from the beginning of the twentieth century until the first Mariner missions in the sixties. Interestingly enough, though, developments in radar techniques were such in the sixties that the first radar maps of the Martian surface were published at almost the same time as the first Mariner photographs – the radar maps were made by Earth-bound instruments, which in effect made a large number of accurate measurements of the distance from the instrument to points on the surface of Mars, a remarkable piece of long-distance surveying.

The first Mariner flights to Mars were simply 'fly bys', when the space probes passed near Mars on their way into the oblivion of deep space. The most useful results came from Mariner 9, which went into orbit round Mars on 13 November 1971, after a flight of some five months from Cape Kennedy. It was the first man-made object to orbit the Red Planet, and carried six different experiments on board, the most important of which was a sophisticated set of television equipment. The pictures that were transmitted back to Earth were initially something of a disappointment to the scientists concerned, because all that they showed was that the surface of the planet was obscured by an immense dust storm. This itself, however, was interesting, since it demonstrated that Martian dust storms were much more extensive affairs than had been suspected previously and that dust was far more prevalent on the Martian surface. The observation led immediately to the suggestion that the seasonal changes in the dusky surface markings were more likely the effects of shifting wind-blown sand deposits than any form of 'vegetation', however lowly. By December 1971, the great dust storm was abating, and visibility began to improve. At the beginning of 1972, Mariner 9 began systematic photographic mapping of the surface.

## The structure of Mars

Only the preliminary results of the many thousands of photographs taken by Mariner 9 were available at the time of writing, but it is already obvious that Mars is a geologically 'live' planet, which has experienced volcanic activity in its recent past. Some scientists believe that Mars is in a stage of evolution intermediate between that of the Moon and the Earth, and that therefore internal processes of a sort are operating at the present day.

The surface of Mars is heavily cratered, but to a lesser extent than the Moon, and there are also areas which are relatively free from impact craters. These are interpreted as being geologically 'youthful' areas, where volcanic activity has occurred in the recent past. Much more conspicuous than these, however, is the great Coprates Rift, which forms a 3,600-kilometre-long slash along the planet's equatorial region. This rift, which would more than span the United States, is eight kilometres deep and over 200 kilometres across at its widest. It is believed that it represents a primitive stage in Martian Plate Tectonics, in some ways akin to the East African rift system. There do not yet appear to be on

Mars any distinct areas of 'continental' or 'oceanic' crust, though future space probes may cast more light on this.

Nor is it yet known what the internal structure of Mars is. This will have to await the data sent back by soft-landing spacecraft of the Viking series, due to land in 1976. Preliminary data from remote sensing instruments aboard Mariner 9 indicate that the surface rocks on Mars have a high silica content, around 60 per cent. This means that they are highly-evolved, and have formed from differentiation processes in magmatic rocks. One would therefore expect to find far more acid volcanic rocks on Mars than on the Moon, and, as a consequence, a wide range of interesting volcanic phenomena such as Plinian pumice deposits and ignimbrite flows.

## Volcanoes on Mars

About half of Mars appears to be covered with volcanic rocks, and twenty separate major volcanic centres have been identified. Most of these are shield volcanoes, built up by thin lava flows of low viscosity accumulating to form very gently-inclined slopes. The best-known volcanic area is a large plateau, parts of which were observed to be poking up through the swirling dust-clouds early on in the mission. One part of this plateau was identified with a feature known previously from telescopic work, and named in the old-fashioned, slightly romantic way *Nix Olympica* (the Snows of Olympus). Three other parts of the plateau had not previously been known, and these were christened in the modern, boringly prosaic way, North, Middle and South Spots.

Now the important thing about Nix Olympica and the three Spots (sounds like the name of an old music-hall turn) is that each is an elevated, shield volcano, and each has at its centre a cluster of large craters. The floors of the various constituent craters are all at different levels and were formed by successive events. South Spot is different from the others in that it has only one main crater, but that is over a hundred kilometres in diameter, with a flat floor and terraced walls. This enormous feature is different from any Earthly volcanic structure, but it's also different from the large lunar craters, since it does *not* appear to have the same kind of blanket of ejected debris around it, but it *does* have a complex series of minor craters on its rim, some of which form arcuate chains, and a series of peculiar cratered valleys which extend north-east and south-west of the main crater.

The crater complex of Nix Olympica is itself about sixty-four kilometres in diameter while the whole massif measures 500 kilometres across the base, and, according to one estimate, rises

62. *A close up from Mariner 9 of Nix Olympica, the largest volcano in the solar system. At least five separate craters clustered together can be discerned at the centre of the complex. The complex as a whole appears to be bounded by a circle of steep cliffs or scarps.*

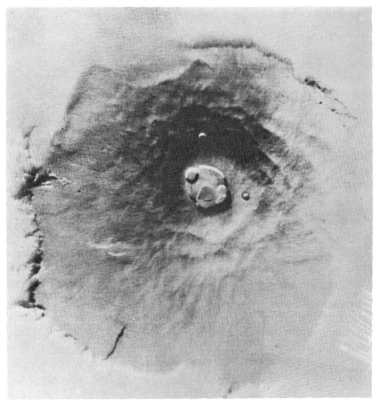

twenty-five kilometres above its surroundings. This makes Nix Olympica easily the biggest volcano in the solar system, and it dwarfs even the largest terrestrial volcanoes. The Hawaiian complex, for example, is about 225 kilometres across at its widest, and rises only some nine kilometres above the Pacific Ocean floor. Taken as a whole, the shapes and sizes of the large craters in the Spots have led scientists to think that they are the Martian equivalent of Earthly calderas, the result of large-scale collapse following major eruptions. Whether or not the extensive plateau on which the Spots are built up will turn out to be made of ignimbrites or their Martian equivalents will be something for the first astronauts on Mars to decide.

The scale of the Martian volcanic mountains is impressive, but, even more stimulating, there is a distinct possibility that some of them may be active. The quality of the Mariner 9 photographs is such that even thin, tenuous clouds can be detected in Mars's thin tenuous atmosphere (the atmospheric pressure on the surface is only about one two hundredth of that on Earth). These are *not* the yellowish dust clouds such as those which were observed during the early part of the Mariner mission, but 'ordinary' white clouds believed to consist of water and carbon dioxide. They have been observed to accumulate during the Martian afternoon round some of the very high volcanoes, and it has been suggested that they result from the condensation of volcanic gases exhaled during the day. If this suggestion is right – and it is *only* a suggestion – then it would be evidence for *present day* volcanic activity on Mars.

## Mercury

Mercury is one of the most difficult of planets to observe directly from the Earth. Since it orbits so near the sun, it can usually only be seen against the background glare of the setting or rising sun. As a consequence, even the biggest telescopes could only reveal a few indistinct, dusky markings on the surface. The close-up pictures taken by the Mariner 10 spacecraft were therefore eagerly awaited by the world's scientists. They were not disappointed.

63. *The planet Mercury, photographed from Mariner 10 from a distance of about 210,000 kilometres. The similarity to the Moon is obvious, but there are no large* mare *basins. The Caloris Basin is just visible on the day–night terminator, slightly below the equator.*

64. *A close-up view of the Caloris Basin, showing the concentric structure of ridges and plains. The cause of the intense fracturing and ridging in the plains is not understood, but the structure as a whole is probably a compound of impact and volcanic phenomena.*

Those who were fortunate enough to be in the receiving laboratory in September 1974 were privileged to see the unique, unrepeatable sight of a stream of pictures flooding in from what was in effect a totally unknown planet. The first photographs were transmitted when the spacecraft was still far distant from Mercury, and others continued to come in while it passed only 7,000 kilometres above the surface. They were of a far higher quality than those taken by Mariner 9 of Mars, and, to the surprise of many scientists, they showed that Mercury looks remarkably like the Moon.

Analysis of the photographs of Mercury had only just begun at the time of writing, but it is already clear that there are no volcanoes of terrestrial, or even Martian, type on Mercury. Most of Mercury is generally similar to the lunar highlands in appearance, with much heavily-cratered terrain, but no large *mare* basins. As on the Moon, the major craters are undoubtedly of impact origin, which triggered off volcanic side-effects. A few features very like lava flows are visible on some pictures. Perhaps the most impressive single feature is the Caloris or 'hot' Basin (so-called because it lies in one of the hottest regions of Mercury nearest the sun). This is strongly reminiscent of the Orientale Basin on the Moon, since it consists of a similar series of concentric ridges and terraces, and it too was probably formed by a huge impact event, after which basaltic magmas came welling to the surface.

There we must leave Mercury, and our brief review of the volcanoes of the solar system. The Mariner 9 and 10 missions have provided man with his first glimpses of worlds outside his own, and have demonstrated that volcanism has probably played as important a part in the history of the inner planets as it has on Earth. Our knowledge of the planets is still in its infancy and it is clear that there will be a number of fascinating discoveries to make and problems to solve in the future. But exactly the same is true of our tired old Earth; we know a great deal more about it now than we did a hundred years ago, but each fresh advance in our knowledge has only opened up fresh fields for investigation. It is probably true to say that there are more questions to answer about vol-

canoes now than at any time in the past. But, whatever we discover about volcanoes in the future, we can be absolutely certain
that volcanoes will still be erupting on the Earth long after man
himself has become quite extinct.

# Index